About this book

Against an international context where NGOs are still
seen, in contrast to many official development agencies, as
the saviours and sources of hope for an otherwise disap-
pointing development process, Dorothea Hilhorst provides
for the first time an empirically rooted and theoretically
innovative understanding of the everyday politics, actual
internal workings, organizational practices and discursive
repertoires of this kind of organization. Her evidence and
insights lead to a different picture of NGOs from the one
prevailing in the literature. And her model of NGOs not
as clearcut organizations, but often with several different
faces, fragmented, and consisting of social networks whose
organizing practices remain in flux, is helpful to understanding not just these bodies, but official development
agencies too.

Critical acclaim

This study of the everyday politics of a Philippine NGO is both entertaining and hard-hitting. It reveals the ongoing dilemmas, divergent interests and ideological oppositions in the social life of one 'progressive' NGO, exposing both the cut and thrust of everyday office relations as well as its dealings with clients and donors. The result is a highly readable and powerful story underpinned by discourse and actor concepts. While researchers will be fascinated by the way the author steers her way through the labyrinths of NGO life, it acts as a warning to practitioners who believe the effectiveness of NGOs can be improved through introducing 'rational' modes of control and accountability. The beauty of this book, then, is the way it combines a theoretical and pragmatic understanding of the 'multiple realities' of organizational practice. *Norman Long, Wageningen University*

Hilhorst goes beyond an unravelling of simplistic notions about NGOs and brings to life a detailed picture of everyday practices within them. If development policy makers and practitioners read it – to understand more about what NGOs are; the roles played by local history, language, social ties and politics; and how multiple meanings are negotiated by NGOs and their funders – then both would have a better chance of building good partnerships and being accountable to those living in poverty. *Emma Crewe, University College London*

The Real World of NGOs challenges us to revisit continually our own assumptions and discourses. It allows the reader to have a better understanding of the day-to-day dynamics within an NGO as it works to achieve the transformative agenda it shares with the indigenous peoples' movement and the women's movement. This story of indigenous women involved in transformation work provides significant insights for social activists and social scientists. *Victoria Tauli Corpuz, Executive Director, TEBTEBBA Foundation (Indigenous Peoples' International Centre for Policy Research and Education)*

In this well crafted ethnography of a Philippine NGO, Dorothea Hilhorst has put forth a set of arguments as important as they are necessary for understanding the political dynamics of contemporary social movements. She makes a compelling case for treating civic institutions not as things but as open-ended processes shaped by the practices and discourses of various actors ranging from grassroots activists to foreign-based funding agencies. In its nuanced analyis of the perils and promises of NGO organizing, this book makes a vital contribution to a critical anthropology of development and the comparative study of everyday politics. *Vicente L. Rafael, author,* White Love and Other Events in Filipino Politics, *Professor, University of Washington*

Hope this may inspire, but mostly hope it will make you laugh too!

The Real World of NGOs

Discourses, diversity and development

Dorothea Hilhorst

Best wishes,

Zed Books Ltd

LONDON • NEW YORK

The Real World of NGOs: Discourses, Diversity and Development was first published by Zed Books Ltd, 7 Cynthia Street, London N1 9JF, UK and Room 400, 175 Fifth Avenue, New York, NY 10010, USA in 2003.

www.zedbooks.demon.co.uk

Cover designed by Andrew Corbett
Set in Monotype Baskerville and Univers Black by Ewan Smith, London
Printed and bound in Malaysia

Distributed in the USA exclusively by Palgrave, a division of St Martin's Press, LLC, 175 Fifth Avenue, New York, NY 10010.

A catalogue record for this book is available from the British Library
Library of Congress Cataloging-in-Publication Data: available

ISBN 1 84277 164 7 cased
ISBN 1 84277 165 5 limp

Contents

Figures and Tables

Figures

Tables

Acknowledgements

For three years, I have enjoyed the warm friendships and hospitality of numerous colleagues, friends and villagers in the Philippines. It was wonderful to live with them and share the precious experiences of doing research and raising a child. I am most grateful for the companionship of Joan Carling throughout these years, and would like to mention in particular Vicky Tauli Corpuz and Tita Lubi, who were pivotal in making this project possible. As I explain in the epilogue of this book, my research was in the end criticized by a group of people in the Cordillera. Although we disagree on a number of issues, I would like nevertheless to reiterate my heartfelt appreciation for the space I was given to accomplish the project and for the dialogue on its merits.

I would also like to thank my academic advisers to whom I owe so much of my intellectual development, Dirk van Dusseldorp and Norman Long, and my friend and professor Georg Frerks. I thank Ann Long for finding time to edit the book and Robert Molteno and Barbara Clarke of Zed Books for their friendly support and confidence. The book would never have seen the light without my mother, Joke Hilhorst, who has been a tremendous source of inspiration and support, and I thank my brother Pieter Hilhorst for his many valuable comments.

No words can express how grateful I am to have my daughter Iana as my brave and most lovable travelling companion. I dedicate the book to my family: my wonderful partner Fred Claasen and our lovely children Don, Franks, Ellis and Iana.

Acronyms

ADDA	Anti-Dam Democratic Alliance
AIWN	Asian Indigenous Women's Network
Amihan	National alliance of peasant women's organizations
BPO	Binasan People's Organization
CADCI	Regulation under DAO-2 for the registration of ancestral domains
CBC	Cordillera Broad Coalition
CDP	Consortium of Non-governmental Organizations' Cordillera Comprehensive Development Plan
CECAP	Central Cordillera Agricultural Programme
CODE-NGO	Caucus of Development NGO Networks
CPA	Cordillera People's Alliance
CPLA	Cordillera People's Liberation Army
CPP	Communist Party of the Philippines
CWNGO	Cordillera Women's Non-governmental Organization
DA	Department of Agriculture
DAO-2	Government Programme on Ancestral Lands
EC	European Community
EFA	European Funding Agency
GABRIELA	General Assembly Binding Women for Reforms, Integrity, Equality, Leadership and Action
GATT	General Agreement on Tariffs and Trade
ILA	Igorot Liberation Army
INNABUYOG	Regional Indigenous Women's Organization
IP	Indigenous People
Kalayaan	Katipunan ng Kababaihan Para sa Kalayaan (Women's Movement for Freedom)
KLAi	Kayatuan Ladies' Association Incorporated
KMK	Kilusang ng Manggagawang Kababaihan (Women Workers' Movement)
KMP	Kilusang Magbubukid ng Pilipinas (Philippine Peasants Movement)
LUPPO	Luaya People's Organization

Makibaka	Women's movement of the early 1970s, later continued underground as the women's organization of the National Democratic Front
MOUNT	Mountainous Development NGO
MSAC	Montañosa Social Action Centre
NDF	National Democratic Front
NGO	Non-government organization
NPA	New People's Army
NPC	National Power Corporation
PANAMIN	Presidential Assistant on National Minorities
Pilipina	Feminist Women's Organization
PO	People's Organization
PRRM	Philippine Rural Reconstruction Movement
PTA	Parent–Teacher Association
RAs	Reaffirmists
RIs	Rejectionists
RIC	Rural Improvement Club
Samakana	Samahan ng Malayang Kababaihang Nagkakaisa (national alliance of urban poor women's organizations)
SPRINC	Self-help Programme for Indigenous and Tribal Communities
UNA	United Nations Agency
UNCED	United Nations Conference on Environment and Development
WISAP	Women's International Solidarity Affair in the Philippines
WTO	World Trade Organization

Glossary

Ading	address used for younger siblings
Amok	state of murderous frenzy
Apo Dios	Father God
Balasang di kalman	'the girls of yesteryear'
Barangay	administrative unit under a municipality, which is governed by an elected captain and council
Barrio	poor community
Bodong	peace pact (Kalinga term)
Bolo	cutting knife
BONGO	Business-organized NGO (NGO term)
Camote	sweet potato
Carabao	water buffalo
Chica-chica	small talk
Come-'n-goes	Seasonal migrants (village term)
COME 'N GOs	NGOs that never or only briefly operate (NGO term)
Debate*	reference to crisis in the movement that started in 1992
Deep Penetrating Agents*	military infiltrators in the movement
Exposure	staying with poor people to be exposed to their living conditions (NGO term)
Facipulation	facilitation and manipulation (NGO term)
Gangsa	brass gong, central to Cordillera celebrations
Ginebra	gin
GRINGO	Government-run NGO (NGO term)
G-string	A long strip of cloth wrapped around as a waistband with the end-parts hanging at the front and back covering the loins
Hiya	sensitivity, timidity, related to feelings of shame
Ifugao	local vernacular, mainly used in the province of Ifugao
Igorot	generic name for the inhabitants of the Cordillera
Ilokano	regional vernacular, used in the Cordillera as a lingua franca
Imon	jealousy

Kaigorotan	CPA concept in 1996 representing all 'tribes' in the Cordillera
Kakaasi	literally 'the pitiful', the 'indigent' people
Kalinga	local vernacular, mainly used in the province of Kalinga
Kankanaey	local vernacular, mainly used in Mountain Province
Makulit	stubborn
Manang	respectful address for older sister, also used for older women
Manong	respectful address for older brother, also used for older men
Middle Forces	city-based, middle-class professionals (NGO term) ·
Organizer	staff facilitating local organizing processes (NGO term)
Pagta ti Bodong	peace pact agreement
Pakikisama	conform or give concession to group wishes in order to maintain smooth interpersonal relations (Tagalog term)
Pakiramdam	feeling the other; tendency to act according to what one thinks is the desire of higher-ups (Tagalog term)
Pechen	peace pact (Bontok term)
Pinoy	Filipino
Principio*	'principle', refers to the movement's ideology
Pulutan	a popular appetizer made of intestines fried in blood
Querida	mistress
Reaffirmists	loyalist NDF faction after the 1992 split
Rectification*	campaign in NDF to go back to the basics following 1992 crisis in the movement
Rejectionists*	those who abandoned the NDF in the 1992 crisis of the movement
Reformists*	those affecting change within the ruling system without effectively supplanting it
Sitio	a subdivision of a *barangay*
Solid organizing*	community organizing according to step-by-step model
Step-by-step*	principle of organizing model
Sweeping organizing*	superficial work in communities
Tagalog	linguistic base of the national Philippine language
Tampu	a large range of 'sulking behaviour'
Tao	common people
Tsinelas	rubber slippers
Turfing	tendency among NGOs to monopolize clients
Utang na loob	life-long moral obligations
Vochong	peace pact (Kalinga language, synonym of *Bodong*)

* A term used by the National Democratic movement and by NGOs within it

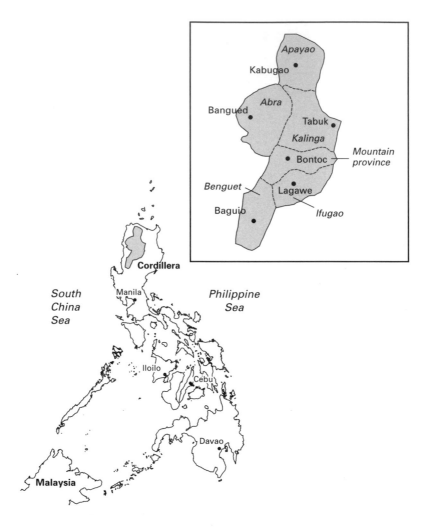

The Cordillera of the Philippines

ONE
Introduction: The Politics of NGO-ing

Helen Fielding, the author who rose to fame with her hilarious accounts of the slightly overweight Bridget Jones searching for true love, has also written a novel about NGO humanitarian assistance to an African country, apparently modelled after Sudan. This novel, *Cause Celeb* (1994), tells of a woman called Rosie, who finds herself increasingly bored with her life as a public relations manager of celebrities in London. Moreover, when her love life reaches a dead end, Rosie follows her impulse to work for a humanitarian NGO in Africa. Several years later an acute emergency arises in the refugee camps, to which the humanitarian community fails to respond. In desperation, Rosie turns to her famous friends in London to set up a 'Live Aid campaign' in order to prevent thousands of people from dying of hunger.

In the novel, Rosie's NGO does what organizations do: it has a mission and clear objectives, staff with differentiated responsibilities, and it works with a budget for planned activities. Yet the novel also brings out how this NGO is shaped by actors in the organization and their surrounding networks. These people carry out activities according to their understanding of the situation and follow the whims of their personalities, motivated by various combinations of sacrifice, self-interest, vanity and compassion. It also places the humanitarian activities in their political context, both in the local situation of a country at war and in the politics of development bureaucracies and fundraising. Finally, the novel delightfully turns the refugees into real people – good *and* bad, lovable *and* pitiful – who actively endeavour to enrol NGO staff members and visitors to provide the necessary assistance.

Fielding's novel is strikingly different from most of the scholarly literature on NGOs. Reading this literature, one is usually presented with a black-and-white picture in which managers play the lead roles, all other actors remain silent and the organizations unfold their objectives in a participatory way. One wonders what these tidy organizations have to do with the other realities that reach us from developing countries, including social and political movements, conflict and fundamentalism. And one keeps wondering what really happens inside the organizations and how this relates to the lives of the NGO staff, volunteers and beneficiaries.

Why would Helen Fielding succeed in giving this real-life account of an NGO where development scholars have failed, apart from the obvious reason that she brings her literary talent to this task? A first answer to this question may be that anthropologists, although well equipped to unravel the internal dynamics of social units, have hardly bothered to study organizations. After they made some breakthroughs in organization studies, starting with the Hawthorne experiments in the 1930s, they seem to have abandoned this interest since the 1950s (Wolf 1990; Bate 1997).[1] Only recently has this interest been revived (see, for instance, Wright 1994 and Fox 1998). Literature on NGOs has by and large taken for granted their organizational properties. As a result, the question of what is *non-governmental* about NGOs has been extensively debated, whereas the more essential one of what is *organizational* about them has largely been ignored.

Sad to say, the second answer to this question is probably that Fielding could do the job precisely because she is not a development expert. Anthropology – and development studies more generally – have been accused of being too much incorporated into development (see, for instance, Gardner and Lewis 1996). Most studies looking into NGOs have indeed been undertaken from within development. As Stirrat and Henkel (1997: 68) charged, these studies 'take for granted the underlying assumptions of the new development orthodoxy and work within that paradigm'. This has been the case as much with academic as with applied studies, and has no doubt been exacerbated by the majority of academic projects that have been commissioned by NGOs or funding agencies, leaving researchers little room for critical exploration outside the formal and expected. There have, of course, been studies that take the language and practices of development as their subject and these have been growing in number.[2] However, NGOs have not been very central to the concerns of such critical development studies. More often than not they escape scrutiny and are simply posited as alternative signs of hope against dominant development discourse.

A final answer to the question of why NGO literature seems so remote from NGO realities may be found in the politics of publishing. In literary prose, the idea that a story about how a few people organize their lives may be of wider public interest is uncontested. No publisher would demand that Rosie's humanitarian work should take her to at least six refugee camps in three different continents in order to avoid the novel's appeal being limited to a small circle of Sudan-loving people. And yet, academic publishers do exactly that. It has become increasingly difficult to find an outlet for ethnographic case studies. Although publishers may privately admit that they appreciate the value of in-depth studies for the fresh insights these can produce, they maintain that 'the market' demands comparative studies in order to reach a wide readership. Hence, published NGO work mainly consists of comparative volumes, which, through lack of space, can only scratch the surface of each of the cases, probably against the better judgement of the authors involved. This book none the less presents the story of one NGO and its institutional surroundings. It could be written because I had the opportunity to work for three years in a local development NGO in the Philippines, while researching the on-going organizing processes.[3] Then, I was lucky to find space in a university to work on the manuscript and a publisher willing to take the risk of an ethnographic case study on NGOs.

Why This Book?

In the 1980s NGOs became a major phenomenon in development, when their enormous rise in numbers even made some speak of an 'associational revolution' (Salamon 1994: 109). As Tvedt (1998) stipulates, the usual answer to why NGOs were formed in such large numbers is that they fill the gaps created by withdrawal of government control under pressure of neoliberal reform policies. Criticizing such functionalist third-sector views of NGOs, Tvedt argues instead that NGOs have to be analysed 'as an outcome of complicated processes where factors like international ideological trends, donor policies and agendas interact with national historical and cultural conditions in complex ways' (Tvedt 1998: 4). Tvedt's approach explains why, on the one hand, so many NGOs in developing countries take the same shape, goals and methods of working, and how, on the other, variations in national conditions account for different NGO histories and practices in each of these countries. However, it cannot explain diversity among NGOs in countries, and more importantly, it cannot explain contradictions and inconsistencies within NGOs. Although Tvedt rightly points to the interplay of international and national processes in NGOs, what remains problematic, to my mind, is the implicit premise that, however complicated, there is none the less a single answer to the questions of why NGOs are formed, how they are given meaning and how they operate. Like other NGO approaches, his work is limited by the implicit assumption that NGOs constitute a single reality.

The central issue addressed by this book is that there is no single answer to the questions of what an NGO *is*, what it *wants* and what it *does*. NGOs are many things at the same time. An NGO may adopt a certain structure, but in practice where are its boundaries? NGOs present different faces to different stakeholders, for instance in relating to donor representatives, clients or colleagues. Which is the real face, or, in case they are all real, what does that mean for our understanding of NGOs? There are always different ideas of what the NGO should be, among and within staff, management and stakeholders. How do these notions compete, and what role do they play in shaping the practice of the organization? To understand NGOs, this book argues that we have to take on board a more dynamic approach to organizations, pay more attention to the working of discourse within them and, above all, accord more importance to the question of how actors in and around NGOs deal with the local, international and global complexities that affect NGOs' shapes, values and practices. Such an approach to organizations and organizational discourse will provide a vehicle to comprehend otherwise unresolved questions about the diversity among NGOs and the discrepancies observed in their histories, ideologies and practices. Most importantly, it brings out the political nature of NGO work. As I will argue throughout the book, everything happening in and around NGOs has a bearing on the politics of power within the organizations, the politics of organizational legitimation and, finally, the politics of (local and global) development.

Much of what NGO people do is inspired by and affects the power politics of the internal and external control and allocation of NGO resources, ideas and activities. This can be called the everyday politics of NGOs (see Kerkvliet 1991: 11). At the same time, NGO actions are geared towards legitimation, which means that, in order to find clients and supportive stakeholders, NGOs have to convince others of their appropriateness and trustworthiness (see Bailey 1971). Finally, NGOs are not just the product of interrelating international and national developments and politics, they also play a role in such politics. Although development policy often continues to lean on the notion of NGOs as value-driven and apolitical, this has increasingly proven not to be the case. Often, contrary to their appearance, NGOs make ideological choices and, wittingly or unwittingly, they do play political roles (Hulme and Goodhand 2000). These different kinds of politics are each important in the realities playing on and affected by NGOs. How they intertwine and work on one another will, in this book, be captured by an actor-oriented approach to the organizations and discourses of NGOs.

An Actor-orientation to the Organization of NGOs

A more dynamic understanding of organizations starts with treating them not as things, but as open-ended processes. Organizations have no fixed boundaries and do not operate in isolation. People act through multiple social settings and turn organizations in overlapping networks that are in constant flux (Nuijten 1998). Moreover, organizations constitute multiple realities: they are many things at the same time (Morgan 1986). It is not clear in advance how the different meanings of an organization coincide, interact, dominate, facilitate or divide. This implies that students of NGOs must shift their attention away from organizational features, structures and reports to the everyday practices of the social actors in and around the organization. Rather than taking organizations at face value, we have to ask and observe how the claims and performances of NGOs acquire meaning in practice. NGOs are not things, but processes, and instead of asking what an NGO is, the more appropriate question then becomes how 'NGO-ing' is *done*.

There is a divide in NGO literature between approaches that view NGOs primarily as being shaped by people – in particular charismatic leaders and participatory methods – and those that view NGOs primarily as outcomes of and steered by situated historical and political processes. Yash Tandon (1996), for instance, considers NGOs as tools of international neoliberal development policies. Similarly, Wiebe Nauta (2001) understands South African NGOs as by-products of apartheid, having lost their significance in the post-apartheid years. More comprehensive approaches, like that of Tvedt discussed above, consider international and national developments while acknowledging the importance of NGO leaders in building NGOs. Yet, when NGO leaders are important, where do they derive their power from and what is the explanation of their success? If it is charisma, how does it work, and would it also work at other times and places? Surely, people and structural processes are both important, but how do they operate together? Again, I think the answers to these questions must be found in the everyday practices of NGO actors.

My insistence on the importance of taking into account everyday practices in organizations is founded on an actor orientation. Such orientation starts with the premise that social actors have agency (Giddens 1984; Long 1992). They reflect upon their experiences and what happens around them, and use their knowledge and capabilities to interpret and respond to development. An actor orientation recognizes that people operate within the limitations of structural constraints, but emphasizes that such constraints operate through people. Constraints only become effective through the mediation of interpreting actors. People in turn are social actors, whose agency is shaped by their life worlds, experience and social networks, among other factors. This theoretical notion about the mutuality of actors and structures has important methodological ramifications for studying NGOs. It means that gauging why and how these organizations come about and operate in the context of local and global developments requires studying their everyday practices. We must follow how NGO actors define the situation, choose their goals and find room for manoeuvre to realize projects. We must try to make sense of people's motivations, ideas and activities by taking into account their past and present surroundings, social networks and histories. And we must observe the way they deal with NGO-ing, because this conveys practical knowledge, implicit interpretations and power processes taking place in these organizations.

This book is based on such research of one local NGO. From 1993 to 1996 I was affiliated to an organization that is concerned with indigenous women and development in the Philippines. I did research for it, travelled with staff members to villages, conferences and donor meetings, shared a house with one of the NGO leaders of the region, underwent – with my baby – local rituals for newborns, shared numerous moments of office and family life, and participated and observed. I followed the actors in different domains of work, dealing in formal and informal ways with one another and with their stakeholders in order to analyse how NGOs come about, acquire meaning, and find legitimation.

NGO as a claim-bearing label Most books on NGOs start by defining or classifying these organizations along a number of dimensions, such as their origins, function, ownership, approach and scale of operation (Clark 1991: 40–41, Farrington and Bebbington 1993: 3–5). Leaving aside the usefulness of these definitions and classifications for different purposes, I think it is important to note that, by identifying properties to distinguish 'real' from 'non-real' NGOs (see, for example, Fowler 1997: 32), these definitions themselves become part of the politics of NGO-ing. In the Philippines, the matter of fake NGOs is taken very seriously. Karina Constantino-David (1992: 138) speaks, for instance, of 'NGOs which *hide under the cover of development* [my emphasis] but are really set up for economic and/or political reasons'. A range of acronyms has emerged for each of the 'fake' NGOs, such as GRINGOs for government-run NGOs, BONGOs for business-organized NGOs, and COME 'N GOs for fly-by-night NGO entrepreneurs who never, or only briefly, operate (ibid; see also Constantino-David 1998).

I found that identifying fake NGOs is not a neutral occupation: it is political. Processes by which organizations attribute 'genuine-ness' or 'fake-ness' to themselves and others are conflictual and power-ridden. Competition over funds, popular support and space in public discourse is strong, and it is common to find NGOs accusing *each other* of being fakes. When I worked with NGOs in the Philippines, it could happen that staff members of X were convinced that Y consisted of 'opportunists looking for self-enrichment', while staff members of Y implied with the same ardour that X represented a 'cover organization for politically subversive activities'. The outcome of these struggles over which organizations are entitled to call themselves NGOs can have far-reaching consequences for the funding, room for manoeuvre and even the very existence of these organizations.

My problem with NGO definitions and classifications is that they pre-empt the question of why and how particular organizations become *NGOs* rather than any other type of association or non-association. The defini-tions put boundaries around the phenomenon. In doing so, they cut across the self-referrals of organizations, and therefore fail to bring out the meaning of the NGO label as such. This study starts from the opposite direction. It considers all those organizations that present themselves as NGOs. Whether these are 'genuinely' working for development, or consist of a 'family business', a 'criminal organization' or a 'political instrument', is not relevant to my argument. What is important is that they adopt the label of NGO. This label is a *claim-bearing label*. In its most common use, it claims that the organization is 'doing good for the development of others'. The label has a moral component. Precisely because it is doing good, the organization can make a bid to access funding and public representation.

The meaning of the label NGO, as an organization that does good for the development of others, is not universal and is contested by two other views of NGOs. One of these is political, seeing NGOs as extensions of depoliticized neoliberal development discourse. It criticizes the political role of NGOs and is found in particular among People's Organizations or social movements that object to being included in 'the NGO com-munity'. A peace advocate aptly expressed this by saying: 'I have always been an activist, until somebody told me I was an NGO person'. The other view comes from within development bureaucracies and has recently gained ground among the public at large.[4] It is a generalized view of NGOs as unaccountable organizations that are primarily concerned with advancing the material well-being of their own staff. I will concentrate here on the dominant label of NGO as an organization that does good.

Conceiving of 'NGO' as a claim-bearing label opens an avenue to studying the everyday politics of NGO legitimation. Through everyday politics, NGO actors negotiate the meaning of their organization and enrol outsiders into accepting it. Acquiring legitimation as 'an organ-ization that is doing good for the development of others' is no easy job. It entails first convincing others that a situation or population needs development. Second, it requires convincing others that the intervention of the NGO is indispensable and appropriate, and that it has no self-interest in the envisaged programme. Third, it requires convincing others that the NGO is able and reliable, in other words, trustworthy and capable of carrying out the intervention. For NGO actors, the legitimation of their organization is a matter of (organizational) survival. The main asset of an NGO is its reputation as an organization doing good for the development of others, and earning and maintaining this reputation is a major occupation of NGO actors.

I must stress that my focus on legitimation processes and politics should not be taken as suggesting that NGOs generally are untrustworthy. Many NGOs, including those I have been privileged to work with, largely live up to their claims. What I do argue, however, is that there is no *necessary* correspondence between an NGO's worth, the way it manages its image and the way it is perceived by the outside world.

Discourse and NGO politics An interest in the politics of NGO-ing takes one invariably to study language and discourse, since, as Fairclough puts it: 'politics partly consists in the disputes and struggles which occur in language and over language' (1989: 23). Discourses are more or less coherent sets of references that frame the way we understand and act upon the world around us. They are an ensemble of ideas, concepts and categories through which meaning is given to phenomena (Gasper and Apthorpe 1996: 2). Due to the influential work of Foucault, discourse has come to be seen as closely interweaving knowledge and power. The effect of discourse is that certain ways of understanding society, including its organization and the distribution of power, become excluded, whereas others attain authority.

In the 1990s, several studies focused on regimes of development discourse that 'identify appropriate and legitimate ways of practising development as well as speaking and thinking about it' (Grillo 1997: 12). Ferguson (1990) analyses, for the case of Lesotho, how development policy constitutes its subject as a 'Less Developed Country'. Deprived of its dynamics, history and politics, this subject becomes a proper target for the technical development interventions that these agencies have to offer. In a similar vein, Arturo Escobar (1995) contends that since the Second World War a global language has emerged that creates development, under-development and the subjects of development. From this language, a whole body of practices has followed centred around planned development interventions. Both authors claim that these discourses are hegemonic in shaping development. Ferguson (1990: xv) likens the discourse to an anti-politics machine, 'depoliticising everything it touches', and Escobar (1995: 39) speaks of 'a space in which only certain things could be said and imagined' (ibid.). More particularly, in the 1990s, many considered that neoliberal discourse was able to attain hegemony because the end of the Cold War largely silenced contesting political themes of socialism and/or Third Worldism (Duffield 1998).

These studies of development discourse also explain the rise of NGOs in recent decades. While some, such as Escobar, seem to view this rise as a counterpoint to the dominant development discourse, others elaborate that the growth of NGOs is in fact an expression of this discourse. NGOs are important to neoliberal policies because they can provide services that receding states are no longer able to deliver. Wood speaks, in this respect, of a franchise state, where 'state responsibilities are franchised to NGOs, mediated to a considerable extent by the ideological prescriptions of donors' (1997: 80). NGOs are also considered to contribute to neo-liberalism because they strengthen civil society, which is conditional in achieving democracy (Putnam 1993). Although many celebrate the role of development NGOs in civil society for its potency to advance human rights and development, this has also evoked a critical view of NGOs as advancing the neoliberal project and collaborating in the depoliticization of development. Yash Tandon, for instance, calls NGOs the 'missionaries of the new [neoliberal] era' (1996: 182; see also Pearce 1993; Arellano-López and Petras 1994).

These works on development discourse may explain the rise of NGOs (or at least explain why so many organizations take on the label), but tell us little about their practical workings. By claiming that they are the outcome of a hegemonic development discourse, it is implied that NGOs operate according to a single discursive framework. This leaves no room to take into account that development organizations may be inspired by alternative ideological or religious frameworks, let alone that their prac-tices reveal how these different frameworks intertwine. The changes that local responses make to development interventions are ignored. Local actors are not merely overcome by development: they interpret, bend and negotiate it.[5] Hence, these works provide no clues as to how discourse works in everyday development situations in communities.

Lately, the very idea of a hegemonic discourse of development has been discredited. In the first place, several authors have asserted that there are always multiple discourses, 'a multiplicity of voices within development, even if some are more powerful than others' (Grillo 1997: 22; see also Preston 1994; Apthorpe and Gasper 1996; O'Brien et al. 2000). Even though one discourse may appear dominant, there are always parallel, residual, emerging or counter-discourses.[6] As Norman Long stipulates: 'since social life is never so unitary as to be built upon one single type of discourse, it follows that, however restricted their choice, actors always face some alternative ways of formulating their objectives, deploying modes of action and giving reasons for their behaviour' (Long 1992: 25). In the second place, studies have shown that discourse gets reinterpreted at the local level. While the idea of hegemonic discourse implies that such development discourse is incommensurable with local knowledge, and therefore no interpenetrating takes place (Hobart 1993), it is now recognized that there is interplay of discourses. Arce and Long conclude that we should abandon 'a binary opposition between Western and non-Western epistemologies and practice, and instead attempt to deal with the intricate interplay and joint appropriation and transformation of different bodies of knowledge' (2000: 24; see also Arce and Long 1992). The meanings of development notions are renegotiated in the local context (Pigg 1992). So, even when a certain vocabulary is adopted it may acquire different and often multiple meanings in the localities. In a remarkable study of discourses of identity in multiethnic London, Gerd Baumann shows how local people have different meanings of the concepts of 'culture' and 'community' that fit into two opposing discourses, a dominant and a popular counter-discourse. They use these meanings contextually in such a way that local usage and practice 'sometimes affirmed and sometimes denied the dominant discourse' (1996: 30). Hence, people find room for manoeuvre within the multiplicity of discourses they have available.

This line of analysis gives a more dynamic interpretation of discourse, acknowledging the multiple realities of development of the agency of people in bending discourse to their own needs and realities. It leaves us, however, with the question of what the Foucaudian idea – that discourse inescapably frames our understanding and practice – means for development NGOs. Are we instead left with a market of discourses, a 'free place of ideas' that people can strategically employ to their own interest and liking? We only need to think of religious and ideological fundamentalism, affecting NGOs as much as other parts of society, to realize this is not the case. Several chapters of this book show that, at certain points in time, particular NGO discourses indeed succeed in effecting a certain closure of alternative readings of situations and relations. More lasting than fashions, these discourses are effective in re-creating the past, stipulating policy for the present, reshaping organizational forms and practices, and including, excluding and reshuffling people's relations. Similar observations can be made for other NGO communities around the world.[7] They may include the 'takeover' of a gender discourse from a class-based language; a fascination with neoliberalism rather than Third Worldism; religious ideas swapped for development notions, or vice versa; the introduction of rational management at the expense of goodwill and solidarity; or the hegemony of kinship obligations and community over NGO and organization. The seemingly contradictory working of discourses whereby, on the one hand, actors have available multiple discourses and, on the other, certain discourses at certain times become dominant in framing actors' notions, calls for a yet further elaboration of the concept of discourse.

My position regarding discourse can be likened to Anthony Giddens's notion of the duality of structure. Paraphrasing this author (1984: 5), one can say that discourses are both the medium and outcome of the practices they organize. This position, the duality of discourse, steps away from the tradition of Foucault, in which discourses work like structures, 'constituting us to our very roots, producing just those forms of subjectivity on which they can most efficiently go to work' (Eagleton 1991: 47). It also steps away from the idea that people can change discourse as easily as a pair of shoes, and manipulate ideas to their liking. Discourses are not innocent, but can become very powerful. The more dominant a discourse, the more it operates as a set of rules about what can and cannot be said and done, and about what.

While recognizing that discourses *can* become powerful by closing options and creating new realities, we should never start an analysis by assuming that discourse is powerful. First, we should ask *when* and *how* particular discourses become more powerful than others (Watts 1993: 265). In the words of Bakhtin (1981/1935: 259–423), we should ask ourselves how and through what centripetal or centrifugal processes do certain discourses become dominant, or, alternatively, lose their central position. Second, when a discourse becomes powerful, we have to ask how it affects NGO practice in the interplay with alternative and everyday discourses.

In order to deal with these questions, the concept of social interface turned out to be very helpful. Studying the interplay of different discourses and how they are negotiated in everyday practices can be accessed by a focus on interfaces. Social interfaces typically occur at points where different, and often conflicting, life worlds or social fields intersect. Since social interfaces are real or imaginary meeting points of different discourses, 'studies of social interfaces can bring out the dynamics of the interactions taking place and show how the goals, perceptions, interests, and relationships of the various parties may be reshaped as a result of their interaction' (Long 1989: 2). Many cases in this book provide such an interface analysis to delineate the strategic use of, negotiations over, and working of development discourse.

Philippine NGOs: A History of Turbulent Politics[8]

The Philippines is a good country in which to study the everyday politics of NGOs. It has probably the largest NGO density in the world[9] and its history brings out clearly the political nature of NGOs and their forebears, civic organizations. Philippine NGOs work on socioeconomic development, community organizing, political campaigns and advocacy, arts and drama, research and publications. They are concerned with issues of poverty, human rights, justice, environment, gender, ethnicity and conflict resolution, sectoral interests of fisher folk, urban poor, farmers, prostituted women, mineworkers and migrants. Some are highly specialized, others combine several of these interests and fields of work.[10] A handful of NGOs have nationwide operations, hundreds of staff and multimillion-dollar budgets, such as the widely known Philippine Rural Reconstruction Movement (PRRM). The vast majority of NGOs in the Philippines, including those figuring in this book, have fewer than 50 staff members (Clarke 1998: 98). Many find their pedigree in social movements or church social action programmes (the Philippines is the only predominantly Christian area in the region, with an estimated 83 per cent of the population belonging to the Catholic Church, the remainder to Protestant churches and Islam). Some are (elite) family foundations. Others are NGOs aligned to politicians, NGOs grown out of state-instigated co-operatives, initiatives born out of academic outreach programmes, local branches of international NGOs, and a vast number of private organizations that ebb and flow with the tides of financial opportunities.

An important ground for distinction among Philippine NGOs is their political identity. Philippine NGOs do not represent a unified development 'community', but mirror the full range of Philippine political interests and contradictions. The NGOs I discuss in this book belong to a radical political movement, the so-called National Democratic movement. This social movement derives its political inspiration from the ideas of the National Democratic Front, an alliance of organizations comprising, among others, the Communist Party of the Philippines (CPP) and the New People's Army (NPA). As we will see, this feature is more important than any other in their relations with stakeholders. To understand this, we have to go back into the history of NGOs in the Philippines. Development NGOs, as we know them today, date back to the 1970s. Their forebears, civic and voluntary organizations, emerged from the 1880s onwards. Gerard Clarke studied the history of these and found the political meaning of voluntary organizations in this country far more important than their socioeconomic impact. According to him: 'Philippine NGOs and their antecedents, civic and political organizations, have long been used in the pursuit of political objectives' (Clarke 1998: 66).

Since the 1880s, civic organizations, either church-based, state-led, or aligned to partisan organizations, have all played a role in the making *and* breaking of revolutions and other political movements. This is well illustrated by the history of women's organizations. One of the first such organizations, the Women's Red Cross Association, was formed in 1899 to provide humanitarian relief to Filipino soldiers fighting the takeover of the Philippines by the United States from Spanish colonizers in 1898. The Americans, once having won the war, likewise used women's organizations in their 'pacification' campaign of the country, in part by forming the Philippines Women's League for Peace (Angeles 1989: 107–29). From 1905 onwards they encouraged the formation of a suffragette movement that, while enhancing women's emancipation, couched their aspirations within the framework of the American colonial apparatus (Jayawardena 1986: 155–66). Civic organizations continued to play a role in the patronage politics that evolved in the post-independence state, and remained instrumental to the state's political projects. The first organizations for rural development, NGOs *avant-la-lettre*, were instituted by the newly independent state, as well as by churches and elite foundations, in order to curb local peasant rebellions that might otherwise turn into Communist insurgencies (see Kerkvliet 1977).

The NGOs discussed in this book belong to the so-called *progressive* NGOs, associated with social protest and oppositional politics. They find some exemplary predecessors in earlier revolutionary movements in the nineteenth century and in the peasant uprisings of the 1950s, but mainly originated in the later 1960s. A protest movement then swept the country, as elsewhere in the world, centred around nationalism and student activism. New organizations sprang up, while existing organizations turned increasingly progressive, such as those of the Catholic Church, where Liberation Theology radicalized the concept of social action (Alegre 1996: 8–9; Labayen 1995: 31–41; Fabros 1987). These years also saw the foundation of the Communist Party of the Philippines (CPP) and its armed branch, the New People's Army (NPA), which in 1971 expanded into the National Democratic Front (NDF).[11]

In 1972, President Ferdinand Marcos declared martial law, marking the beginning of 14 years of dictatorship. All opposition groups and progressive social organizations were banned and numerous activists and community organizers were arrested, tortured and killed. Those who escaped continued their work underground as part of the NDF. Aboveground socioeconomic and human rights organizations resumed from the mid-1970s onwards, mostly under the umbrella of the churches and often staffed with cadres deployed from underground groups (Alegre 1996: 16; Rocamora 1994: 9–43). The murder of Marcos's best-known political opponent, Ninoy Aquino, in 1983, triggered a wave of political protest. A period of feverish mass mobilizations and the upsurge of numerous organizations followed, further eroding Marcos's dictatorship. This culminated in the so-called 'People's Power Revolution' of 1986, after presidential elections in which Marcos declared himself the winner. In the days that followed, a massive uprising, supported by the USA and by the Philippine military shifting their loyalty, ousted the dictator, and Corazon Aquino, widow of Ninoy, became president.

It was in this period, the 1980s, that actors of the protest movement increasingly made a distinction between the different kinds of organizations among their ranks. From then on, the term 'People's Organization' (PO) was reserved for community-based organizations. 'Sectoral Movements' came to refer to 'grassroots' movements, such as those composed of peasants or indigenous people, or the POs of the urban poor,[12] or to thematic social movements such as the human rights movement. In addition, the word 'NGO' started to gain currency, to refer to what Edwards and Hulme (1992: 14) call 'intermediary organizations, who support grassroots work through funding, technical advice and advocacy'. The distinction between POs and NGOs turned out to be of growing importance. In the course of the decade, a greater disparity evolved between the different categories, which increasingly came to correspond to empirical groups of organizations. NGOs became more 'professional': they paid their staff (slightly) higher salaries, required from them a higher education and a good command of English.

Under Aquino's presidency, the state-centralist, anti-NGO policies of Marcos gave way to differentiated state practices. NGOs proliferated. They were given recognition in the Constitution, followed by the Local Government Code of 1991, which provided space for significant NGO and PO representation in local government (Brillantes 1992). While the number of NGOs grew, the progressive NGOs increasingly fragmented into multiple communities and non-communities.[13] The various groups were subject to different treatment by the state, especially by its military elements. The National Democratic NGOs, in particular, experienced ruthless human rights abuses, surpassing even the Marcos years in intensity (Amnesty International 1992). Only towards the early 1990s did the human rights situation start to improve, although pockets of anti-NGO propaganda and human rights violations continue to this day. Notwithstanding the differences, NGOs all engaged in coalition work in order to scale up their activities. Coalitions amalgamated further, until some embraced thousands of organizations spanning the whole political spectrum. The late 1980s thus became the 'golden age' of coalition building (Alegre 1996: 28).

When Fidel Ramos took over the presidency in 1992, the number of development NGOs in the Philippines was at its height. Many of these had no particular political profile, but National Democratic NGOs still comprised a large part of those that had. In the following years, a split in the underground National Democratic Front resulted in a schism within this latter group, which could be traced back to conflicts that had lingered on since the early 1980s (Rocamora 1994: 107–39). Those in the NDF who continued to align with the leadership were labelled Reaffirmists (RAs). Those who did not, and as a consequence abandoned the movement, were called Rejectionists (RJs).[14] Neither friends nor foes of the movement had anticipated quite how much this split would affect the National Democratic development NGOs, which appeared through time to have loosened their ties to the underground movement. What evolved, however, was something close to a battlefield. NGOs and coalitions split apart, accompanied by fierce fights, and staff were ousted by whatever means, including the dragging up of age-old controversies. During a year or more, they competed in every way over office equipment, bank accounts, donor agencies and, of course, over control of the People's Organizations they worked with. After the dust had settled, it was clear that a number of NGOs had not survived and many staff members had withdrawn from NGO work. The 'reject' or breakaway NGOs embarked on a number of different strategies and alignments. For the remaining National Democratic NGOs, their reaffirmation was but the first step in a *rectification* process that was to last for several years. The whole experience of the organizations was summed up, assessed and reassessed, and errors defined and corrected, until slowly a 'new' National Democratic movement took shape. The NGOs in the Cordillera region belonged to this last group. My fieldwork spanned the years of rectification that followed the split. It was a period full of organizational and personal tension: stakes were high and so was the emotional involvement of NGO actors. These were years of intense discussion and reflection on the character of NGOs, their discursive repertoires and organizational strategies. Many of these discussions have found their way into the analysis that follows.

The Cordillera: contested development This book is about NGOs in one of the regions of the Philippines where development has become highly contested: the Cordillera. This mountainous area in the north of the Philippines is comprised of six provinces, with approximately one million inhabitants. The regional capital, Baguio City, is 225 kilometres from Manila. Travelling through the Cordillera is a breathtaking affair. Its one high road has many rough stretches: bumpy and – with a rainy season of eight months a year – usually muddy and prone to landslides. Additional roads are few, and several villages can only be reached by days of hiking. The area is inhabited by the so-called Igorot people with their world-renowned rice terraces. During four centuries of colonization, the

Spanish never succeeded in bringing these people under their control, and apart from some missionary outposts, they were not hispanicized. It was only under the American administration of this century that the Cordillera became incorporated into the Philippine state. The name Igorots was given to them by the Spanish, who erroneously labelled the mountain peoples as tribes. In the course of the centuries several ethnographic maps were constructed of the area, usually distinguishing seven or eight tribes according to the different languages spoken in the region. Not only did they haphazardly omit certain groups (Lewis 1992; Resurreccion 1999), they also assumed levels of organization that did not exist beyond the village communities (Prill-Brett 1989). Nevertheless, in the course of time these labels became reality, to a certain extent as identity markers: being 'Kalinga' or 'Ibaloi' increasingly acquired meaning in peoples' lives (Russell 1983). The term 'tribe' has become part of the local vernaculars, for example in expressions such as 'tribal wars'.

Igorot was a derogatory label, short for 'uncivilized naked savages' (Scott 1993: 55), an image confirmed by publications with titles such as *Taming Philippine Headhunters* (Keesing and Keesing 1934; see also Kane 1933). These images disregarded the intricate institutions that had evolved to regulate conflict and headhunting practices between the villages, as appeared in later studies, when the Cordillerans received more appreciative names, such as *Mountain Arbiters* (Dozier 1966). It is only in the last few decades that Igorot became a self-applied label (although not to all Cordillera inhabitants), as part of an increasingly positive identification with the 'indigenous' character of the area and its cultures. In the Constitution of 1987 the indigenous lobby resulted in a clause granting the Cordillera the status of an autonomous region. Since then, two Organic Acts have been proposed to realize this autonomy, but in both instances these were turned down in plebiscites, in 1990 and 1997 respectively, leaving the matter as yet undecided.

Seen from the outside, the lives of people in the Cordillera are still highly organized through traditional practices and techniques. Viewed from the inside, the area is, however, very diverse, both in cultural terms (de Raedt 1987) and in the extent to which it has been integrated into the economic, political and sociocultural processes of the lowlands. Overall, the pace of change has accelerated considerably over the last 30 years (Sajor 1999), partly through a transition in livelihoods, where commercial vegetable growing has increasingly replaced terraced rice production and shifting cultivation.

The recent history of the Cordillera has been full of conflict. In the 1970s, protests against the construction of hydrological dams in the area spurred the growth of People's Organizations and movements, and the formulation of an indigenous discourse. At the same time, the region became a stronghold for the revolutionary struggle of the National Democratic Front and its armed wing, the New People's Army, enjoying for years much support among villagers but also fuelling existing antagonisms. A high level of militarization by the government, including the bombing of areas until the 1990s, accompanied by extensive propaganda against development NGOs, further sharpened ongoing debates. In the midst of all this the area was hit by a major earthquake in 1991, enhancing the environmental concerns people had developed in response to earlier large-scale logging. It also brought many organizations concerned with relief and the reconstruction of infrastructure and housing into the area. Meanwhile, the Philippine government increasingly pushed for the 'development' of the Cordillera, which in practice mainly meant the exploitation of its natural and cultural riches through dams, mines and tourism. This notion of development has constantly been challenged by NGOs, which supported small-scale projects and introduced concepts like participatory and sustainable development to the communities. Hence, the concept of development in the Cordillera has become highly contested.

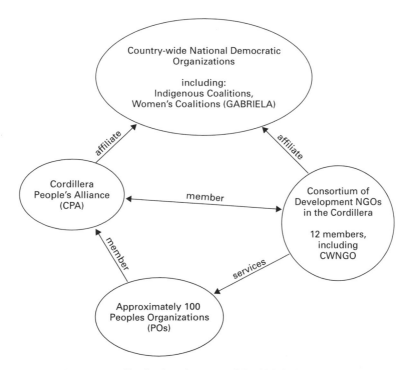

Figure 1.1 Institutional set-up of the NGO Consortium

The NGO central to this book is the Cordillera Women's NGO (CWNGO). CWNGO is concerned with indigenous women and development in the Cordillera region of the Philippines. It was founded in 1984 and works with women in five provinces of the region. Its main office is based in the regional capital of Baguio City, with an additional four small offices in the other provincial capitals. CWNGO is one of the NGOs that appeared from this development cacophony. It belongs to a group of development NGOs that emerged in the 1980s out of social protest in the region. This group of twelve has formed a Consortium of Development NGOs in the Cordillera. Each NGO operates independently, but is accountable to the Consortium, where, to a degree, NGO policies are determined by the National Democratic ideas to which the Consortium adheres. The Consortium is affiliated to a sectoral movement, the Cordillera People's Alliance (CPA). The CPA, in turn, is an umbrella that encompasses 100 local People's Organizations (POs) and support groups in the region. The institutional set-up is such that the NGOs of the Consortium provide services to assist the People's Organizations affiliated to the CPA to organize, educate, and have projects, as represented in Figure 1.1.

Cordillera Day

I like to introduce the CWNGO with an account of an annual one-day event that brings all the above-mentioned parties together: the celebration of Cordillera Day. I could equally well introduce the organization by describing its office, some of its projects in the village, a meeting of its staff or an encounter with its funding agency. Yet I have chosen to start with a window on the wider network of this NGO. In doing so, I am able to bring out the issue of organizational boundaries. Programme proposals, reports and project documents create an imagery of NGOs as clearly bounded entities, whose activities are planned in advance and periodically demarcated. One might be tempted to confound this image with real-life NGOs. However, when looking at NGO practice, the boundaries that surround the organizations and the activities become vague or may evaporate altogether. The NGO may shrivel to the proportion of a mere post box, or conversely, become a barely distinguishable part of a larger whole. The latter applies to CWNGO, which is part of a larger configuration that evolved out of the region's history. What it nevertheless means to be an NGO in this (ever changing) environment is one of the questions addressed in this book.

Cordillera Day is held yearly on 24 April and marks the anniversary of the death of Macliïng Dulag, a hero of the struggle of the 1970s and 1980s. He was killed for his opposition to the hydroelectric dams that were to destroy the ancestral lands of the Kalinga Igorots. Since his death, the Cordillera People's Alliance has organized an annual event in one of the villages or towns of the region. In 1996, the celebration took place in the regional capital, Baguio City, and was attended by an estimated 3,000 people.

Baguio City, 24 April 1996 The event is held in a community of urban poor, on top of a hill overlooking the city. It can be reached by vehicle, but most of the participants climb up on foot. The road is extremely steep, but the climb is facilitated by the swelling sound of the *gangsas*, the brass gongs that are central to all Cordillera celebrations. At the end of the road, on top of the hill, is the basketball court. At its entrance, a large banner spans the road, leaving no doubt as to the political nature of the celebration:

> Live Out The Ideals Of Our Revolutionary Martyrs.
> Unite Against The Intensified Assault Of The US–Ramos Regime.
> Advance The Filipino's Struggle For Self-Determination And National Democracy.

A backcloth to the stage inside the court elaborates on the theme set out on the banner. It is an immense mural depicting the diverse 'struggles of the Cordillera peoples' against exploitation of their natural resources and the human rights abuses of the military.

The setting of the court is like a festival. As far as possible, the place is covered by large pieces of plastic, to protect the participants from the showers that are inevitable during this season. On one side stand large tables from which meals will be served. On the other, vendors have set up their stalls to sell candies, cigarettes and refreshments. There are also sales points for handicrafts. Staff members of the Cordillera People's Alliance (CPA) sell woodcarvings to generate money. At another table, a group of workers dismissed from a weaving company sell picturesque wall decorations, which they produce with support from one of the NGOs. The most festive element of the event is the participants themselves. The expanse of colourful native attire forms an attractive picture: woven wrap-around skirts for women and G-strings[15] for men. These are worn both by the provincial delegates of the People's Organization and by the Baguio-based NGO staff. Participants who come from Manila and other parts of the Philippines wear the usual 'progressive uniform' of jeans and a T-shirt bearing a funny print or political slogan. They honour the indigenous character of the occasion by donning at least an element of Cordillera cloth, such as one of the vests, shawls or bags that are for sale in NGO offices in Manila. The variety in footwear indicates the different socio-

Figure 1.2 The Cordillera of the Philippines NGO map of the province of Ifuago (drawn after a banner presented at Cordillera Day, 1996)

economic background of participants. Cheap sandals dominate, alongside *tsinelas* (the rubber slippers worn by all Filipinos inside their houses and the fields, but only taken into the streets by poor people), hiking boots and shiny leather shoes.

Around nine o'clock in the morning, all participants sit down on the concrete floor in a semi-circle in front of the stage, on which CPA officers and speakers are already seated. The programme customarily opens with prayers, the national anthem and the reading of solidarity messages from within and outside the Philippines. It culminates in a 'banner-dance', a combination of a flag parade with an indigenous Cordillera dance to the rhythm of the continuing gong music. By the end of the dance, the music swells and hundreds of people join in, waving dozens of flags above their heads. The five provincial delegations then present the situation in their own areas. Each delegation consists of 60 to 100 people, who present their reports through songs and skits. Without exception, they denounce the government policies and development programmes implemented in the region as part of the government's goal to join the ranks of the Asian Tigers with their booming economies. First, they express their opposition to the development of open-pit mines that 'will destroy the livelihood, environment and water sources of the Cordillera'. Other protests concern the construction of a dam and the promotion of tourism in the region, such as through the banner depicted in Figure 1.2. An officer of the CPA summarizes:

> As we see, brothers and community-mates gathered here to celebrate Cordillera Day, all these projects and programmes are clearly in the interest of the foreign imperialists, joined by the rich in the Philippines, to control and continue to deplete the resources of the Cordillera.

After this, a speech is delivered by a Manila representative of a National Democratic organization to which the CPA is allied. In contrast to the pleasant cultural presentations of the provinces, his address clearly aims to agitate. Standing in front of the stage, shouting into the microphone, he explains the latest developments within the National Democratic movement. He ends his speech by calling on people to 'intensify the struggle against feudalism, imperialism and bureaucratic capitalism'. While most people listen attentively, others chat, and despite the heavy tone of the speech the atmosphere remains light. I am standing to the side with a small group of CWNGO staff, all women. They giggle and challenge me to step forward and take a close-up photo of the speaker. The excitement is not caused only by his status as a national leader of the movement. We all agree about the handsome looks of this (unmarried) man, and the picture I finally take is later displayed in the office.

After the speech, everybody starts to mingle, looking for relatives and friends in the crowd. The women quite naturally group together, and I find myself in the company of current and former staff of CWNGO and other NGOs, and several village women enjoying the festive atmosphere and admiring one another's children. Long queues form in front of the tables, from which lunch is served from huge cooking pots full of pork stew with cabbage. Banana stems and coconut shells serve as plates and soup bowls respectively. While people eat and talk, rain pours down almost without interruption. If anything, it seems to add to the mood, especially when the plastic sheets cannot hold the assembled rainwater and splash it onto some unlucky people, to the great amusement of the rest. After lunch, everybody is supposed to go downtown for a rally that will be held in the city centre. This is delayed for some hours due to lack of transport, but the participants don't mind. They use the time to continue their exchange of the latest stories and gossip. Since there is no telephone network in the Cordillera provinces, the day is also used extensively by members of NGOs and People's Organizations to pass on messages, set schedules for meetings and activities, or relate some project's progress or organizational problems.

It takes until after dark before, finally, the rally starts. In a column four abreast, the march is impressively long as it moves along the main street of Baguio. At the end of the march, we gather in the square. One of the elders, wearing nothing but a G-string despite the rain, starts to chant. He keeps us spellbound. No microphone, no music to accompany him, just the melancholic sounds of the chanted story. After this, the crowd moves for a war dance around the effigy of a crocodile – the widely used symbol for politicians as hypocritical and all-devouring animals – representing President Ramos. The men from Ifugao, the most 'indigenous' province of the Cordillera, lead the dance. With careful and concentrated moves, they throw and spin their spears up in the air at every step. It is an eerie sight, illuminated by dim streetlights and reflected in the rain puddles. The dance ends by torching the effigy until it is burnt, surrounded by a mass of yelling people. Around us, the flow of the city in rush hour continues, except for a circle of curious spectators who have stopped to watch the scene.

After everyone has returned to the site, and eaten dinner, the 'solidarity night' starts. All provinces and 'sectors' (miners, workers, students, women) present something. Most of the groups called to the stage perform a dance accompanied by *gangsas*, each of them using the rhythms and steps particular to their area. Some have prepared skits. Watching the performance of the skits, it becomes clear that, for these people, 'progress' and 'development' have become terms of opprobrium. In one skit, Ramos, easily recognized by the big, unlit cigar, comes to a community and declares that he will bring 'progress', only to be kicked out by the community folk. The same happens to a man with a high hat painted with the American stars and stripes, who says he will bring 'development'. The songs reiterate: 'We don't want progress, we don't want development.'

The 'observers', participants who are not from the region, are also asked to present something. The foreigners there, around fifteen of them from different nationalities, are compelled to sing a song from their country. Some of us are prepared for the request, obviously used to the Philippine 'solidarity night' practices; others feel completely embarrassed, and take a long time to find a song that can possibly be sung. The night turns more and more into a party, with people chatting, joking, gossiping, and dancing. To the relief of the organizing committee, only a few men get drunk. After midnight, people slowly start to leave to get some sleep. However, faithful to what has become one of the Cordillera Day traditions, some of the men continue the dances until morning, and then go around with their gongs to wake up the community.

On- and off-stage: actors' networks and discourses The speeches, appearances and acts of Cordillera Day provide a window on the use of multiple discourses in the network of the People's Alliance of the Cordillera. The political language of the National Democratic movement dominates the event, but there are traces of various other discourses too. Some of these are deliberate, others simply seep in. Central to the political language is the trio of anti-feudalism, anti-imperialism and anti-bureaucratic capitalism. These have been the catchwords ever since the National Democratic movement was founded in the late 1960s, but far from being perfunctory, they are brought out passionately and explained as if new. This is related to the fact that this year's Cordillera Day took place in the midst of the rectification campaign, referred to above. One aspect of this campaign was to reinvigorate the original language of the National Democratic movement.

Then there is the indigenous discourse, as a second voice enriching National Democratic parlance. It envelops the senses through its use in clothes, dance and music. It also appears in the strong attention to topics related to ancestral land and other natural resources, and in the constant appeal to insider/outsider categories and the anti-development, anti-progress rhetoric. Third, there is the language of participation and development projects. When the provincial delegates present their reports during the programme, this is done in a cultural manner, through skits and songs. They reminisce about the participatory development techniques promoted by NGOs throughout the 1980s. The language of development projects is not part of the official programme of Cordillera Day, but often slips into the off-stage conversations in the interactions between NGO staff and PO women.

The political, indigenous and development discourses are the three pivots around which NGO work in the Cordillera region is shaped. They all provide rationales for the work, all appear in NGO writings and all contain points of reference to guide the numerous decisions and actions taken in NGO work. To some extent they are complementary, and can be applied strategically by NGO staff and management. For example, a narrative couched in development language is predominant when talking to funding agencies (ensuring the use of fashionable concepts), authorities, or those villagers who are wary of politics. The indigenous discourse gets emphasized when the NGOs deal with regional or national politics, and guides their operations in international activities and United Nations events. The National Democratic discourse is brought out in gatherings like Cordillera Day, and guides much of the interaction between the NGOs, the POs and the Cordillera People's Alliance. However, when we turn our gaze inside the NGOs, the use of multiple discourses leads to contest and conflict. As history has twice proven, during the struggle for regional autonomy and again during the episode of splits in the National Democratic movement, these conflicts can endanger the very existence of the organizations (see Chapters 2 and 3).

The picture becomes even more complicated when we take into account the discourses that dominate Cordillera Day in the off-stage interactions. Paramount among these is the language of kinship. During the day, everybody spots relatives and bits and pieces of family news form a major topic. Other such discourses concern the 'hardships of life' and 'village politics'. The relation between the on-stage and off-stage discourses is not always the same. Sometimes they are plain contradictory. Note, for example, the singing of the national anthem at an event of a movement that denies the legitimacy of the Philippine state symbolized by this anthem. They can also be translations from one another. The language of kinship, for example, has found its way to the stage in the habit of speakers to create a sense of family among the participants by addressing the audience as 'brothers and fellow townsmen'. In other instances they can be parallel or counter-narratives. 'Indigenousness', for example, turns out to have different faces. Where indigenous unity is celebrated on stage, village conflicts are relegated to the off-stage gathering. During the day, one of the participants was sitting to the side, carrying his *bolo* (cutting knife). His village was engaged in a 'tribal war' with a neighbouring village, and he was on guard to protect himself against a possible attack to revenge a murder committed by one of his fellow villagers.

The informal, off-stage interactions during Cordillera Day provide as much a window on NGO work in the region as the on-stage activities. There were many NGO staff members among the participants, both Baguio-based and from the provinces. In appearance and behaviour they did not stand out. Many originated from the region, speak the dialects and find numerous relatives and friends among the participants. Some actually live in the urban poor area where the event was held, since NGO staff are often not significantly better off economically than their clients. The man with the knife was also an NGO staff member. Staff members bring their social networks and concerns to their NGO work. Clients are also relatives, colleagues also godparents of one's children, and government officials also former colleagues. This has implications for the meanings attached to the organizations and their everyday practices. It impinges on NGO operations, albeit in a far less deliberate way than the 'official' discourses of national democracy, indigenousness and development. Everyday discourses remain largely invisible from project reports and other statements on NGO work. Nevertheless, they pattern meetings, interactions with beneficiaries, dealings with the funding agencies and other NGO activities.

By studying the interactions of NGO actors with relevant others, the dynamic interplay of official and everyday discourses becomes apparent.

Organization of the Book

The first chapters elaborate on NGO history, social embeddedness and discursive repertoires. Chapter 2 discusses the relevance of social movement theory for understanding NGOs and deals with the protest movement for regional autonomy, from which the development NGOs of the book originate and continue to be part. Chapter 3 addresses the question of how, in a situation of multiple realities, a particular discourse becomes dominant, even leading to fundamentalist tendencies. It portrays the struggles of a political movement aiming to restore its grip on development NGOs that increasingly form a depoliticizing alternative to their radical project. It particularly brings out how women's organizations endeavoured to accommodate gender issues in the National Democratic movement, but eventually subsumed their particular interests to the dominant political discourse. While the first three chapters examine how development NGOs emerge from and fare in the waves of regional political turmoil, Chapter 4 enters the everyday life world of local village women. It discusses how local people use different notions of development in order to manipulate development interventions, but also shows how a particular development discourse unwittingly changes their lives. Chapter 5 asks the pertinent question of how much room for manoeuvre NGOs can muster locally, in order to implement their programme? By reviewing a number of cases, it concludes that organizing in villages is negotiated, and that villagers are much more decisive in the outcome than NGOs. The next chapter discusses how social actors outside of the locality can make sense of NGO activities and gauge their value. This question hits at the centre of debates on NGO accountability. A theoretical analysis of this concept leads to the conclusion that transparency is a myth. The ability of NGOs to enrol others to believe their accounts and accept their trustworthiness is more important in this process than their ability to implement projects.

Chapters 1 to 6 all testify to a conception of multiple realities of NGOs, through political and discursive processes on the one hand, and local diversity and power processes on the other. The remaining chapters explore how NGO actors shape and accommodate these realities in their organizational practices and at interfaces with funding agencies and other stakeholders. Chapter 7 addresses a strikingly ill-researched topic, namely, how NGO actors in their everyday practices give meaning to the organization. This question turns out to be much more complex than simple ideas of 'management-directing-the-organization', or 'management-versus-the-rest' perspectives, can account for. The chapter shows how, through the symbolic use of particular locales, social networks and cultural institutions, a certain coherence none the less emerges. Chapter 8 looks at NGO leaders. These 'unusual human beings' have attracted much attention and usually have a lot of power attributed to them. The chapter asks where this power comes from? NGO leaders appear as brokers of meaning: they enrol stakeholders to acknowledge their position, and accept their representation of situations, organizations and themselves. Chapter 9, the final empirical chapter, deals with one of the most contested NGO stakeholders – the funding agencies. An extended case study[16] is presented of the (eventually broken) relation between CWNGO and a UN-related programme. It points to the politics of partnership as a main source of conflict and calls into question the generalized complaints about efficiency and account-ability that, to this day, dominate the discussions regarding local develop-ment NGOs. Chapter 10 rounds off the arguments advanced in the book and outlines their implications for some of the ongoing debates regarding development NGOs. The epilogue discusses some methodological con-siderations in response to a critique on my work by representatives of the NGOs in the Cordillera. The critique raises major questions that have worried anthropologists and their subjects in recent decades: the association with (neo-)colonialism, the ownership of research and the use of ethno-graphy.

Notes

1. For exceptions, note the use in the 1980s of anthropological methods and concepts by organization specialists in empirical studies, in particular the work of Pettigrew on rituals in organizations. Also, in the early 1990s a number of im-portant works theorized on organizations, for instance that of Czarniawska-Joerges (1992), who links language and action through social drama analysis.

2. Anthropology of development has a long pedigree, starting with works like Tony Barnett's analysis of the Gezira Scheme (1977; see also Porter, Allen and Thompson 1991), to numerous works discussing development practices and inter-ventions at the interfaces of development (see note 4), and especially in the 1990s studies on development discourse (see section on development discourse).

3. The complexities involved in this research setting, in particular the critique it evoked from local NGO representatives, are dealt with in the epilogue to this book.

4. For a discussion of these, although focused on Northern Development NGOs, see Sogge (ed.) 1996 and Smillie 1995.

5. See Long and van der Ploeg 1989; Long 1992; de Vries 1992; Arce 1993, 1989; Mongbo 1995; Grillo and Stirrat (eds) 1997; Villarreal 1994.

6. Certain counter-discourses have also penetrated world development in-stitutions, see Woost (1993) and Feeney (1998) for participatory development;

Willets (1992, 1996) for NGOs in the United Nations; Wilmer (1993) for indigenous voices in world politics; and Princen and Finger (1994) for global impact of environmental organizations. For NGO influences on Philippine policy, see Clarke (1998: 6) and the Ethnic Studies and Development Centre Research Team (1997).

7. See Rutherford 1995 for a biography of a Bangladeshi NGO moving from a political activist People's Organization to a highly specialized NGO providing development financing. The biographical approach taken in this book brings out the ramifications of these changing identities for the organization, its clients, the composition of the staff and, not least, the understanding of poverty. Poverty moves from its origins in social injustice and exploitation to signify a lack of knowledge and capacities. It is also interesting to note how discourses that have been abandoned continue to linger in strategic discussions in the NGO, through the influence of different generations of staff.

8. This section does not refer to Mindanao, where Moro-Christian politics account for a different NGO history not dealt with in this study.

9. The Securities and Exchange Commission records an exponential growth of NGOs from 23,800 in 1984 to 70,200 in 1995. These figures are blurred, since they contain thousands of organizations not engaged in development work, as well as organizations that ceased operating but were not removed from the statistics. A 1992 study estimated the number of actively operating development NGOs at 10 per cent of the SEC figures (Clarke 1998: 70). In 1992 CODE-NGO, the largest NGO alliance, did a countrywide survey and counted 7,000 NGOs, including an unknown number of People's Organizations. After 1995, the number of NGOs may have dropped slightly. In 1998 CODE-NGO comprised around 3,000 NGOs and co-operatives. They estimated this to be more than half of the total of active NGOs in the Philippines (interview with Dan Congco, January 1999).

10. For an overview of Philippine NGOs, see Silliman and Noble (eds) 1998.

11. This Communist Party, founded by José Maria Sison, was in fact formed by a split from an earlier Communist Party.

12. The distinction between POs and sectoral movements is not always clear. Large grassroots umbrella organizations are, in everyday parlance, often included under the label of POs.

13. These labels were Nat-Dems for National Democrats, Soc-Dems for Social Democrats or those working closely with the government, and Pop-Dems for Popular Democrats or those favouring non-aligned participatory development strategies.

14. For a review of the different positions, see the special issue of Kasarinlan (Kasarinlan 1993).

15. A long strip of cloth wrapped around as a waistband, with the end-parts hanging at the front and back covering the loins.

16. Most of the cases in this book take the form of 'extended case studies' (van Velsen 1967). Following or reconstructing projects or relations over a longer period of time can provide a 'close-up view of social interaction and confrontation' (Long 1989: 251). This enables one to observe how meanings are constructed in practice and how social relations are reshaped or confirmed in the process.

TWO

Damning the Dams: Social Movements and NGOs[1]

Why have a chapter on social movements in a book about NGOs? NGO documents rarely refer to publications on social movements, and vice versa, and that is a pity. NGOs and social movements may have much more in common than we have come to believe in the 1990s. Several decades ago, organizational interest in developing countries often focused on political or social movements, from revolutionary groups and Third World activists to struggles for land reform and squatter movements of the urban poor. From the 1980s onwards, this interest was slowly overtaken by studies of NGOs, often without asking how the two kinds of phenomena were related. NGOs appeared as value-driven and development-oriented and seemed to belong to a different domain from social movements. The NGOs discussed in this book, however, clearly defy such a separation. They have grown out of a regional movement for autonomy, and throughout their history continued to be associated in different ways with this movement. The same may be the case for numerous other NGOs in the developing world. This merits a consideration of social movements in the study of NGOs, as much as it should invite students of social movements critically to review the effect of the rise of NGOs to their movement (Fisher 1997: 451).

Besides, social movement theorists have for a long time puzzled over many of the questions raised on NGOs in the previous chapter. NGO actors need to legitimate their organization as doing good for the development of others. This is not very different from the need for social movement leaders to frame their cause in such a way that people will join it. Followers of social movements must be motivated and convinced to participate since these movements always demand sacrifices and, at best, promise insecure benefits. In their quest for legitimation, NGOs and social movement leaders alike have to ensure that they have no personal interest in their cause. In the same way that NGOs claim space in public arenas and request funds on behalf of their clients, social movement leaders enter politics on behalf of their followers. The issues of internal dynamics, everyday politics and discourses that I find pertinent to the study of NGOs, have thus always been part of the agenda of social movement researchers.

Clashes between social movements, states and development institutions like the World Bank have in many countries been occasioned by the construction of large dams (Gray 1998). While dams are meant to solve development problems by regulating floods, providing electricity and en- *Dams* abling irrigation downstream, they are normally opposed by those people living in the direct vicinity of the river who have to be resettled because their lands are inundated. These people ask what kind of development the dams deliver, for whom, and who bears the social and environmental costs? Such was the case in 1973, when the Philippine government started a project to build a series of hydroelectric dams in the Chico river of the Cordillera. There was immediate opposition in those villages where exploration work for the dams started. Villagers tore down the camps of the exploration teams, and sought the help of local priests to write petitions to President Marcos asking him to relocate the dams in another area. This localized protest turned out to be the beginning of a social movement for regional autonomy. This chapter first traces how the movement that emerged from resistance to the Chico dams acquired its shape. How did it transcend local opposition, and why did it become a movement towards regional autonomy rather than blend into the national movement against the Marcos dictatorship that simultaneously swept the country? The chapter then brings out how struggles over the proper way to frame collective action have major ramifications for issues of leadership, control and representation of social movements.

Social Movements: Theoretical Perspectives

New theories of social movements (and theories of new social movements), began to flourish by the end of the 1960s. These were triggered by the prolific rise of such movements in Europe and the United States among groups that were outside the classic class categories, such as students, blacks and women. Two strands are usually distinguished in theories of social movements: new social movement theories that have their centre of gravity in Europe, and resource mobilization theories that were particularly developed in the United States.

New social movement theories sought to understand the logic of new movements, such as the student, peace, women's and environmental movements, in the context of post-industrial societies and emphasized their cultural components. These movements were different from their forerunners in the labour movement. They were based on the new middle classes, had a loose organizational structure that was averse to traditional *SM* party politics, emphasized lifestyle and values instead of material demands, and were anti-modernistic (Alan Scott 1990: 16–19; Klandermans and Tarrow 1988: 7). New social movements were originally defined in the context of Europe and the USA, but the concept has also been applied in the southern hemisphere, mainly in Latin America. There, social movements such as urban, women's, indigenous and peasant movements were considered to share many of the above characteristics, with the notable exception that their main constituency was found among poor people, not the middle classes, and that their demands were partly material (Escobar and Alvarez 1992). The label of 'newness' attached to such social movements provoked endless debates about whether one could truly speak of new movements, or whether they shared much in practice with older movements. Academic debate was also concerned with the question of how the new social movements fitted into post-industrial societies. As one critic later stated, Touraine, Habermas and other new social movement theorists of the 1970s 'searched for a substitute for the working class, and a new focus of opposition to society in its totality' (Scott 1990: 80).

The other strand of social movement thinking since the 1970s was formed by resource mobilization theories. It focused on the question of how social movements came about, in particular how obstacles to collective action were overcome. Resource mobilization thinking originated with Olson, who coined the problem of 'free-riders' to refer to those who tend not to commit resources to struggles for collective benefits, since they enjoy the fruits of collective action regardless of their individual participation. Olson has been extensively criticized for the lack of explanatory power of his model. It made non-participation understandable, but his theory failed to explain why people often do participate in collective action, sometimes at great personal risk. In Olson's line of thinking, people's needs and goals are treated as given, and the social processes through which their motivations become shaped are ignored (Scott 1990: 109–31). Moreover, the individualistic basis of Olson's decision-making model was discredited by research showing the importance of social networks in movements for processes of identification and mobilization (Tarrow 1994: 21). Discontent does not automatically result in resistance, nor does resistance automatically result in collective action, as was demonstrated by James Scott (1985). One of the themes of resource mobilization theories later became the search for the conditions under which collective action actually emerges. The argument was advanced that collective action does not come about in response to deprivation, but in response to changes in political opportunity structures (Tarrow 1994). Another important element in the development of social movements was found in the role of 'sympathetic third parties' (Klandermans and Tarrow 1988: 4–7).

The two strands of new social movements and resource mobilization theories converged towards the 1980s (Klandermans and Tarrow 1988; Scott 1990; Escobar and Alvarez 1992). This marked the advent of a more constructivist perspective on social movements, such as that put forward by Alberto Melucci, among others. According to Melucci (1988), the earlier debates on social movements were all hampered because they treated collective action as a unitary empirical datum. Instead, he proposed viewing such movements as a process in which actors produce meanings, communicate, negotiate and make decisions (note how closely this corresponds to my own view of NGOs).

Identity or identification? Once the notion of relatively unitary movements is abandoned, or taken as a product rather than a given, the question of how a 'collective' actor is formed and maintains itself becomes a problem of analysis (Melucci 1988: 331). This renders the construction of a collective identity an important aspect of social movement studies, since, according to Melucci, people need such a shared identity to enable them to 'construct their own script of the social reality and compare expectations and realizations' (ibid.: 340). In the case of the Cordillera, this would mean that we have to ask how the collective identity of the regional indigenous people came about. However, as we shall see, this identity was contested and fragmented, and it might be better, therefore, to speak instead about identification. Although the concept of identity has considerably changed and incorporates notions of fragmentation and contingencies (Tilly 1995), it still remains difficult to assert that collective action is based on one particular identity.

The Cordillera regional movement, for instance, appears at first sight to be based on a regional, indigenous identity. As Finin (1991) described in much detail, an embryonic regional identity came about prior to the Chico Dams struggles, which was a product of the administrative grids imposed by the Americans during their colonial rule in the first half of the twentieth century. Finin traces the emergence of an 'imagined community' (Anderson 1991/1983) to the protective policies that the Americans under Dean Worcester extended to the 'tribes' in an area they demarcated as the Cordillera. During colonial rule the Cordillera gained a certain 'reality' through, for example, the introduction of segregated workforces in the mines and separate education institutes for Cordillera residents. These processes fostered among Cordillera residents an occasionally expressed experience of difference with outside areas and, even more unlikely at the turn of the century, a sense of internal commonality (Finin 1991). As Finin stipulates, the opposition that started against the Chico dams was able to build on the seeds of this emerging regional identity.

However, what happened in the regional movement in the Cordillera, as we will see, cannot be explained as the maturation of a regional or indigenous identities. The regional identity became the most visible for some time, but was always contested by others. Moreover, it was also clear that many people who formed part of the movement had no indigenous identity at all. The movement attracted many followers, varying from national politicians, a range of anti-dictatorship activists, an organization for national liberation, to international advocates. What these people shared was not an indigenous identity, but rather a sense of identification with this movement. A great number of people started to make the concerns of this movement of 'others' their own, and at considerable risk to themselves.

We cannot assume, therefore, that the sense of 'we' inspiring collective action stems from a collective identity, or even that there always is a shared, singular sense of 'we'. Following Long (1997), I think it more appropriate to speak of processes of identification rather than collective identity, in reference to an issue or movement.[2] Identification, according to Long:

> allows one to consider a wide range of self definitions, some more fixed and continuous, others more fleeting and highly situational. How people make and attribute identification to themselves and others offers a key for understanding cultural and socio-political orientations and commitments.

Discourse in social movements Discourse is a key notion of social movement theories, since it is through discourse that people define their situation and assess possibilities for action. Social movement theory often refers to social movement discourses as 'collective action frames'. The term is derived from the work of Snow and colleagues, who contend that social movements function as signifying agents that carry, transmit, mobilize and produce meaning for participants, antagonists and observers. They call this signifying work 'framing' (Snow and Benford 1988: 198). The emerging collective action frames have a mobilizing appeal: they serve to 'dignify and justify' the movement (Tarrow 1994: 99). Tarrow explains framing as follows: 'Out of a toolkit of possible symbols, movement entrepreneurs choose those that they hope will mediate among the cultural underpinnings of the groups they appeal to, the sources of official culture and the militants of their movement – and still reflect their own beliefs and aspirations' (1994: 122).

Notwithstanding the valuable insight that actors' experiences need to be linked to prospects for action in order for (collective) action to occur, I find Tarrow's position problematic. First, he presents collective action frames as carefully plotted by entrepreneurs. By separating the entrepreneurs from the constituency of movements, he denies agency to non-entrepreneurs, and excludes them from an active role in the process of framing. Although this picture may reflect certain moments of certain movements, it does not capture those moments of a movement when framing is 'everybody's' business and concern. Second, Tarrow's presentation implies that each social movement has one discourse and, moreover, that this discourse originates before the movement 'takes off'. In his model, the entrepreneurs and their objectives are given outside of, and prior to, the collective action. This position overlooks the contestations that occur in the framing of collective action and, as a consequence, misses out the power struggles accompanying these contestations.

Social movement discourses, in my view, are not given, but are negotiated and evolving. They are emergent properties that evolve out of the practice of social movement actors, including leaders and ordinary participants (see Boudreau 2001). The frames of social movements always draw on multiple discourses, some official and others developed 'off-stage', like hidden transcripts. The notion of hidden transcripts was developed by James Scott to denote those 'speeches, gestures, and practices of sub-ordinate people that confirm, contradict, or inflect what appears in open interaction between subordinates and superiors' (Scott 1990: 4). Discussed in private, whispered about in public, hinted at through jokes, hidden transcripts are narratives shaped among peers. The forging of hidden transcripts could be understood as the social construction of discourse in people's everyday life. Framing discourse as an everyday occupation of people should complement the concept of framing as the craft of the entrepreneur. The development of discourse, then, should be viewed as a negotiating process in which the distinction between entrepreneurs and constituency and the objectives of collective action are not preordained, but get constructed through a process. The following narrative on the Chico river struggle in the Cordillera exemplifies this perspective. The first part focuses on the relation between educated political 'entrepreneurs' and villagers, and the second on the contests between different groups of 'entrepreneurs' who started to compete for leadership of the movement.

The Chico River Struggle

The Chico river is the longest and most elaborate river in the Gran Cordillera mountain range, flowing through Kalinga and Mountain province. As early as the 1960s, the Philippine government started to explore means of generating electricity within the country, in the face of increasing urbanization and industrialization. The initial plans, however, were shelved because they were not economically and politically feasible.

This situation changed drastically in the early 1970s. World prices for crude oil increased sharply and, with the declaration of martial law, President Marcos concentrated such power under his authority that strong implementation of the project could be expected. A German contract firm conducted a World Bank-financed pre-feasibility study in 1973, and came up with a proposal to build four dams on the Chico river, named simply Chico I, II, III and IV. According to the study, the best way to proceed was to start with Chico II in Sadanga, Mountain province. Following the study, the National Power Corporation (NPC), was charged with continuing survey work. The actual construction of Chico II was scheduled to start in 1978, to be completed in 1982 (Cariño 1980: 3).

The people along the Chico only became aware of the plans when survey teams entered their areas. Before long, they recognized the threat the projects posed to their communities, and the survey team's first two camps in Basao were soon torn down by the villagers. In a third effort to erect a surveyors' camp, the personnel of the National Power Corporation were backed up by military escort. The escorting unit of the Philippine Constabulary began to intimidate the villagers, forcing local boys to join a William Tell game, which involved shooting coconuts off their heads (Anti-Slavery Society 1983: 103). The villagers, alarmed by the behaviour of the constabulary and the material damage done by surveyors to crops and fruit trees, began to seek the intervention of the president. They brought six petitions to the president in the course of 1974, hoping that President Marcos would withdraw the project once he realized its impact on local residents. Each petition, the costs of which were borne by the community, with church support,[3] was taken by a delegation of village elders to the presidential palace, but none of them got the chance of actually meeting Marcos. A letter from the president in response to the first delegation labelled their arguments as 'sentimental' and called upon them to 'sacrifice themselves for the sake of the nation' (ibid.).

Until this time, opposition to the dams had been localized. Local, village-based resistance to intrusions had been a regular response in the region's history. The Cordillera had been little integrated in the country's colonial history with Spain, and stands therefore to a certain extent apart from the lowlands. Being apart from the lowlands did not, of course, automatically mean that it formed a region in any political, cultural or social sense. Notwithstanding a certain degree of regionalization brought about by the Americans, the Cordillera in the early 1970s remained predominantly an area of 'village societies' (see Prill-Brett 1989). Competition was a major element in everyday village relations, regularly developing into inter-village warfare, which was regulated through the institution of peace pacts, to which I shall return later.

It is therefore not surprising that the villages affected by the dam did not initially co-ordinate or unite much beyond village level. One of the early petitions to the president, for example, actually expressed support for the dam, as long as it would be built in the area of another village (Berg 1996: 50). Later petitions were signed by more villages, and took a completely oppositional stand against the dams.

Contours of a movement In April 1975, the Catholic Bishop Francisco Claver, of Bontok origin, aligned himself with the Chico basin residents in an open letter to the president. I shall quote at length from this letter, since it draws on several themes that came to be central in the opposition to the dam:

> Mr President,
>
>   I came here because I was summoned by my people ... They do not accept your decree – if decree it is. They will not accept it. This is the message they want me to convey to you, with respect, yes, but with firmness, too. Deep down in their guts they know damming the Chico is a *decree of death for them as a people*. This they cannot, will not accept ... My people are giving serious thought to armed violence and they are asking whom they should approach for arms. Mr President, when a Bontok has to turn to a people not his own for help, this only means he has tried his supreme best to solve his problem by himself, and he realizes his powerlessness in the face of overwhelming odds. In short, he is desperate. *Armed violence is the only answer, and he knows his spear and head-axe are no match for your guns* ... It is my prayer that their message will get through to you and you will grant them the least of their requests: a hearing, a real hearing at some future date. This is all they ask – for the moment (cited in Anti-Slavery Society 1983: 104, emphasis added).

The bishop's phrase that the dams meant *the death* of a people expresses the vital symbolic meaning of land. Land, as a central element in the ancestral worship of people in the Chico valley, became a focal point of the struggle. As one of the later advocacy papers explained:

> All the many ancestor and spirit gods are associated, in the people's minds, with the land of the home region. The remains of all who die, even those who may die many miles away, are brought home. The home region – the land and all its improvements [a reference to the rice terraces constructed in the area over centuries] – as it appears today, is largely the accumulation of the collective efforts of deceased ancestors, of generations of co-operation between the spirits and the living. The living are the guardians of this inheritance and, therefore, have strong responsibility for the care of the

land and the dead. The ancestral spirits will hold the living accountable for any neglect in this awesome responsibility. (Cariño 1980: 5)

The 'land is life' theme was to become the most pronounced in the course of the struggle. This does not mean that it had been so from the start, or that it was equally shared by everybody. For example, in about 1977, 20 families from the village of Tanglag accepted the government's offer to relocate. They came back after some months, however, because the government had not delivered what it promised (Berg 1996: 58).

The other element implicit in Bishop Claver's letter was the threat of violent resistance. By mentioning the spear and the head-axe he evoked the formally eradicated headhunting days that continued to linger – if not in practice, certainly in local memory and in lowland conceptions of Cordillerans. While the image of fierce headhunting warriors exacting retribution for the desecration of their lands hovers over the letter, their capacity and preparedness to play according to the rules of the game of 'modern', lowland politics is clear in the conventional and non-violent demand for a hearing with the president. The threat of violence remains, while at the same time the bishop makes it clear that these are 'reasonable people' to be taken seriously in the negotiations concerning the dams.

The multilateral peace pact The increasingly integrated opposition movement, consisting of many villages in the area as well as predomin-antly church-based 'outsiders', became institutionalized in 1975 through the creation of a multilateral peace pact. This instrument was developed during a church-sponsored conference in Manila that brought 150 village people from the Chico valley to the capital. The peace pact, called *vochong* or *bodong* among the Kalingas and *pechen* among the Bontoks, is a tradi-tional institution regulating relations between two villages. Although there are many variations, essential elements of such peace pacts are that each village assures the safety of residents of the other village when they come within its boundaries, and that the pact holders take responsibility for violence or crimes committed by anyone of their people against somebody from the other village. One of the implications of village responsibility is that violence can be avenged against any person from the other village (see Barton 1949: 167–208; Benedito 1994; Dozier 1966: 197–239).

The peace pact made at the conference differed in two respects from traditional ones. First, the signatories of the pact consisted of a great number of parties, not just two villages, and included outsiders who extended their solidarity to the struggle. Second, the content of the pact clearly aimed to unite villages against the government. The pact stipulated, for example, sanctions against anyone who co-operated with the National

Power Corporation. In order to avoid conflicts between villages, two sections of the *pagta ti bodong* were included to place struggle-related violence outside the jurisdiction of the existing peace pacts among villages:

2. Should a Kalinga or Bontok from the dam areas be killed while working on the dam project, the peace pact villages opposed to the dam will not be held responsible, nor will they have to answer for the victim.

6. A peace pact already existing between two barrios will not be affected in any way when one of the members of a peace pact village dies or is killed as a consequence of his working with the NPC. Relatives will claim his body quietly but are prohibited from taking revenge.

(cited in Anti-Slavery Society 1983: 105)

These sections thus made exceptions to the practice of village responsibility for violence committed in their area. The conference peace pact, then, laid down and regulated the inter-village character that had developed in the oppositionist struggle. I will later elaborate on how this peace pact, both in its conceptualization and in its enforcement, partly depended on the intervention of the New People's Army.

Government strategies: divide and rule Several weeks after the *vochong* conference, Marcos abruptly ordered the National Power Corporation to cease all operations and withdraw from the area. No explanation was offered, but it was believed that his government, in the light of the Muslim war in the south of the country, wanted to avoid a second front of open rebellion in the north (Anti-Slavery Society 1983: 106). The relief at the suspension of the operation was, however, short-lived. By October 1975 it became clear that the government wanted to pursue the activity, and it started project work on another site, in Tomiangan, Kalinga, where Chico IV was planned. Chico IV would submerge six other barrios, with a total number of between 670 and 1,000 families, according to different estimations (Cariño 1980: 4). By choosing another site, the national government apparently believed that it could divert the opposition. This turned out to be a miscalculation. Those villages in Mountain province that were no longer directly affected by the project continued their involvement with the opposition in co-operation with the Kalinga villages.

In order to break the opposition, and in particular the inter-village co-operation, the government now brought the Presidential Assistant on National Minorities (PANAMIN) onto the scene. The head of PANAMIN was Manuel Elizalde, a son of one of the richest families in the Philippines. Elizalde arrived in Kalinga in November 1975, accompanied by a convoy of four freight trucks, three buses, a helicopter and eight other vehicles. His entourage of 60 people included fully armed soldiers, doctors, lawyers, cinema operators, 'hospitality girls' and two magicians (Rocamora 1979). Apart from trying to impress people by handing out money, rice and other items, PANAMIN's policies to 'pacify' the Kalingas were based on divide-and-rule tactics, including the fuelling of local conflict by supplying arms to a village at 'war' with two of the oppositionist villages. Through a combination of tricks, bribery and promises for development projects, Elizalde was able to enrol a number of community leaders into supporting the dam project (Winnacker 1979). In his own way, Elizalde thus also built his strategies on cultural heritage and practices in the area. While the opposition maximized the regulating mechanism of the peace pact, he tried to exploit the underlying competition between villages.

Despite, or perhaps because of, the rather crude interference of PANA-MIN, local resistance to the work of the National Power Corporation continued. The villagers in Kalinga responded in ways similar to those in Bontok: by physically obstructing the surveying work and by petitioning the president. While villagers tried to stop the NPC from constructing buildings, the government responded with increasing military intervention. During one of the villagers' raids on the camps, around one hundred villagers, mainly women, were detained and taken to an unknown military camp. The search for detainees took several months, during which villagers' networks in Manila expanded. They enrolled the assistance of several NGOs and senators, among others.

At the local level, the struggle received an impetus when some people from the New People's Army (NPA), the armed wing of the underground Communist Party of the Philippines, arrived and offered to assist villagers in fighting against the dams. The villagers readily accepted the offer. As one of them explained during my fieldwork:

> We had a strong opposition. First, we took a clear position to stop the dams. So, we didn't allow any materials or constructions into the area. Later, we were outnumbered by the military, so we wrote petitions. But the president of the organization who went to Malacañang was tempted by Elizalde's offer and changed his position. A neighbouring president was also bribed, so we began to get frustrated. Then the NPA came. We didn't know what to do any more by ourselves, so we thought maybe the armed group could help us further. (Field notes, February 1996)

Entry of the New People's Army The New People's Army was established in 1969 as the armed branch of the Communist Party of the Philippines, which had been formed one year earlier. After the imposition of martial law, when many legal opposition groups were forced underground, the CPP/NPA expanded to become the National Democratic Front with a total of twelve organizations. Following the Chinese example, they envisaged a revolution that was waged from the countryside. From the outset, the Cordillera provinces were considered very suitable for expansion, because of the strategic advantages of a mountainous area. As early as 1971 a first NPA group was established in Ifugao, and in 1972 a Montañosa Party Branch was formed (Castro 1987: 27).

Although these first NPA cadres did not get involved with the Chico river struggle, their experiences will be considered briefly, because they shed light on later developments in the organization. The NPA leadership in the Cordillera consisted of cadres originating from the region, but educated in Manila. They were primarily involved as activists in the nationalist movement. During the 1970s, however, they became increasingly influenced by a revival of interest in indigenous culture and values. This was partly triggered by a publication of the historian, William Scott, who presented the history of the Cordillera as one of a string of episodes of united resistance against outside forces (William Henry Scott 1993/1972; see also Finin 1991). His rather romantic representation of the cultural heritage of the area[4] provided activists with a historic foundation for emerging Cordilleran discourses of a united 'we'.

Their (renewed) exposure to Cordillera life led these cadres in 1974 to initiate debates within the Communist Party on how to assess the regional situation in relation to the revolutionary analysis, and what approach would be appropriate for the CPP/NPA in the area (Castro 1987). The NPA found specific conditions in the area that made it difficult to apply the general guidelines laid down in *Philippine Society and Revolution* (Guerrero 1979/1970). According to this handbook, 'the correct policy toward all the national minorities is to take a proletarian standpoint and make the necessary class analysis' (ibid.: 274). The NPA had tried to follow this approach, but after some time came to believe that it was not suitable for the Cordillera. They proposed to change the Party's style of work in the Cordillera and form a separate army, named the Igorot Liberation Army (ILA). This proposal was turned down by the central leadership of the Party. The controversy led to a temporary suspension of village-based work in the province of Ifugao until 1976 (Castro 1987).

In the meantime, an NPA unit from Isabela province had to retreat under military pressure to the neighbouring province of Kalinga. They stayed in the area and gained acceptance, especially after their leader, Ka Sungar, married a Kalinga woman. As opposition to the dams grew, the unit of seven NPA cadre decided to move to Tinglayan and offer their help (Finin 1991: 435). The NPA gained much popularity when they started to ambush the battalions based in the Chico area. Yet the initial numerical involvement of the NPA remained modest. The NPA members in Kalinga had grown to 33 by 1979, but then more and more local men and women started to join (ibid.: 453). This took the form of village contingents, with all villages of the Chico line sending a number of youth to join the NPA.[5]

NPA involvement coincided with an increasing military presence in the area. Faced with growing opposition to the dam, the central government withdrew PANAMIN, which had enjoyed little success in 'pacifying' the Kalingas, and started to send in more military troops. In the years that followed, the NPA took responsibility for armed aspects of the struggle, although strongly supported by the population. The NPA, which sat down with villagers as equals and whose lifestyle and discipline generally formed a strong positive contrast to the behaviour of government troops, remained very popular. Apart from the many Kalingas who actually joined the NPA, most villagers were involved in one way or another, either as messengers or by providing food for the cadres.

With intensifying military operations in the area and the involvement of the NPA, the anti-dam opposition set into a kind of rhythm. On the one hand, the everyday routines of villagers were marked by harsh policies from the military side, including curfews that placed restrictions on agricultural work, and on the other, by the need to provide daily food for the cadres. This routine was intertwined with regular military operations, ambushes, dialogues and other forms of struggle. The estimated death toll related to the struggle was 100 by 1980, with the majority on the side of government troops, collaborators and National Power Corporation personnel (Cariño 1980: 14).

We can conclude that the involvement of the CPP/NPA in the local struggle against the dams was the result of a blending of different interests. For local villagers, the NPA represented a resource that could be mobilized for their struggle. For the CPP/NPA, on the other hand, the controversy over the dams in the Chico river provided the political opportunity to gain a foothold in the area, in order to further their revolutionary struggle.

Window on the emerging discourse of the movement   The discourse of the struggle gradually changed under the influence of National Democratic politics propounded by the NPA and other organizations. It remained close to the issue of the dams, but became increasingly outspoken about themes that pointed to a 'broader analysis'. In 1980, a group of Kalinga village leaders had dialogue with Itchon, the president of the National Power Corporation. The meeting, transcribed by observers from the Montañosa Social Action Centre (MSAC), provides a window on the emerging opposition discourse. The following excerpts are cited and partly summarized from the MASC transcription (appendix to Cariño 1980).

The meeting took place in an open space in Binga, Benguet, in the presence of Itchon and six other NPC officials. After the opening, the first Kalinga to approach the microphone was Macliïng Dulag, the most renowned leader of the opposition. He said:

> I have only one thing to state here: your project proposal of building dams along our rivers will mean the destruction of all our properties on which our very life depends. We Kalingas were once known for our well-kept place, but your dam project has brought only trouble among us. We, therefore, ask you: forget your dams, we don't want them.

A second village elder, Balucnit, added:

> I have travelled through the lowlands and noted that people there could perhaps own pieces of land from two to five hectares. But they can get hungry, as they depend only on the production of rice from these few hectares. This is not so with us in Kalinga. We don't go hungry. We have whole mountain sides for other crops besides our rice ... The electricity that you produce here ... where does it go but to factories and the houses of the wealthy?

The statements of Macliïng Dulag and Balucnit reiterated the 'land is life' theme, and the implication of death resulting from the dams. By this time, however, the argument was couched in a comparative way. The Kalinga 'way of life' was compared, favourably, to that of the lowlands. If development meant following the path of the lowlands, they were not interested in it. In questioning the purpose of the dams, for (predominantly foreign-owned) factories and the houses of the wealthy, their denunciation had become partly incorporated into nationalist and class-based arguments.

After another seven statements by Kalingas, Itchon replied in a mixture of Ilokano and Tagalog why they had to persist with the dams, pointing to the energy crisis that threatened the nation. He ended his speech by saying: 'I hope you can understand the answer to your question: we have no choice but to go ahead with it.' The first Kalinga to respond to Itchon brought up another theme that had emerged, that of discrimination against indigenous peoples: 'If you decide in favour of dam construction, are we not in this way being considered non-Filipinos? Or are we third class?'

In the discussion that followed, Itchon challenged the value that the Kalingas attached to their lifestyle and land. He argued that because of a growing population, their way of life was jeopardized anyway: 'This was your problem too, long before the NPC went there.' Furthermore, he referred to the many Kalingas who had already left the area to make a living elsewhere and added: 'God gave us brains, not just hands. And so it is not true that when you move out of your places to go elsewhere, you will die there. We use our brains to work out our way to live.'

To this a Kalinga responded: 'God gave us our brains in Kalinga. God gave you yours in Manila. Keep to yours!' In no clearer way could he have indicated that the oppositional discourse had partly evolved an ethnic identity. Lowlanders (in particular Manila people) are here presented not just as different species of God's creation (the notion of God remaining the only shared understanding), but as completely incongruous to Kalingas. Anticipating the section below, it is perhaps equally interesting to note that the categories being compared are lowlanders versus Kalingas, not lowlanders versus 'Cordillerans'.

Macliïng added to their defence:

> While it is true, as you said, that people who have moved to other places may have been able to survive, such people voluntarily left their original barrios in search of land. But for any of us to be moved forcibly away from our homegrounds ... that is quite a different matter.

Macliïng here explains the prominence of the 'land is life' theme in the struggle. He acknowledges that out-migration and/or selling of land is an accepted and often adhered to part of Kalinga practice. However, he points out the crucial difference between voluntarily leaving, with the option of coming back or at least being buried in the 'homegrounds', and being forced to leave and completely losing the 'homegrounds' to inundation. In discussing peasant resistance in Peru, Gavin Smith described a similar process where peasants had to defend their livelihood. In the course of the conflict,

> heightened discourse engaged people intensely in the 'production of culture' and in so far as membership and meaning were not just abstract notions vaguely linked to identity but rather were essential to the continuation of livelihood, participants were intensely committed to the outcome of this debate. (Smith 1989: 26)

In the case of Kalinga, the sacred value of land was part of local concepts prior to the struggle, albeit among more varied practices and values in relation to land. However, once faced with the threat of completely losing their land, the equation of land to life and something worth dying for became the dominant transcript of villagers.

Two-way influences: debates within the vanguard The CPP/NPA substantially influenced the development of opposition discourse and the organization of the movement, but the ideological influence worked both ways. The experiences of NPA cadres in Kalinga also led to debates within the Communist Party. As in the preceding years in Ifugao, the CPP/NPA leaders deployed in the region began to review the relation of the struggle in the Cordillera with the national revolution. In 1979, the NPA chapter in Kalinga made a proposal for the establishment of an Anti-Dam Democratic Alliance (ADDA, meaning 'there is') that would comprise a broad coalition of anti-dam activists, within the NPA as its army. The proponents of ADDA thought the issue of the dam was more important than feudalism, and wanted to incorporate indigenous concepts in organizing work (Castro 1987: 29).

History was, however, repeated when the regional secretariat of the Communist Party turned the proposal down. The secretariat was concerned that the proposed changes would eventually lead to a replacement of the Party by ADDA. Moreover, it considered the proposal ideologically flawed. According to the secretariat, the issue of the dam was in fact a manifestation of feudalism, albeit with the government as landlord (ibid.). This ideological discussion was far from semantic or academic. If the dams controversy was a regional issue, there was no need for leadership beyond the regional level. If, on the other hand, the dams were an expression of feudalism, this legitimized the integration of the regional opposition into a nationwide and centrally co-ordinated resistance movement. Hence, the ideological discussion was ultimately about the leadership role of the Communist Party. Although ADDA was never formed, debates within the NPA continued to simmer beneath the surface until eventually, in 1986, one group would break away from the CPP/NPA to form its own regional movement.

Clearly, then, ideological and organizational influences during the struggle were two-way processes. The CPP/NPA strongly influenced local opposition discourse, but at the same time became engrossed in debates about its own 'project' through its experience in the region. The key to understanding this two-way process are the changing conceptions of NPA actors. Although deployed as agents of the National Communist Party, many of them were personally attached to the region, either through birth, or, in the case of Ka Sungar, through marriage. Their attachment increased through their exposure to the villages and, before long, they were transformed from 'self-interested outsiders' to 'committed brokers', whose identification with the national revolution was in competition with their equally strong identification with the region. Although seeds of conflict were soon to erupt, it seems that the double identification of the CPP/NPA leaders contributed for some time to the coherence that characterized the protest movement until 1986. Visitors and observers during these days were impressed – according to many enthusiastic testimonies in the press – by a vibrant movement that was carried both by educated, Manila-bred participants and the local population, and characterized by a close co-operation between legal and underground modes of organizing.

Movement for Regional Autonomy

In the period from 1980 to 1986, the protest movement grew significantly all over the Cordillera. Apart from the Chico dams controversy, another hotbed of resistance had emerged in the province of Abra, against a government-sponsored wood company. From these two centres of resistance the movement spread to other places, increasingly acquiring a regional character. The regional movement also expanded through legal organizations, both at local and regional levels. In 1984, the Cordillera People's Alliance (CPA) was formed. The initial membership of 25 organizations doubled within a year. The CPA embodied the village organizations as well as NGOs and other support groups that had been formed, including human rights, media and anti-dictatorship groups.

The CPA was dedicated to greater Cordillera unity and self-determination. One of its activities was to co-ordinate the growing international support networks that the regional struggles had attracted. Lobby work by international advocates led the World Bank to suspend its financial support for the Chico river dams, which all but meant the end of the project. Some time later, under the Aquino administration, the project was officially cancelled. Another effect of international work was that it enlarged the 'exposure' of Cordillera activists to international discourses on indigenous rights, for instance at gatherings of the United Nations. The international links served to strengthen the regional movement's emphasis on its 'difference' from the lowlands, and its agenda became increasingly formulated in terms of indigenous people's rights.

The formation of the CPA announced the change that had taken place from a movement against particular government interventions towards a movement for regional autonomy. The movement had changed from 'protest to proposal' (Fals Borda 1992: 305). Moreover, through the experience of struggle at local level, exacerbated by international developments, the 'proposal' concerned the region and focused on indigenous rights, rather than on the nation state. This transformation meant that the movement became centred in Baguio City and was more dominated by educated people.

Political opportunities opened up in 1986 to enter negotiations with the national government. When Corazon Aquino replaced Marcos, a new Constitution was formulated and the CPA successfully lobbied for regional autonomy. A tedious negotiation process developed in the years that followed, in which it became clear that the national government was trying to maintain as much control as possible over the region's natural resources and its military and financial policies. As it turned out, the proposal for an autonomous region resulting from the negotiations vested little power in the regional level, so that it resembled more an administrative than an autonomous region. Autonomy was not realized, because the proposal was turned down twice in a plebiscite, which led to an as yet unresolved impasse in the process towards autonomy.

One of the reasons why the autonomous region did not eventuate was that the autonomy movement had lost its coherence. Three factions emerged within the movement during the negotiation process. The resulting groups devoted much of their energy to struggling with one another in the arena of autonomy negotiation. Fierce competition arose over matters of representation in the negotiations, as well as in the public bodies to be created in the autonomous region. With the emergence of different factions, debates concerning the movement's discourse intensified.

Factions in the movement for autonomy One group was the faction aligned to the National Democratic movement: the underground CPP/NPA and the legal Cordillera People's Alliance. In their analysis, the struggle for autonomy could 'only be successfully waged in conjunction with the overall Filipino struggle for national freedom and democracy' (CPA 1989). The CPA's bid for representation of the Cordillera people was based on its formal membership of People's Organizations. In 1987, the CPA had 124 member organizations, representing an estimated 25,000 individuals (Cariño 1987: 169). The CPP/NPA, although never formally involved in the negotiations for autonomy, none the less maintained a presence in the process by, among other tactics, releasing statements through the press. They claimed their status on the basis of their involvement in the regional struggles:

> The people themselves will tell you that they could not have organized massive and sustained resistance against the Chico River Dam project, the Cellophil Resources Corporation, logging and mining concessions, land grabbing, graft and corruption and militarization if not for the Communist Party's painstaking and unremitting efforts to foster unity among the various tribes and lead the struggle against the common enemy. ('Ka Benjie', in an interview with Malaya, May 1986, cited in Finin 1991: 571)

A second faction emerged in 1986, when an NPA group headed by a rebel priest, Conrado Balweg, broke away and formed its own 'Cordillera People's Liberation Army' (CPLA). The CPLA was a result of ongoing debates within the regional CPP/NPA. Its major grievance, according to press releases, was the 'Party's failure to understand and accommodate the differences between the Cordillera and lowland society'. The CPLA envisaged an autonomous region, governed through extended traditional peace pact structures. Its claim to represent the Cordillera people was based on its grounding in the regional culture. As a CPLA spokesperson explained during a press conference:

> We call [the CPLA] the legitimate army of the Cordillera, based on its history. If we recall, the NPA only entered the Cordillera in 1972. And the CPLA, although it was not yet called CPLA at that time, was already there. When I say the CPLA is already established, I say it in the fact that during our, even before the Spanish came to the Philippines, our tribal warriors, or I mean clan, are already there. Although it is not yet throughout the whole Cordillera … So, the history of the CPLA begins with the development of this tribal society. (Mailed Molina 1986, cited in Finin 1991: 778)

The National Democratic camp (CPP/NPA and CPA) and the CPLA soon became each other's arch-enemies, with their competition extending even to ambushes against each other's leaders.[6] Both factions maintained an underground, armed component. An increasing number of advocates for regional autonomy distanced themselves from armed struggle altogether, deeming it unnecessary after democracy was formally restored under Aquino. These people came to form a third faction when they organized the Cordillera Broad Coalition (CBC). Many of its members were professionals, or local government officials in the Cordillera (Rood 1987: x), and its core was associated with one of the earlier indigenous lobbying organizations in the region (Casambre 1991: 61; Finin 1991: 260–68).

The CBC, more than other groups, emphasized the diversity of the region, which they presented as 'unity in plurality'. By their own claim, they wanted to represent the voice of the 'silent majority', and thus placed a strong emphasis on democratic procedures:

> There are varied and equally legitimate voices of the Cordilleras. These voices speak a 'host of tongues' and articulate a greater range of issues and concerns. In any 'peace talks' for the Cordilleras, the silent majority cannot and should not be ignored. This is the challenge to and of the Cordillera Broad Coalition. (From a CBC statement, presented in Rood 1987: 163)

The three factions that emerged employed different discourses, with varying assessments of the regional situation and correspondingly divergent proposals for collective action. Underlying their debates about how to understand the situation were struggles over the proper way of handling it and parallel struggles over leadership and control of the movement. Once the conflicts had erupted, each of the factions reconstructed a past that gave it particular credit for the struggle and for the people's 'victory' against the dams. The National Democrats maintained that their contribution lent them the status of representing the people, whereas the CPLA wanted to derive its status from its cultural embeddedness. The CBC, in turn, challenged the singular representation of both the other groups, maintaining that a plurality of voices should be heard and credited, a plurality that it, moreover, claimed to represent. The struggle for control over the movement was thus not limited to competing discourses about the action at hand, but also focused on a question of 'who owns the history and can therefore represent the movement?'

The missing link: from local to regional identification Before concluding, let me return to the question of the relation between movement 'entrepreneurs' and villagers in the social construction of discourse during the years of autonomy negotiations. Although villagers remained involved, the influence of the educated leaders with a base in the city increased. A gap clearly emerged between discourses formed within organizations at the regional level, and the villagers. This was particularly clear for the CPA and the CPLA, since these two groups had an outspoken vision of the region, and both maintained a popular base in the villages to which they were accountable one way or another. Despite their differences, the CPA and the CPLA had several themes in common. In particular, they both condoned the idea of the Cordillera as an appropriate unit for an autonomous region. Both the CPLA and the CPA formulated a vision of bringing the diversity in the Cordillera under one regional denominator. Both encountered objections from their popular base organizations in the provinces of the Cordillera.

The CPLA focused its regional vision on the institution of the *bodong*. It wanted to transform the *bodong* into an extra-local and even regional institution. The *bodong* was not, however, practised all over the Cordillera. Moreover, in those areas where peace pacts were part of local institutions, they operated under different names, with *bodong* referring to peace pacts only in Kalinga. The proposed transformation of the *bodong* provoked a fear among people outside *bodong* areas that CPLA proposals meant that the Kalingas would 'take over' the region (PIA 1989; Rood 1994: 11; see also Prill-Brett 1989). The CPA, on the other hand, introduced the concept of *kaigorotan*. *Kaigorotan* was represented as a kind of tribe encompassing all 'tribes' in the Cordillera. It was the CPA's proposed expression of the Cordillera people as one population with a common identity. However, the CPA had to abandon the concept when they found during their congresses that many highlanders could not identify with the label of Igorot (Loste n.d., Casambre 1991: 58).[7]

One could thus say that both CPLA and CPA efforts to 'translate' localized discourses into a regional one were not very successful. Apparently, villagers' identification with the region was not such that they accepted a public regional identity. Another indication of this missing link was the eruption of internal conflicts between Kalingas and settlers from Mountain province in the 1980s. These settlers had, since the 1960s, been buying land in Kalinga. Inspired by the discourse on ancestral land, the Kalingas started to reclaim this land from its legal owners, whom they forced to return to Mountain province. Apparently, the land discourse had escaped the confines of its application in the conflict with central government, and had been redirected to legitimize conflicts with a group of fellow Cordillerans.

These conflicts clearly point to a dilemma of the 'indigenous movement' in the Cordillera. The movement acquired its regional character in response to the government's treatment of the region as a resource base for national development. This common ground for opposition against the central government did not, however, replace or exceed the differences within the region. Although a regional 'we' emerged, it remained fluid. Rather than a regional identity, it was an identification with the region that appeared in a common defence against the impositions of national government. As it turned out, this identification did not congeal into a lasting regional identity, to the detriment of the regional autonomy advocates. This underscores the point made earlier that we should be careful to confound identification with a social movement with the development of a 'we-identity'.

Discourse and Power

When the Philippine government started exploration work for dams on the river it was unimaginable that local opposition would lead to a region-wide autonomy movement whose influence affected the entire country, and whose mobilization networks reached the United Nations' headquarters as well as numerous countries in the North. Yet this is exactly what happened. In the first years, the struggle was localized both in its organization and its discourse. In a second phase, the movement vastly expanded. It attracted a wide range of actors and organizations. The organizational constellations that emerged were dynamic; boundaries were vague between different organizations and there were no clear distinctions between insiders and outsiders, leaders and followers. The CPP/NPA seemed to lead much of the struggle, but was in turn largely composed of local village cadres. These entanglements resulted in changes in thinking among the respective groups of actors. Villagers came to think more in national terms, while NPAs started to bring local issues into Party discussions. An oppositional discourse evolved, where inter-local and national interests found a combined expression in the movement for regional autonomy. This illustrates well the duality of discourse elaborated in Chapter 1. When the CPP/NPA entered the area, it strategically adopted the 'land is life' discourse, but their ultimate objective was gradually to transform the villagers into National Democrats. However, once exposed to village life, the NPA actors increasingly attributed reality to the local indigenous notions. In the third phase, the movement broke into different factions, as the combined result of discursive struggle within the movement and changes in the 'political opportunity structure' following Marcos's downfall. When the arena of struggle increasingly moved to political deliberations in the city centres, the distance between educated leaders of the movement and the villagers increased.

The case of the Chico dams struggle reveals how discourses emerge in collective action. They arise from the practice of everyday resistance in complex processes of negotiation involving different groups of actors. Rather than fabricated by movement entrepreneurs, discourses of collective action are produced through continuous iteration between entrepreneurs and participants, engineering and spontaneity, myth and 'reality'. In the Cordillera case, these tension-ridden tendencies met at some junction halfway through the 1980s, producing a moment when the movement attained its most irresistible or, depending on the observer, its most terrifying vibrancy. The material presented here further underscores the point that issues of power and control are at the heart of conflicts over discourse. As the next chapter will elaborate, fights over discourses are power struggles that can significantly reshape the relations between groups of actors, in social movements as well as in NGOs.

Notes

1. An extended version of this chapter was published in *Images and Reality of Rural Life*, edited by Henk de Haan and Norman Long, see Hilhorst 1997.

2. Another question is whether identification is accessible to the observer, or in other words, how to measure or observe consciousness. In dealing with this dilemma, Anthony Marx proposes to rely on elite pronouncements and evidence of collective actions as indicators of identity formation (Marx 1995: 165). So will I. It would be useful, however, to bear in mind the nature of the 'elite' of the Cordillera movement, especially when village leaders are concerned. Although perhaps more affluent and influential than their co-villagers, these were people fully engaged in everyday village life, usually semi- or non-literate, whose state-

ments have been transcribed by movement advocates or recorded during my fieldwork.

3. On the significance of churches as supporters of indigenous organizing in the Philippines, see Rood 1998.

4. Florendo, for example, in discussing Cordillera involvement in the Philippine revolution of the end of the nineteenth century, concludes that: 'An ideology that transcended tribal boundaries was definitely not in accord with the conditions in the Cordillera at the outbreak of the Revolution. The *tribus independientes* were reacting to the crisis because of the need to ward off threat to their tribal integrity' (Florendo 1994: 88).

5. For an interesting account on the motivations, incentives and costs of peasant household participation in the NPA on the island of Negros, see Rutten 2000.

6. In 1987 the CPLA killed Daniel Ngayaan, one of the leaders of the dam opposition. In December 1999, Conrado Balweg was killed by the NPA in revenge for 'his crimes against the people of the Cordillera', including the killing of Daniel Ngayaan, which he admitted having ordered.

7. Interestingly, debates about regional autonomy were mainly concerned with the way highlanders related to each other. The question of how lowlanders living in the Cordillera, estimated to comprise almost half of the Cordillera population, would be integrated in the autonomous region played only a minor role (Rood 1987, 1994: 16; Finin 1991: 672).

THREE

The Power of Discourse: NGOs, Gender and National Democratic Politics[1]

This chapter delves into the history of NGOs in the Cordillera of the Philippines, in particular the intimate relation between NGOs and regional politics. NGOs in the region originate from and continue to be part of the National Democratic movement discussed in Chapter 2. During the time of this research, from 1993 to 1996, the movement was experiencing a major political crisis. In 1992, the leadership triggered a split in its ranks by calling upon members to 'reaffirm the principles and rectify the errors'. Loyalists to the leadership became known as Reaffirmists (RAs), while the secessionist individuals and organizations were called Rejectionists (RJs). Little is known of what happened within the National Democratic movement during the years that preceded and followed the split, and especially about the role of NGOs and the women's movement, a gap that this chapter intends to fill. First, the so-called rectification process, through which a group of NGOs in the Cordillera reaffirmed its ties with the movement, is discussed. Second, the chapter focuses on the women's movement, where women grappled with tensions between their feminist and National Democratic political positions. The chapter elaborates how the political crisis in the National Democratic movement may partly be viewed as an effort of its leadership to bring development NGOs back under its reins. It also suggests that the call to go back to basics may partly be understood as a 'patriarchal' reaction to expansions in the space that women were finding to manoeuvre in.

I use this case of the National Democratic movement of the Philippines to explore questions of dominant discourse. As discussed in previous chapters, the discursive repertoire of NGOs in the Cordillera region includes the national democratic key ideas, indigenous rights discourses and the language of participation and development, as well as a number of everyday discourses, such as the language of kinship and traditional village politics. Before the political crises of the split in the movement,

NGOs used these discourses simultaneously and strategically, deriving from their multiplicity room for manoeuvre to deal with everyday affairs. The ensuing crisis can be understood as an effort to restore the dominant position of the National Democratic discourse in the practice of NGOs. The question addressed, then, is how and when a discourse can become powerful and the dominant frame of reference. Why did NGO actors submit to this process, when it was going to restrict their room for manoeuvre? As will be seen, this question defies a simple answer. Discursive power works in different ways: it coerces, convinces and seduces until a (temporary) closure of alternative readings and discourses is reached.

Stories of NGOs in the Cordillera

In the 1980s, a number of NGOs emerged in the Cordillera as offspring of the political movement. Development work *avant-la-lettre* in the region had sporadically been organized throughout the twentieth century. Churches normally organized voluntary associations to assist the clergy, and some of these engaged in projects to raise living conditions in the villages. Government agencies initiated (mainly women's) associations to promote their programmes, starting with the Rural Improvement Clubs of the Department of Agriculture in the 1930s (Miralao and Bautista 1993: 21; see also Po and Montiel 1980). Finally, cadres of the New People's Army (NPA) during the 1970s facilitated small-scale projects as part of their organizing work, such as the construction of pig pens, and health education. As one former NPA explained to me, they did this because 'when you came to these villages, the need for such work was very clear'. This desire to improve life in the remote areas coincided with the ideological approach of the NPA, which, following Mao, sought to embed armed struggle through organizing activities in the villages.

In 1979, the first NGO was formed as part of the National Democratic movement in the region. After this, NGOs were set up one after another, and in 1986 ten of them formed the Consortium of Development NGOs in the Cordillera.[2] There were three reasons why activists of the National Democratic movement resorted to the formation of NGOs in the region. First, the struggles against the Chico river dams and other resource-extracting projects had led to an interest in alternative development, based on small-scale, local, people-centred, and environmentally friendly projects. Second, setting up NGOs was a way to straighten out some of the institutional tensions in the social movement, where churches and the National Democratic organizations partly coincided but to some extent competed with each other. The first NGOs in the region were set up by activists working in a church community development programme, and were intertwined from the start with the organizational structures of the National Democratic movement. A final impetus to form NGOs came from outside, when it became clear in the early 1980s that international donor agencies tended to favour NGOs over People's Organizations.

The formation of the NGO Consortium in 1986 was a response to new development opportunities in the region following the installation of President Aquino. Under her government, the Cordillera became a popular site for large international development programmes. One of these was the European-sponsored Central Cordillera Agricultural Programme (CECAP). The story of CECAP deserves some attention, since it shows how development projects may become a tool in political conflict.

CECAP: political struggles over a development programme The Central Cordillera Agricultural Programme (CECAP) became for some years an important issue in development politics in the region (see Figure 3.1). In a struggle parallel to the negotiations for regional autonomy, CECAP became one of the arenas where contestations over which organizations to include in the ordering of the region's development were decided. CECAP aimed to facilitate a wide array of small-scale projects for infrastructure, agricultural production and marketing in the communities of the Central Cordillera.[3] The Department of Agriculture was selected to be the Philippine counterpart. From the start, it was clear that one of the objectives of the programme was to curb the Communist-inspired resistance movement in the region (Severino 1994: 1, CRC 1989: 10). Despite reservations prompted by this political agenda, the Cordillera activists were initially interested in co-operating with the EU, because it would give the NGOs an opportunity to expand their socioeconomic activities. They decided to form a consortium of development NGOs, with the explicit aim of entering into a relation with the proposed CECAP project.

The Consortium, with the assistance of a Manila-based consultancy firm, drafted a proposal that was endorsed by the Cordillera People's Alliance (CPA). The format and presentation of the proposal clearly showed that the associated NGOs were intending serious and competent development work, centred around the key concepts of: participation, social justice, self-reliance, environmental conservation and utilization of local structures and institutions (CDP 1987). Although the EU representatives and the ministry responsible for CECAP had invited NGOs to become partners of the programme, they never entered discussion with the Consortium and simply ignored its 86-page proposal. When the project was approved in October 1987, there was no provision to include the CPA, the Consortium or any other NGO.

When a journalist asked EC and DA representatives in 1994 why they had barred the participation of the CPA-related NGOs, they pointed to the political nature of the NGOs. The undersecretary of the Department of Agriculture (DA) said: 'Why should we deal with the brokers in Baguio, when we already talked to the front-line groups?' He referred to a meeting in September 1986, when the NPA had abducted an EC delegation and held them for six hours to discuss the CECAP project. The DA representative used this enforced meeting with the NPA as an excuse for not consulting the NGOs. The EC representatives, in turn, declared that the EC would rather work with 'project-oriented' than with 'politically-oriented' NGOs (Severino 1994).

Apparently, the government and EC representatives viewed the CPA

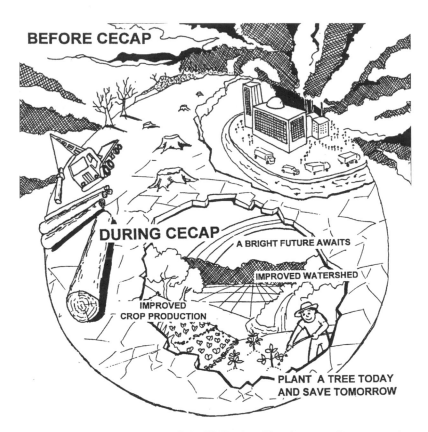

Figure 3.1 The Cordillera of the Philippines Development Programme's map (drawn after a poster of the Central Cordillera Agricultural Programme, displayed in Cordillera villages in 1994)

and related NGOs as belonging to the underground National Democratic Front. From illegal, but widely accessible, readings from the revolutionary movement, it was clear that the movement extended to legal activities. Although it was seldom expressed openly in the discussions, many people believed that the CPA-related organizations formed a supportive mechanism for the underground movement – if not for their ideological resemblance to the NDF, or because of continuing military allusions and propaganda, then on account of the reputation of key actors in the organizations. In a relatively small region like the Cordillera, informed actors (who were one way or another engaged in regional affairs) normally thought they 'knew' who belonged to the underground movement, either through their past involvement, or by deducing it from the people they were seen with, or simply from rumour. Apparently, no amount of effort, statement, or democratic practice of the CPA-related organizations could overcome this alleged and tacit 'knowledge' among their opponents. The professionally crafted proposal of the NGO Consortium did not convince the DA and the EC that they were dealing with real development organizations. It did not outweigh the reputation of the NGOs as political agents. If anything, the effect of the EC attitude was that the CPA-related groups, experiencing their lack of room in the newly created 'democratic space', saw their ideological stances confirmed and maintained, or even strengthened their allegiance to the National Democratic movement. By doing so, it seems that the EC underestimated the genuine desire of the NGOs to work on socioeconomic development.

The CECAP débâcle did not mean the end of the NGO Consortium. The NGOs continued their development work in diverse socioeconomic fields. They were able to access a variety of short- or medium-range funds with foreign donor agencies. What happened next is an ironic affirmation of the multifaceted nature of NGOs. The same organizations that were deemed too political by the government and the EC to be credible as development organizations became, in a few years' time, too 'developmental' and 'professional' for the taste of their political counterparts in the National Democratic movement.

Cordillera NGOs 1986–92: expansion   In the period from 1986 to 1992, the work of the Consortium of NGOs proliferated and changed. Leaving the political organizing to the CPA, the NGOs increasingly concentrated on socioeconomic work in a greatly expanded area. International work, organizational alliances and co-operation with government agencies continued to change the nature of NGO work. The following account of the Cordillera Women's NGO (CWNGO) is illustrative of these trends.

From 1984 onwards, there were instances of women organizing, especially in Baguio City, as part of the anti-dictatorship struggle. In 1987, CWNGO was formed, initially as a Baguio organization and, within a year, region-wide. CWNGO started with three part-time staff members, who engaged in research activities. The first year it operated without funding, except for 'loans' from other NGOs. When in 1988 a European funding agency decided to support CWNGO, the organization expanded rapidly.

CWNGO started with research workshops, contact building, and organizing and educating women's organizations. By directing efforts to already existing church women's organizations and women's People's Organizations, CWNGO developed within three years a constituency of more than a hundred local women's organizations. All of them were given an education seminar and invited to join the women's movement. In 1991, this culminated in the formation of a Cordillera-wide women's federation. CWNGO had now expanded its staff to more than twenty, and opened four additional offices in the provinces. Two years later there were 35 staff members. The main office in Baguio developed a number of separate 'desks', with projects as diverse as functional literacy, co-operatives, human rights, violence against women (with a separate crisis centre), research and documentation, and a day-care centre. The diversification of the NGO was accompanied by an increasing specialization of staff. CWNGO continued to receive its basic funding from the European funding agency, but several other projects were taken on with different funding agencies, including projects on women's reproductive health, integrated pest management and women's co-operatives.

In these years, the NGOs in the region also expanded into international work. The CPA in the 1980s already represented the Cordillera peoples in United Nations circles and became a popular guest at international events. The international work reached a climax in 1993, which was the Year of Indigenous Peoples of the United Nations, when more than sixty international trips were made by CPA affiliates. As an officer of the CPA, the director of CWNGO undertook a number of these trips and soon established a name for herself, receiving many personally addressed invitations. The international dimension was further shaped through the large number of foreign visitors who continued to come to the region, being sent for the experience of exposure to the villages. Through this international work the NGOs started to focus more on issues of indigenous people's rights. This became apparent from the education material that CWNGO, as well as other NGOs, produced on these issues for the People's Organizations.

CWNGO's work in the villages expanded further through alliance work and collaboration with government agencies. The organization was allied to a number of NGO networks, some of them with technical specializations, such as the environment and small-scale trade. These networks offered skills training to NGO staff members, further contributing to their professionalization. The networks (as well as funding agencies) often initiated activities that relied on the contacts of NGO staff members in the villages. By obliging these demands, CWNGO regional staff members increasingly set the agenda of the People's Organizations, instead of the other way round. This rapid expansion was not without difficulties. The fast growth of NGO work, as well as changing political conditions in the region, led to increasing problems towards the early 1990s.

Juggling with development discourses Rapid expansion and diversification had many implications for the organization. While new and often inexperienced staff had to deal with large numbers of village-based activities, CWNGO management was largely absorbed in report writing. International and alliance work often took them away from the office, leaving little time to become personally involved in village-based work. Another implication was that the NGOs' work increasingly drew on a multiplicity of discourses. They continued to echo their own political language, but increasingly used notions derived from the international indigenous movement and development agencies.

Following how the language of development was incorporated by the organization illuminates some of the processes occurring during these years. In the time of CECAP, the adoption of 'development-speak' had a clear strategic undertone. This even continued when most funding agencies were no longer as interested in political NGO activities as they had been during Marcos's dictatorship, and only wanted to fund socioeconomic projects under the heading of poverty alleviation. NGOs felt obliged to couch their proposals in terms favoured by donors. The NGOs also introduced a politically neutral development language in the villages. At the height, and in the aftermath, of intense militarization in the region, NGOs were often branded as Communist organizations. In order to avoid problems, NGO staff members started to censor their choice of language, carefully omitting words like imperialism and even human rights, since these phrases instilled fear among villagers, who would think they might be dealing with the NPA, which would lead to military retribution.

In the course of time, however, the strategic nature of the use of the language of international development faded. Before long, as funding came in and projects were implemented, development work gained reality in the everyday practices of the NGOs. NGO management and staff alike became increasingly absorbed in the implementation of projects, and took pride in their results. One of the things that changed was that NGOs started to demand educational qualifications from their staff, and people with less than a college degree were either not hired or received a salary lower than that of their colleagues. This was demoralizing for former activists among the NGO staff, who had often interrupted their college education to attend full-time to political work and were now discredited.

Nevertheless, management remained highly aware of the priorities and history of development thinking. When one CWNGO manager was asked in 1993 what she meant by sustainable development, she replied: 'I really mean social revolution.' When I subsequently asked her about her ideas on participation, she smiled and said: 'Then I also mean social revolution. Everything we do is for a social revolution.' For this management actor it was still clear that development was a pseudonym for radical social change. However, it soon became obvious that for newer staff, many of whom had no history of political work and were assigned to specific tasks, the development discourse had become natural. These staff members had no idea or had forgotten what the underlying political meaning of the NGO was.

By the end of 1993, the management of CWNGO and the other NGOs of the Consortium had begun to recognize the effects of the fast pace of change in their organizations. They felt alarmed by the signals that the work had become too thinly spread. Some People's Organizations began to complain about expectations not being met. Many felt that the NGOs had begun to lose their distinct identity in the eyes of the villagers, who increasingly viewed NGOs as project deliverers.

Changing state–region relations In the 1990s, NGOs found it increasingly difficult to position themselves in relation to the state, due to the changing nature of state–region relations. During the Marcos era, NGOs opposed a government that was demonstrably anti-people. After the transition to democracy, relations and identities had to be redefined.[4] Immediately after the transition to Aquino, a short period followed in which the NGOs tested the ground for democracy. When it became clear that the CPA was marginalized in the regional autonomy talks, that the Consortium was excluded from CECAP, and that Aquino, moreover, had declared 'total war' against the insurgency, leading to heavy militarization in the Cordillera, the NGOs resumed their opposition to the state. In the 1990s, militarization in the region subsided, and space was created for NGOs and People's Organizations to participate in local government, through the installation of Local Development Boards.[5] Although the Consortium NGOs of the Cordillera did not, in most cases, become involved in these boards (in certain areas boards did not function; in others they were excluded or chose to opt out for various reasons), they increasingly engaged in joint projects with government agencies. CWNGO, for instance, co-operated with the government over its reproductive health project and in setting up village day-care centres.

Such co-operation blurred the distinction between government and NGOs in the eyes of villagers and even for a number of NGO staff members. The identity of NGOs relative to the state became all the more unclear as government agencies increasingly adopted NGO features and vocabulary: they entered into direct funding relations with international agencies and used the language of sustainable and participatory development. A pamphlet of peasant organizations produced at this time hints at the mounting frustration among National Democratic NGOs:

> NGOese like 'sustainable', 'people empowerment' and other developmental jargon culled from the so-called third sector (the PO–NGO community), have been liberally adopted as their own by government after Marcos in their unceasing doublespeak to deceive and perpetuate neo-colonial rule. (KMP 1994)

The ensuing perplexity became even more problematic when the government developed a number of policies for the region in 1994, beginning with a number of projects to register and acknowledge claims to ancestral lands. According to the NGOs, these projects were empty gestures because they did not grant property rights to the claimants. The government then announced a new hydrological scheme, the San Roque dam, which was to be much larger than the Chico dams were ever going to be. A new Mining Code, moreover, allowed foreign companies to explore large tracts of land, with rights to open mining, the use of timber and water, and even to demand the relocation of people. This convinced the NGOs that the government was still treating the Cordillera as nothing but a region to extract resources from for the national economy, and they resumed their total opposition to the state. At this time, however, the NGOs found it difficult to explain their position to the People's Organizations they worked with. It was not easy to explain to people what was wrong with policies that seemingly met the demands they had been making since the 1970s, especially when people could no longer see the difference between the government and NGOs. There were thus mounting problems resulting from the proliferation of NGOs on the one hand and political changes on the other. When, at this same time, the leadership of the National Democratic movement summoned the organizations to reassess their work and 'rectify their errors', many of the NGO managers were ready to do so.

Rectify the errors: the split in the underground movement   The underground National Democratic Front (NDF), spearheaded by the Communist

Party of the Philippines (CPP), went through a difficult time after the 1986 watershed events. Just before the so-called EDSA revolution, the NDF had grown into a major revolutionary force. It reportedly had a mass base of ten million and a membership of 35,000 cadres at its disposal. It operated on 60 guerrilla fronts in 63 provinces of the Philippines. With the EDSA revolution, the NDF saw much of the gains of years of organizing being reaped by an elite government and its middle-class followers. Uneasiness in defining its role under the democratic government of Aquino, increased military harassment and mounting internal problems resulted, according to the movement's own assessment, in a reduction of its mass base by 1990 to 40 per cent of its 1986 level. The organization had also been seriously damaged by purges within its own ranks, following the unmasking of a number of military infiltrators into NDF organizations. Suspicions that several so-called 'deep penetration agents' had joined the ranks of the NDF organizations led to the killing, detainment, torture or expulsion of hundreds of NDF people between 1985 and 1991, especially in Mindanao and southern Luzon. Disagreement over military tactics and the leadership of the National Democratic movement finally caused a split in 1992. This was triggered by a document, authored by Armando Liwanag, called *Reaffirm Our Basic Principles and Rectify the Errors*. The document was intended to bring the movement back to its pre-1986 shape by 'going back to the basics' (Liwanag 1992).

Armando Liwanag is commonly assumed to be a pseudonym for Jose Maria Sison,[6] founder of the CPP, who modelled the movement by combining Marx's class-based analysis with the Leninist call for a vanguard organization leading the proletarian masses and Mao Zedong's rural-based revolutionary tactics. Sison continued to lead the Party throughout several years of detention and, from 1986, as a political exile in the Netherlands. The *Reaffirm* document is the outcome of, and at the same time the reason for, a split in the organization and leadership of the movement. For the most part the document concerns the ideology, strategies and organization of the Party and the armed struggle (see Weekley 2001). Some sections, however, explicitly focus on above-ground (legal) offices, including the NGOs. One paragraph in particular applies to these:

> There has been a proliferation of legal offices and institutions in conjunction with the increase in staff organs and a continuous build up in them of dropouts or near dropouts from the Party and the mass movement. An increasing number of political prisoners have also been lured into these offices instead of returning to direct work among the masses and the countryside where they are badly needed. Party work and Party life in them are often buried in office routines and office work away from the

masses and the mass movement and where petty bourgeoisie [sic] views, habits, loose discipline and craving for comfort are strong and often go unchallenged. (ibid.: 326)

It seems the Party leadership increasingly viewed NGOs as competition instead of instruments of the NDF. The Party had supported and even initiated the formation of many NGOs since the 1970s, but always had difficulty in defining the role of socioeconomic work. This work was considered instrumental to the creation of the revolutionary mass base. On the other hand, it was considered dangerous because it could become 'reformist', that is, could bring about change *within* the ruling system, without systematically supplanting it. With the proliferation of NGOs after 1986, this fear seemed to be coming true. In addition, it has been suggested that Party revenues from NGOs (directly or through revolutionary taxation) started to decline towards the end of the 1980s, because NGO management negotiated to retain larger sums of their funding actually to implement programmes. Finally, NGOs began to provide institutional space for outright opposition to the Party leadership, both by providing venues for discussion in the period leading up to the split, and by serving as a basis and platform for alternative 'progressive' agendas in the period thereafter (Clarke 1998: 113–18; CDP 1991).

Rectifying Cordillera NGOs *Reaffirm* called upon the movement to 'go back to its basics'. It led to a split between those accepting the document (the Reaffirmists) and those rejecting it (the Rejectionists). Neither friends nor foes of the movement had expected how much this cleavage would affect the National Democratic development NGOs. What evolved, however, was an intense conflict. Splits in NGOs and coalitions in Metro Manila and several other regions of the country were accompanied by fierce struggles. A number of NGOs did not survive, and many staff members withdrew from NGO work. The breakaway NGOs embarked on a number of different strategies and alignments. For the remaining National Democratic NGOs, the reaffirmation was the first step in a rectification process that was to last for several years. The NGO Consortium in the Cordillera belongs to this latter group.

In the Cordillera, NGO managements decided to go along with the call to 'rectify' their errors. Certain individuals decided to resign from office, but on the whole, NGOs stayed loyal to the National Democratic movement. For a time, the debate demoralized many NGO actors, who saw their movement set back by years, and were confronted with the 'betrayal' of many National Democratic leaders who had long been friends and respected leaders. Nevertheless, the regional movement, including the

NGOs of the Consortium, started to work seriously on the rectification campaign by the end of 1993.

The rectification campaign was to last for several years. With admirable stamina and thoroughness, round after round of evaluations were held, using the *Reaffirm* document as a term of reference. Experiences from the start of the movement in the 1970s were meticulously summed up and analysed, submitted for discussion and fed back to the different organizations. Once the assessment was completed, policies had to be reformulated and the work reorganized. The new directions had to be disseminated through education sessions, and co-ordination procedures between organizations and education material for the People's Organizations were all redrafted. For some time, the rectification was so time-consuming that NGO work in the region virtually stopped, except for routine follow-up of ongoing commitments to People's Organizations and funding agencies. By the end of 1995, however, it was felt that the movement was sufficiently back in shape to respond proactively to developments in the region and to implement new programmes. Painful as the evaluations were at times (punctuated by criticisms and self-criticisms), many revived their enthusiasm and motivation in the process. By early 1996 many NGO actors, especially from management echelons, felt that the rectification process had succeeded in better tuning their policies and practices, and in strengthening their organizations.

Evaluation of NGOs during the rectification campaign led to the identification of several 'errors' of a reformist nature. The term 'NGOism' captures the critique. The 'malady of NGOism' as it was called, is defined by the National Democratic peasant movement as 'a state of being engrossed in unholistic developmentalism leading to bureaucratic tendencies in dealing with the people that the NGOs have sworn to serve' (KMP 1994: 13). In a statement about reformism in the Philippine NGO community, the peasant movement charges that:

> NGOs afflicted with this malady have a concept of development segregated from the people's movement, focused on welfare, productivity and sustainability concerns and unmindful of challenging the base structures responsible for the people's emiserization [*sic*]. Victims of NGOism also magnify the NGO position in social transformation. (ibid.)

The pamphlet identifies seven major symptoms of the malady of NGOism:

• Loyalty to the funding agency rather than to the people's movement.
• Socioeconomic work without the need for class struggle and changes in the social structure.

- Bureaucratism.
- Corruption of the NGO service orientation.
- Professionalism.
- Adoption of corporate practices and standards.
- Competition or 'turfing'. (ibid.: 14–17)

All in all, it was concluded that in the period from 1987 to 1992 certain basic principles had been lost. To rectify this, a large number of measures were taken that profoundly affected the organizational structures, practices and discursive repertoires of the NGOs. Thorough political education was to ensure that NGO staff members (re)mastered the proper language of the movement. To avoid confusion, the oppositional stance to government policies was no longer to be watered down by simultaneously co-operating with government line agencies, which would be limited to a minimum. Another important measure consisted of the devolution of NGOs. In order to break down the top-heavy structures of NGOs, with too many specialist staff members in the office compared to organizers in the field, as many staff as possible were redeployed from the Baguio offices to the provinces. Office-based management was to be much more selective in taking on alliance work and international assignments. Travelling abroad was to be restricted. In order to better integrate and co-ordinate local work, NGOs pooled their staff in area-based teams, largely setting aside their separate specializations. The teams primarily focused on the (re)building of People's Organizations in the villages.

Not all NGO actors in the region were equally involved in and happy with the rectification process. Some NGO leaders opted out of it, other individuals withdrew completely from NGO work. Others, who were not fully convinced of the rectification, were none the less motivated to move along for several reasons. Some did not want to leave the movement for reasons of belonging. Others took the rectification movement in their stride, anticipating that once the movement was consolidated it would open up again to alternative ideas. The response of NGO staff members who were not part of management varied. The broad lines of the rectification were explained to them through education sessions. Some found the change of work meaningful, others merely followed the instructions of the management. There were also quite a few who did not like the turn of events. They silently looked around for other job opportunities. The number of staff decreased substantially. Particularly dissatisfied were those who had been involved in politics for several years, but at a low level, for example through participation in study groups. They felt excluded from the discussions of the rectification movement, and many reconsidered their affiliation to the movement and the NGOs.

Yet most NGO management did endorse the rectification. They wanted to achieve ideological coherence and to systematically design structures and practices in line with this ideology, so that they would become organizations with an unmistakable and clear identity. The question remains as to why NGO actors wanted to make these changes. After all, the measures had vast implications for their relative autonomy as well as for the individual room for manoeuvre of NGO managers. Moreover, some explanation is required for the reason why NGO people, who had been exposed to and had come to believe in a multitude of ideas, resorted again to an ideology that reduced the problems of society to the three themes of 'feudalism', 'imperialism' and 'bureaucrat capitalism', defined as central in the 1960s. Why would actors operating in a globalized world convert to such a reductionist scheme?

Responses A number of factors appear to have been relevant for those NGO managers who, wholly or half-heartedly, reshaped NGO work in the region. One source of consent or inspiration was found in the legacy of the National Democratic movement before 1986. A large number of NGO managers had grown up as activists in the 1970s and 1980s and were excited at the prospect of reviving those years. 'Finally,' exclaimed one of them after a meeting, 'we will step away from socioeconomic work. I really missed the social activism.' Among some of the younger managers this legacy acquired mythical proportions. They were ardent admirers of Jose Maria Sison and looked upon his writings, if not as the gospel, at least with a lot of goodwill.

Second, the critique embodied in the *Reaffirm* document found clear resonance in the disappointment among leaders with the meagre and dispersed NGO performance in the region, both concerning their socio-economic work and their political aspirations. There had indeed been a lot of problems. The straightforward analysis of these problems provided in the document gave a clear indication for strategies to remedy them. Although they looked back at a period of errors, they now had their work clearly cut out for the period to follow. In regard to this, I was often struck by the enormous sense of personal responsibility NGO leaders felt for past mistakes. I remember in particular one provincial manager. He was a professional man with a full-time job, who co-ordinated NGO work in his spare time. He seemed dragged down by perpetual fatigue, and over a beer I asked how he was doing. He then presented me with an awesome list of tasks for the near future, to which he added an equally awesome list of problems and obstacles he foresaw. When I asked him where he found the motivation to move on with this herculean workload, he responded:

There is the option to simply continue with my ordinary work. Especially since there is family pressure to do so. But I am still motivated. I feel responsible for many of the mistakes that were made. So I have a duty to take part in correcting them. We just have to start again.

Finally, a strong impetus to believe in the rightness of the 'back-to-basics' ideology was provided by government policies. Despite economic growth, the majority of the Philippine population continued to live in abject poverty. In the Cordillera, military oppression and the violation of civil human rights had decreased in the last years, but were replaced by economic policies that were possibly even more devastating. For the National Democratic activists, these developments contained ample evidence that, politically speaking, nothing had changed: the country was still ruled through imperialism and bureaucrat capitalism.

Before thinking through what NGO actors' responses to the rectification campaign mean for our understanding of development discourse, I will elaborate on gender and the role of women in the National Democratic movement.

Stories of Gender in the National Democratic Movement

A central question is how National Democratic women's organizations fared in the rectification. CWNGO belongs to a nationwide women's movement called GABRIELA, formed in 1984. This coalition has always emphasized class and nationalist dimensions of women's oppression, in the belief that 'equality with men is meaningless if we can only be equal with them in poverty and oppression' (Dacanay 1998: 10). For this reason, the major issues addressed by GABRIELA are land reform, labour exploitation and human rights abuses, with special reference to the gender dimension of these. They also address body politics such as the export of female labour, sex trafficking and prostitution. These are high on the agenda for good reason, considering the enormous number of women affected and their often heartbreaking experiences. Gender relations in the household, on the other hand, receive far less attention, and are rarely considered a priority. Nevertheless, this section focuses on how domestic violence against women is addressed by the women's movement, and on gender issues within the National Democratic organizations. This choice of topics should be seen as a methodological device. More than any other issue, the treatment of gender in the family and in the organizations reveals conflicting positions and power relations in the National Democratic movement.

The history of GABRIELA is locally specific yet related to global developments in women's or feminist movements. In 1984, Robin Morgan launched the slogan 'Sisterhood is Global'. Like many feminists in the 1970s, Morgan asserts that women share a common worldview as a result of a common condition. This idea has since been thoroughly discredited, with women pointing to divisions based on class and race. It has also become common sense that there is no one singular kind of women's movement. Just as gender has come to be seen as evolving at particular historical junctures and constantly subject to negotiation (see Lamphere 1987; Moore 1988), so feminist movements must be contextualized to be understood. As Mohanty (1991) argues, there are many feminist agendas and movements.

It is one thing to assert that feminist movements, like other social movements, have a constructed and emerging character. However, at the same time, we have to acknowledge that particular frozen images of women's movements continue to play a role in discussions and practices of women engaged in collective action. One such idea is that feminism is a product of 'decadent' Western capitalism and of no relevance to (poor) women in the Third World. Notwithstanding the work of people like Jayawardena (1986), showing that many early feminist struggles arose in the Third World, the *image* of feminism as a Western concept has deterred many Southern women's movements from adopting the word (Johnson-Odim 1991: 315; Basu 1995: 6–9). Time and time again, dividing lines have been drawn during international conferences where women from the South emphasize that women's oppression should be understood in a framework wider than that of gender only, to include class, nationality and race. These dividing lines have a certain justification in differing women's practices, but are just as much related to habits of pigeonholing 'others' in fixed positions (Wieringa 1996: 1–23). It is difficult to talk about women's movements without feeding into stereotyped notions of feminism or anti-feminism.

The Philippine women's 'movement' consists of a large number of organizations divided according to their position regarding women's oppression and running along two axes: cultural and political.[7] The cultural axis originates in debates on the issue of complementarity of gender in South-east Asia, which stipulates that gender roles in this part of the world are not so much ranked hierarchically and accorded differential status, but are organized in a complementary way.[8] Positions range from stating that women in the Philippines are not oppressed, pointing to their relatively high status compared to other cultures, to claiming that women *are* none the less oppressed. The latter view is arrived at by referring to the cultural ruptures caused by the introduction of inequality in the colonial period, or by referring to evidence that the nature of South-east Asian complementarity is such that 'the prerogatives and prestige of men typically exceed those of women' (Ong and Peletz 1995: 7). Those organizations stressing complementarity denounce those speaking of women's oppression as 'anti-male', with the charge of being 'Western biased' always around the corner. This position has been more pronounced in organizations of indigenous women, who are thought to have retained more remnants of pre-colonial, complementary culture.

The political axis refers to debates regarding the positioning of gender *vis-à-vis* other sources of women's oppression. It ranges from locating women's oppression solely in their gender, to viewing women's oppression as stemming exclusively from class and national factors.[9] Organizations move along this axis trying to define their own position, while at the same time being boxed into the extremities of the axis by other women's organizations, mixed organizations and the media. The first women's organization that explicitly tried to combine a gender approach with a political outlook was Makibaka. It was formed in 1970, and sprang from the student movement that raged in the Philippines in the late 1960s. Makibaka's first public activity was the picketing of a major beauty contest, echoing a similar picket held earlier that year in London. Immediately, Makibaka was scorned in the press as a bunch of 'anti-male', 'bra-burning' Western feminists propagating 'free sex', and was practically denounced by comrades in the student movement. However, the manifesto that accompanied the picket made it clear that Makibaka translated its feminist standpoints for the local context by placing the event in the political context of the Philippines:

> Women have a far more important role in our society than participation in such inane activities as beauty contests. Makibaka believes that in these crucial times women of the Philippines should participate in the struggle for change towards a just and equitable society.

It further said that women should be emancipated from 'feudal restraints which prevent their full participation in the struggle for National Democracy' (Taguiwalo 1994). Debates between Makibaka members and their student comrades were soon cut short by the imposition of martial law in 1972, when all such organizations were banned. Makibaka lived on as the underground women's organization, and one of the member organizations of the National Democratic Front. Lorena Barros, who founded the organization, joined the NPA guerrilla fighters. She became one of the heroes-cum-martyrs of the revolution when she was killed by government troops in 1976.

In the early 1980s, new women's organizations began to emerge from the National Democratic-dominated anti-dictatorship struggle.[10] In 1984, the nationwide coalition of women's organizations, GABRIELA,[11] was formed. The coalition was named after Gabriela Silang, a heroine of the Philippine resistance against Spanish colonizers. The backbone of the coalition was formed by large alliances of peasant women (Amihan), urban poor women (Samakana), and women workers (KMK). From the start, GABRIELA took a firm political position as part of the National Democratic movement. In 1992, the coalition consisted of 80 organizations, with a total membership of 40,000 women. The treatment of gender issues within GABRIELA as part of the National Democratic movement continues to be problematic, however. The National Democratic women's organizations started in the early 1980s with the aim of involving more women in the anti-dictatorship struggle, with the bonus that women were effective in attracting funding. Long-time GABRIELA leaders remember the International Women's Conference in Nairobi in 1985 as a turning point in this instrumental approach, towards a more feminist perspective. One of them said in 1994: 'When the GABRIELA delegation came back from Nairobi the talk was all about Global Sisterhood and women's oppression.' For several years, GABRIELA sought to continue dialogue with international women's organizations, in part through the organization of a number of WISAPs, 'Women's International Solidarity Affair in the Philippines'. At the same time, the coalition maintained a critical distinction from Western feminism, by strongly emphasizing that feminism should be embedded in nationalist and class issues.

Violence against women   Ideologically, GABRIELA women increasingly identified with socialist-feminism. They defined their coalition as 'distinct but integral' to the National Democratic movement. The organization's effort to strike a balance between the socialist and the feminist becomes apparent when we consider how it organized International Women's Day over the years. Every International Women's Day on March 8 is surrounded by a campaign. The themes for these campaigns are derived from ongoing political struggles, to which GABRIELA adds a gender dimension. In 1987, for instance, the organization adopted the political slogan 'Peace, Based on Justice' with a focus on human rights abuses against women. In 1993, however, GABRIELA broke away from this tradition and chose a theme with a clear gender connotation: 'Violence Against Women'. The country was shaken at the time by a series of highly publicized rape killings and GABRIELA was involved in lobbying for an anti-rape bill. Moreover, through research and education activities GABRIELA leaders came to realize that many women in the Philippines experienced domestic violence, with estimates as high as 60 per cent of all women. As one GABRIELA leader told me:

Our 'Violence Against Women' campaign started with education with women. When we told them about the military abuse of women, they responded that they had no experience of that. Their problem was with their own husbands who beat them.

In the brochure that GABRIELA disseminated for the campaign, only one or two sentences are devoted to men as perpetrators of violence. The remainder of the text blames violence against women entirely on the Philippine government. The state is held responsible because it maintains anti-women policies, such as 'the indiscriminate selling of Filipino migrant workers', through 'its own officials and agencies violating women's rights' and by its 'lack of interest in pursuing cases of violence against women'. The brochure concludes that government must be held accountable for the prevalence of violence against women (GABRIELA 1993). Despite GABRIELA's careful political setting of the issue (to the extent of inviting criticism from other feminist organizations), the campaign was criticized by a number of National Democratic organizations. One organization reacted by saying the issue was too personal, and asked why GABRIELA did not choose instead more poignant issues such as difficulties with the provision of electricity resulting in frequent 'brownouts'. The youth sector complained that the brochure designated men first as responsible and the state only second.

From the start, the need for a separate women's movement was regularly questioned by people from the 'mixed' National Democratic organizations. This put the women of GABRIELA always on the defensive (Angeles 1989: 213–16). The National Democratic leadership endorsed the women's movement, but in practice it seemed that raising gender issues was allowed only as long as it added to anti-government protest. The tolerance for gender issues stopped short when men were implicated as agents of women's oppression. This was even more so when this concerned men *within* the movement. This became clear from responses to an interview given by a leader of the peasant women of Amihan in 1992. She mentioned that several men, *even those who were organized*, prevented their wives from participating in Amihan activities, or harassed women organizers (Balmaceda-Gutierrez 1992: 34). In response to the interview, the regional branch of the farmer's organization of KMP, which is the 'mixed' counterpart of Amihan, wanted nothing more to do with Amihan. As one Amihan officer said: 'We could not understand why they were so furious, because it is common knowledge that wife battering happens. But they said it is baseless.'

The discussions triggered by the 'violence against women' campaign were soon overtaken by the debate between the Reaffirmists and

Rejectionists. As a nationwide coalition GABRIELA was heavily affected by this debate, and a number of its national leaders left the organization.[12] But the core of the coalition continued to work within the framework of the National Democrats. In the rectification campaign, GABRIELA went back to basics and reiterated its priority for class-based and anti-imperialist struggles. In particular, the evaluation concluded that the adoption of a socialist-feminist framework was an error, because it implied a kind of equal importance to both elements instead of prioritizing the socialist side. In 1995 GABRIELA again went to the International Women's Conference, in Beijing. This time they were not searching for new ideas, but had a clear mission to meet like-minded women and to bring anti-imperialism back on the agenda of the international women's movement. Makibaka was also in Beijing, distributing a pamphlet warning against the 'gender trap', which portrayed the Beijing Platform for Action as an 'Imperialist Scheme for Co-opting the World's Women', excluding the possibilities for empowerment of women through revolution (Makibaka 1995: 40). The two organizations had some very well-attended activities and rallied the support of hundreds of women in a protest march during the talk of Hillary Clinton before the NGO forum.

Rectifying gender in the Cordillera CWNGO was from the start a member of GABRIELA, and adopted a similar socialist-feminist view. However, to the trinity of national, class and gender oppression, CWNGO added a fourth dimension, ethnic oppression, to characterize the condition of indigenous women. In the early years, CWNGO was outspoken in claiming that gender issues should be addressed within the National Democratic organizations. The initial feminist position of CWNGO was also apparent from what may be called one of the 'founding myths' of the organization. This was the oft-repeated story (with slight variations) of how the organization acquired its first funding:

> In 1987, a woman from a European funding agency came to attend a conference in Manila. She had written a letter to another NGO of the Consortium to say she wanted to talk to women in the Cordillera. Though we had been working for several years as CWNGO, we were never told about this letter. We only found out by sheer accident. And so we asked to meet her. But they said: 'we will talk to her ourselves, because most of us are women after all'. In the end they grudgingly arranged a short meeting just before she was leaving. Her plane left at 9, and we were meeting her at 7. And she was so happy to meet with us. She then asked us for a proposal. So, that is how it all began.

The story brings out an image of determined women who, despite obstructions, had successfully established their institution. CWNGO managers were also fond of recalling how male companions in mixed organizations had not taken them seriously until the NGO acquired its own financial base, proving, in their opinion, how important economic independence is for women.

The first time that CWNGO ran into problems because of its gender focus was, again, around the issue of domestic violence. In 1989, CWNGO conducted health research among women in a small-scale mining area. One of the findings was that 50 per cent of the women experienced wife-beating. Among the husbands were several leaders of the miners' organizations, and these men objected to the publication of the findings. According to them, CWNGO had damaged their reputation by reporting such findings. In the first instance, CWNGO emerged more defiant from this experience, relating the protests of the miners during several public occasions to substantiate their idea that a separate women's movement was needed apart from, but integral to, the 'mixed' National Democratic organization. As we shall see, this interpretation of the event would later be changed.

CWNGO continued to work on issues of violence against women. Approached by women victims or their relatives, it set up a number of campaigns relating to cases of rape and sexual harassment. In writing about these cases, CWNGO emphasized that violence against women was either alien to indigenous culture or met with strict community sanctions. Public campaigns were launched in cases where the perpetrator was either a lowlander, an educated government official or a member of the military. After some time, CWNGO decided to open a Women's Crisis Centre, which attracted two staff and several volunteers. The centre provided counselling and legal advice and engaged in lobbying government agencies to get them to become more proactive in regard to violence against women. Deliberately, CWNGO located the Crisis Centre in a separate office in town. The reason given was that women needed to be able to go to there unobserved and in private. Prominent among the projected clientele were NGO staff members and wives of men in the NGOs and regional organizations. The Crisis Centre thus contributed to acknowledging that violence against women also occurred within NGOs and National Democratic organizations.

Towards the end of 1993 there were increasing complaints about CWNGO's education seminars, in particular a two-day Basic Women's Orientation, which laid the groundwork for their nationalist feminist position. According to CWNGO and other NGO staff members, this education was considered divisive in the community. This led to considerations among CWNGO staff to redesign the training for women and men together. However, by this time the damage had been done and the Basic Women's Orientation and CWNGO had acquired a reputation in the wider NGO network of being 'divisive'. As mentioned, when the rectification came, women's work in the region was largely deemed an error, and the socialist-feminist approach was abandoned as a 'dis-orientation' because it implied that class and gender oppression were equally important. Instead, referring to Marx and Engels, it was stated that patriarchy was, in fact, a derivative of class formation. Women's work was also considered to be culturally inappropriate for the indigenous population. At the time of the rectification a story gained mythical pro-portions, of how Manila-based feminists had come to the region to give a so-called 'women's orientation' in the province: 'When the session came to women's bodies, they suddenly removed their shirts, showing their breasts, saying: "look how beautiful women's bodies are". And these women in the villages were just so embarrassed.'

After careful evaluation, CWNGO management reconsidered its opinion about the conflict with the miners' organizations. It was now said that it had been wrong to publish the findings, because it had not helped women: 'The men were so angry that the women had told us stories, that instead of stopping they hit them even more.' When some months later mixed NGOs complained to CWNGO about an interview they were about to publish, in which an NGO staff member stated that her husband failed to help her with household chores even though they were both full-time activists, CWNGO withdrew the publication without much ado. Hence, the rectification gave a strong message about gender issues, stipulating that attention to gender was still possible, even important, but should not be divisive. As long as women's organizations continued to address state or economic oppression of women, it was all right. But they should refrain from addressing gender relations within the household and especially gender relations within the organizations. This ideological shift had several ramifications for the organization of women. Thenceforth, villages were going to be organized with teams from mixed NGOs addressing men and women simultaneously; maintaining separate women's organizations was no longer a priority and was sometimes actively discouraged. Women orientations were being revised, and when the regional women's federation was revived, a major policy point was not to be divisive. The Crisis Centre was closed.

Informal gender repertoires So far, I have dealt with the ideological struggles regarding gender and how the more or less formal relations between women and mixed organizations informed these. However, there is another side, relating to more informal, cultural changes. It is the story of how NGO women started to break away from the cultural prescriptions for middle-class women in the Philippines and how this was resented by men in the NGOs (and a number of women too), including the male leadership of the National Democratic movement. It is more tentative, constructed from reading certain trends, from pieces of conversation and observations. It is nevertheless an important story to tell.

From Makibaka's beginnings, members increasingly addressed a large range of gender issues through their everyday practices and discourses. Their practice over the years became replete with statements about women's roles and gender relations. In the first place, they focused attention on the implications of motherhood and other issues pertinent to women activists in the National Democratic movement. Some women comrades considered pregnancy mainly as an interruption of their political work, and left their children with relatives as soon as they could. Many, however, felt there was no sympathy for the problems related to pregnancy and child-rearing or felt excluded by virtue of their motherhood. The women of the underground Makibaka thus regularly raised the issue of the lack of attention or the trivialization of issues relating to childbirth and child care (Siapno 1995: 232).

At the same time, National Democratic women in the NGOs were rapidly expanding their room for manoeuvre, especially after 1986. A sign of those times is the growth of lesbian organizations within the National Democratic Women's Movement. While lesbianism in the mid-1980s was associated by many with Western women trying to 'seduce' Filipinas during international events,[13] this was quickly overtaken by the emergence of explicit lesbians in the women's organizations, writing and organizing seminars on the issue as well as introducing it as a normal aspect of personal relations and office life that was largely accepted, or at least openly discussed. Married women, on the other hand, increasingly explored ideas of women engaging in extramarital affairs. It is common and quite accepted among Philippine men to have a *querida* (mistress). Now women joked it was their turn, and some of them actually put this into practice, either with a Filipino or with one of the many foreign visitors.

NGO women, fully absorbed in their work, spent practically all their time with their office mates, extending into occasional beer-drinking sessions. Such sessions were full of jokes and teasing about gender relations and sexuality. Those women who were neither married nor lesbian joked about their autoerotic sexuality, referred to with that wonderful activist sense of humour as 'armed struggle'. When I went to Beijing, one of my NGO friends in Baguio asked me to buy her a copy of Mao Zedong poems, as well as some pieces of silk underwear. When I told one of the

GABRIELA leaders on our way to the airport about this funny combination of orders, she heartily laughed and exclaimed: 'Now, that is the Filipino woman activist!' Not only did these women step away from the ideal picture of the 'good soldier' of the National Democratic movement, but in their songs, political statements and lifestyles they had travelled very far from Maria Clara, the sweet, docile, obedient and self-sacrificing character in Rizal's famous novel *Noli Me Tangere*, which for a long time epitomized middle-class Filipinas.[14]

My interest in the significance of these everyday practices of women is twofold. In the first place, I am interested in knowing what role such changes played in the way the debate manifested itself and, in particular, how women's organizations were dealt with in the rectification. When Liwanag condemned the 'habits, loose discipline and craving for comfort in the offices' (see above), I wonder to what extent he was referring to the changing identities and roles of women. In a volume edited by Valentine Moghadam (1994), it was suggested that the upsurge of nationalist or fundamentalist ideologies (Hindu, Islamic and Christian alike), effecting restrictions on women, could partly be explained as a reaction against changing roles for women. Likewise, I suggest that Liwanag's 'back to basics' call, apart from being the reaction of a revolutionary losing ground, was also a patriarchal reaction against changing everyday gender relations.

This was never openly stated, but is based on impressions, informal comments, frowning faces and other small indications of male redress when confronted with signals or charges from these self-conscious women. This is not limited to the leadership of the movement, but also concerns men in local organizations opposing separate women's groups, or resenting the influence GABRIELA had on women's behaviour. One example, among numerous small events, happened during a seminar in September 1993, when NGO workers had to identify a core gender problem in groups. One male group started their presentation by introducing their group as the Diego group. Named after Diego Silang (the husband of Gabriela Silang), the acronym stood for D'organization for the Immediate Elimination of all GABRIELA Organizations. The core problem they presented was the 'gender insensitivity of women'. When I asked one of them why he was so opposed to GABRIELA, he explained that a local GABRIELA organizer had advised the wife of a friend to abandon her husband. Further probing on my part revealed that the man was a repetitive wife-beater, but nevertheless this man thought GABRIELA had no right to meddle in family life.

In the second place, the temporary closure in discourses on female sexuality and women's oppression in the household and organizations during the rectification process appears much less definite if we take into account the everyday negotiations of gender. In informal practices and interactions, women continued to enact and defend their newly acquired freedoms and lifestyles. Often this materialized in the form of jokes. The nature of jokes and irony is double-faced. During the rectification campaign, jokes seemed first to be a confirmation of the rectification, a ground where people could play out the new directions and show off their political correctness. However, it was also through jokes that negotiations continued over gender values in everyday life. When somebody commented about the jeans and short hair of my baby daughter: 'she might become a lesbian', somebody else replied 'never mind her gender, as long as she has the correct class position'. These and similar jokes point to the complexity and interrelation of discourses in everyday life. Even though discursive order appeared to be restored in the NGOs, women's issues could not be equally 'boxed in' in everyday practices and confrontations.

Discourse at Work

The timing and direction of the rectification campaign of the National Democratic movement as described in this chapter is not so difficult to explain. The campaign, with its call to go back to basics, can easily be read as the defensive move of a threatened leadership. The movement lost much of its strength after 1986: it had difficulty in defining its role in a democratic country, there were internal contestations over power and many people simply lost interest in the revolution. Given the changes that had taken place both in the NGOs and the women's movement, it is also understandable why they were primary targets of the rectification. What remains a fascinating question, however, is why the rectification campaign was successful in enrolling a large part of the National Democratic movement membership. Examining the process whereby the political rectification discourse became dominant among NGO actors sheds light on the interplay of discourse and power.

The question of how discourse becomes powerful is important (think of present-day resurgent nationalist, ethnic and fundamentalist ideologies), and defies a simple answer. What happened in the Cordillera was so complex that I became convinced that power could not be reduced to a single principle. Instead, I contend that the renewed National Democratic discourse became dominant in the Cordillera through a combination of coercion, conviction and seduction. Let me elaborate on this.

The fact that the rectification campaign was not accompanied by violence does not mean that there was no coercion involved. The *Reaffirm* document was popularly said to have evoked a 'debate' in the National Democratic movement. In reality, this was not the case. The document put forward one 'truth' that could be accepted or rejected, but was not up for debate. By leaving no space between 'correctness' on the one hand and 'error' on the other, a 'take it or leave it' situation was created. One either consented or left. Although many organizations and individuals took the exit option, the pressure to stay was considerable in those areas where the leadership had taken sides with the Reaffirmists.[15] To understand this, the nature of the actors' commitment to the National Democratic movement has to be understood. This movement was close to what Goffman calls a 'total institution' (1961). Membership represented many things at the same time. A person operated in closely knit groups, where work, leisure and family life were concentrated in the same people. Entering this movement often implied a virtual break with one's family and former friends, so that comrades became colleagues, friends and relatives at the same time. One believed in the cause of the movement, and it was at the same time one's life project, embodying aspirations and career prospects. While a good record could result in a higher position in the movement, it was hardly saleable in job hunts outside it.[16] In this situation, peer pressure and the prospect of having to leave the movement when opting out of the rectification exerted a strong hold on people.

Second, the rectification was also convincing to a large number of people. Subjects of ideology, ranging from capitalism to present-day fundamentalist movements, have often been associated with 'false consciousness', where people are thought to internalize certain interpretations that have no 'objective' connection to their actual situation, needs and desires. However, as stipulated above, the arguments put forward by the *Reaffirm* document were quite convincing. It was not difficult to find empirical evidence to corroborate the notion that essentially nothing had changed. NGO problems hinted at were not mere inventions of Liwanag, but illuminated growing concerns of NGO management both within and outside the movement (Constantino-David 1998). Once accepted, the ideas of the rectification became indeed a powerful ideology with a high 'ability to intervene in the consciousness of those it subjects, appropriating and reinflecting their experience' (Eagleton 1991: 45). Increasingly, the interpretation of events and processes was filtered through this compelling prism. Sealed off from alternative readings and ideas that were *a priori* considered worthless when originating from somebody without the 'right framework', the rectification discourse became an ahistoric, 'naturalized' representation of social reality. What started as a convincing analysis thus turned into a discourse that increasingly shaped reality.

Finally, the rectification discourse was also seductive. Actors were seduced by it in two ways. In the first place, the rectification did not only present a coherent picture of social reality and errors in earlier strategies, it also provided a clear solution by 'going back to basics'. Emery Roe states that in cases of high ambiguity and pressure to act, organizations tend to resort to broad explanatory narratives and standard approaches (Roe 1991).[17] The *Reaffirm* document was just such a narrative on which to base organizational policy. The rectification was seductive in a more symbolic way as well. The process of identifying and rectifying errors resembled the road to redemption of Catholic sinners. People had committed errors, had wandered from the right path, which was analysed and 'confessed' to in a rectification, after which they could resume with a clean slate, as if they were absolved from their errors/sins. The willingness of people to undergo criticism and self-criticism, accompanied by intense emotional outbursts and a drive to make up for past errors, indicates that they attached a high symbolic value to the rectification.[18]

The mechanisms that lent the rectification discourse its power – coercion, conviction and seduction – worked in different combinations and with different weightings through time for different people. Actors did not simply enact the rectification discourse. They responded differently to the various pressures, accorded different meanings to the discourse and valorized it in varied ways. While for some the discourse represented absolute truth, others used it merely as a reference point. What one person embraced with dedication left his or her comrade largely indifferent. Where some felt the coercive properties of the rectification, others were challenged by opportunities to gain leadership. Some merely subjected themselves to the rectification, others explored the room for manoeuvre it provided. As a result, the rectification campaign never came to a definite closure, as discussions continued about appropriate strategies and a proper balancing of alternative approaches.

Through this chapter I have shown how the rectification process in the National Democratic movement in the Philippines was partly affected by, and in turn strongly affected, developments in NGOs and the women's movement. Due to its contracted nature, the rectification process magnifies, to my mind, certain other processes of constructing and working of discourse in relation to power. The range of responses shows that even a powerful ideological discourse does not operate outside of people's agency. Through their everyday practices, people evoke, empower, challenge and reshape discourses. At the same time, the responses illustrate how discourse, once established, may be a forceful element in creating people's realities.

Notes

1. This chapter is published in *Asian Studies* (Hilhorst 2001).

2. This chapter deals in detail only with this group of National Democratic NGOs. There are many other kinds of NGOs in the Cordillera. A 1990 survey enumerated 60, most of which operate locally (Reyes-Boquiren et al. 1990). As in the wider Philippines, NGOs differ in their political ideologies and affiliations. A small number have a clear indigenous or environmentalist focus, many lean towards the government, and some NGOs were set up by mining companies. For a comparative study on NGO interventions in open-pit mining communities, see Cariño 1992; 1990.

3. This could amount to literally dozens of small projects in one village. For a village case study on CECAP, see Rovillos 1996.

4. The problem of NGOs having to redefine their identity after transformations in the state, for example, from military rule to democracy, has been widely documented. Particularly for Latin America, see the volumes edited by Clayton 1996, and Edwards and Hulme 1992. For Central America see Biekart 1999, Borgh 1999, and Schlanger 1996 on Brazil. The Peruvian case is interesting, since NGOs face a double identity issue – in relation to the state and in relation to avoiding being associated with the Shining Path (Scurrah 1996).

5. See Tigno 1993; Zialcita et al. 1995; CODE-NGO and DILG 1998; George 1998.

6. For an authorized biography of Jose Maria Sison, see Sison and Werning 1989; for an unauthorized account of Sison and the revolutionary movement, see Jones 1989.

7. An additional axis, ranging from practical gender interests to strategic interests (Molyneux 1986; Moser 1993), or feminine versus feminist interests (Stephen 1997), issues that were subject to intense debate in Latin American women's movements, was never very prominent in the Philippines.

8. This complementarity is symbolized in the oft-cited Philippine creation myth, where *Babaye* (woman) is considered to have emerged from the nodes of a bamboo as a whole person, separate from, yet born together with, *Lalake* (man) (Santiago 1995: 110).

9. For analytical clarity these factors are presented as separate. Although they sometimes appear as such, Philippine women's organizations often take into account (explicitly or implicitly) the notion that these forms of difference are not additive, but that the experiences of race or class alter the experience of gender (see Moore 1988). GABRIELA considered the articulation of forms of oppression by consistently raising the question of 'how it is to be female and poor in a country dominated by foreign powers and interests' (Angeles 1989: 65–70).

10. For a comparative account of women's movements springing from revolutionary or liberation movements in El Salvador, see Stephen 1997.

11. GABRIELA stands for General Assembly Binding Women for Reforms, Integrity, Equality, Leadership and Action.

12. Apart from ideological stances, it has been suggested that 'personalities, political maneuvering and self-interest' were additional factors influencing women to take one side or the other (Fumerton 1995: 63).

13. During my first visit to the Philippines in 1986, my hair was cut short.

Several NGO women told me later during my stay that they had initially thought I was a lesbian and had been afraid I might 'approach' them.

14. The class element here may be very significant. I am referring here to changes observed in women movement leaders. Although explicit talk about sexuality is considered shameful among middle-class women, it is, I believe, quite different among peasant women, whose openness I have always found strikingly frank, including detailed comments about their husbands' performances in bed, quite contrary to the commonly cited demureness of Filipinas.

15. One reason why in the Cordillera the leadership did not divide over the debate was perhaps that the movement had already experienced a split in 1986.

16. Research into post-movement careers of CPP-NPA cadres, on the other hand, brings out how people in a region that did not align with the Reaffirm movement found employment using their skills acquired underground (Rutten 2001).

17. See also Hilhorst and van Leeuwen 2000.

18. Returning home from the women's oppression seminar mentioned above, one CWNGO staff member, for example, burst into tears because, as she said: 'If I think back on all the erroneous things I have been teaching these women, how I poisoned their brains, my heart feels too heavy.'

FOUR

Village Experts and Development Discourse: 'Progress' in a Philippine Igorot Village[1]

NGOs intervene in communities with particular ideas about development and the way that its costs and benefits should be generated and distributed. They work, in other words, with a particular development discourse. However, little insight has been gained into how such discourses work in everyday development situations and how they order social relationships in local communities. To answer these questions, this chapter argues that we have to study the use of development discourse in practice. At the centre of the chapter lies a puzzling situation concerning a literacy project for 13 women in Kayatuan in Mountain Province, which I studied on behalf of the sponsoring organization and as part of a one-year ethnographic study in the village.[2] The project was initiated by an NGO to empower illiterate women. The ability to read and write would help them in their everyday life, if only to guide transactions in the market or to travel to the big city. It would also empower the women politically, since being able to write would allow them to participate in elections. After training a volunteer, the local partner organization recruited a class of participants and the programme took off. Two years later the project concluded its first phase and held a graduation party. Seventy guests, including a number of provincial government officials and the municipal mayor, attended it.

As it turned out, there was only one problem with the project: it made no sense. The participants were illiterate, but they were also very old. Most of them were teenagers during the Second World War and they were hardly capable of learning to read and write. They wrote with thick markers to see the letters, and with their arthritic fingers it took them minutes to note down a word. Week after week the same letters were repeated, and on graduation day some could still not spell their first names. It is understandable why the old women liked the literacy class; after all, it was lots of fun. But why did the officers of the organization,

especially the volunteer teacher, put so much time and effort into a training
that was not going to make the participants literate? Why did they consider
it important to organize such a major event for the 'graduation'? If the
purpose was not to teach the women, what did the project do? What
happened to the envisaged empowerment of women? I use the literacy
project as an entry point for examining the question of how development
works in a community. What can the literacy programme and other local
development initiatives tell us about local actors' projects, the meaning
of development, and social change in a village?

Development Discourse

In Chapter 1, I discussed how discourse analyses of the 1990s claimed a
certain development discourse has emerged that is hegemonic in nature
because it 'identifies appropriate and legitimate ways of practising development as well as speaking and thinking about it' (Grillo 1997: 12).
These claims about the existence of a hegemonic development discourse
fall short on two grounds. First, 'there have always been a multiplicity of
voices within development, even if some are more powerful than others'
(Grillo 1997: 22; Preston 1994; Apthorpe and Gasper 1996). Kayatuan is
the object of intervention by government development agencies, politically
radical NGOs, election-minded politicians, a variety of religious groups
and participation-loving academics. All of them have interests, approaches,
languages and styles in promoting 'development' at the local level. Local
discourses, on the other hand, are equally diverse. Even in a geographically
compact locality such as this village, one cannot detect a single meaning
of development. Development actors are therefore not moulded within a
single discursive frame, but avail themselves of alternatives. Even where
one discourse appears dominant, there are always parallel, residual or
emerging alternatives. Second, the relation between dominant and
counter-discourses is dynamic and leads to renegotiations at the interfaces
of discourse encounters. The meaning of development notions is renegotiated in the local context (Pigg 1992). Thus a vocabulary acquires
different and often multiple meanings in the localities. It is not very helpful,
then, to think about discourse in terms of hegemonic structures. Instead,
I proposed to look at the duality of discourse.

To understand the duality of discourse, one must take into account
the notion of agency. Agency endows actors with the knowledge and
capability to process social experience. This means that even though actors
are affected by (dominant) discourses, at the same time they reshuffle,
circumvent and accommodate these. The other side of the duality of
discourse prompts one to look into processes by which discourses become

powerful. Discourses are not innocent. The more dominant a discourse, the more it operates as a set of rules about what can and cannot be said and done and about what. Hence, the issue of dominant discourses remains relevant, but instead of assuming their existence and operation, one has to study when and how they become dominant in relation to other discourses and what this means in practice. Chapter 3 considered how discourse became dominant in a situation of political crisis that centred explicitly on discourse. This chapter, on the other hand, explores the duality of discourse in the everyday practices of village organizations. Here we will see how discourse can order social relations in ways much more unnoticed and seemingly innocuous.

Studying discourse The puzzle posed by the literacy training in Kayatuan cannot be solved when the project is understood as an isolated encounter between two separate bodies – the NGO and the villagers. Instead, it is shaped in the context of the ensemble of development interventions at the local level. How villagers perceive a project is informed by their experience with development, and they respond to programmes in relation to one another (Borgh 1999; Crewe and Harrison 1998: 155–75). Hence, to know how villagers accord meaning to development and reshape power relations in the process, one has to take into account the amalgam of external social relations and development interventions. This is not as complex as it sounds. Development interventions do not pour down on a village like a rain shower; they are mediated by local development brokers (Olivier de Sardan 1995; Mongbo 1995). Development enters Kayatuan through three social networks, each of which is embedded in community organizations. Core actors of these networks represent the village *vis-à-vis* outside development agencies. In the processes of accessing, allocating and implementing development activities, these actors become nodal points where knowledge about development is concentrated. That is why I call them village experts. They speak the languages of the different intervenors and have a definite knowledge advantage over these outsiders. These people are well aware of and reflect openly in interviews on their strategic use of a multiplicity of discourses.

Studying the duality of discourse, and analysing how discourses become realities through actors' practices, is more complicated. These are subtle processes, occurring over long stretches of time and difficult to isolate in the complexities of everyday social life. I approach this by starting out with identifying three discourses on development in Kayatuan. Embedded in the everyday practices and conversations of villagers are fragments of discourses that hint at different and sometimes contradictory notions of development. Since these are not spelled out explicitly, they are defined by mapping different meanings people attached in speech and practice to 'progress', 'community' and 'project'. Here, meaning is a kind of intermediate concept. It denotes what certain phenomena signify to actors. In according meaning, actors draw on different discourses. Hence, studying meanings is a device for analysing how actors use and reshape different discourses.

To delineate the dynamic working of development discourses in Kayatuan, interface analysis is then used. According to Norman Long:

> [i]nterfaces typically occur at points where different, and often conflicting, lifeworlds or social fields intersect, or more concretely, in social situations or arenas in which interactions become oriented around problems of bridging, accommodating, segregating or contesting social, evaluative and cognitive standpoints. (Long 1999: 1)

Since social interfaces are real or imaginary meeting points of different discourses, their analysis can show how the goals, perceptions, interests and relationships of the various parties may be reshaped as a result of their interaction. I made it a special point to attend and analyse meetings and public events, such as the graduation party of the literacy project. These events can be defined as 'occasions that people undertake in concert to make more, less, or other of themselves, than they usually do' (Handelman 1990: 3). Such events are highly revealing for someone interested in the meaning that actors accord to their projects, since, in the words of Geertz (1973: 448) they contain stories that people 'tell themselves about themselves'. During these occasions I observed the enactment of these stories as well as the dynamic between on- and off-stage interactions. Through interviews, I tried to assess how these events fitted in to the everyday life of the actors involved.

By ethnographically identifying discourses and studying their use at interfaces of development, the literacy project could be interpreted. In the end, I found that the project, which was meant to empower the participants, contributed instead to eroding the status of these women. Through the project they came to be defined as women who lack something, namely, literacy. In everyday conversation they were literally referred to as the 'no-read-no-write women'. The officers of the organization, on the other hand, further established their position as bearers of development. Before elaborating on how literacy training became one of the constitutive elements of social change in Kayatuan, I will introduce the village and bring out some of the more salient contradictions in local meanings of development by exploring the local concepts of progress, organization and project.

Meanings of Development in Kayatuan

Kayatuan is a *barangay* in Mountain province. A *barangay* is an administrative unit under a municipality, which is governed by an elected captain
and council. It is situated along the Halsema Highway, a two-track road
only partly cemented and mainly consisting of rough and bumpy stretches.
At the time of fieldwork (1995), there were around 750 inhabitants in
Kayatuan, divided among 150 households. Three features of Kayatuan
are particularly relevant: migration patterns, the changing nature and
composition of labour and the presence of building contractors in the
village.

A rather narrow resource base and a growing population made out-
migration necessary throughout the twentieth century. Before the Second
World War, men sought seasonal work in the forest or mines, coming back
after some months. After the war, whole families often moved, either to join
the fathers at their workplace or to farm in the lowlands. Although many
left on a permanent basis, most practised a variety of temporary forms of
migration, leaving and returning to the village – hence the local term used
for them as 'come-'n-goes'. There was also in-migration from nearby
villages of families who wanted to live near the school that had been built
in Kayatuan in 1956. In the 1980s, international labour migration became
another possibility. In 1995, 27 people out of the 150 households in Kayatuan were working abroad. Of these, 23 were women: daughters or wives
doing domestic work in 'Saudi'[3] or Hong Kong. Migration, then, is firmly
engrained in Kayatuan life.

Another feature has been a rapid move away from subsistence agriculture. Merely two decades ago, it was almost everybody's main activity.
Today, this holds true only for 40 per cent of the adults. Most of these
combine subsistence rice and sweet potato growing with commercial
vegetable farming. Another 40 per cent have paid employment (including
working abroad) or are engaged in shopkeeping, trading or other kinds of
business. Quite a few are professionals in the government bureaucracy or
work as teachers. This development has different implications for social
relations in the village. Gender roles have been affected. Previously, men
were considered the providers for the family, since they could generate
income through road, forest or mine work during agricultural low seasons.
Today, increasingly, women have paid jobs. There is more overseas employment for women and few men are professional. This development
has shaken local gender ideology. Remarks like 'today, women are the
providers' have become commonplace in the village.[4] Moreover, it has
resulted in a widening gap between professionals and peasant women in
the village. The increasing differentiation among women, and the loss of

status of peasant women in particular, reflects power processes at the intersection of the wider society and the community.

A third factor of note is the presence of contractors. Four men and a woman make their living in infrastructural work contracted out by the government. It is common knowledge that these contracts are lucrative, generating incomes for the contractors that sometimes amount to as much as 80 per cent of the entire budget involved. These people are successful in landing contracts because of their proximity to the provincial governor, to whom they are linked through kinship and/or a history of work relations. The practices surrounding contracts are intimately related to the organization of government finances and the way in which Philippine bureaucracy operates (see Coronel 1998). Contract applications should be filed by a community organization, and the contractors are therefore officers of civic organizations such as the Parent–Teacher Association. This has particular repercussions for how local people perceive progress, projects and community organizations.

Progress in Kayatuan Progress in Kayatuan is related to being adventurous and daring to take opportunities. Kayatuans take pride in their history of migration, which is associated with an inclination towards 'progress'. For example, when a group of migrants from Kayatuan ran into conflicts with local residents where they had settled, they derided them as 'not liking progress'. Alternatively, villagers use the term progress to refer to material advancement, as in the remark: 'There is no progress in Kayatuan, only in Baguio. Here, only the contractors have progress.' A third meaning of progress is related to becoming modern. It refers to modernizing the village by obtaining electricity, water systems and cemented pathways, but also in adopting modern values. This is particularly salient in the importance attached to cleanliness.

Painfully aware of their origins among the 'headhunting tribes' of the Igorots, and even more of certain traditional practices now considered 'dirty', many Kayatuans go to great lengths to convince themselves and outsiders that they have broken with their past.[5] Different people told the same story to introduce Kayatuan to me, namely: 'If you had come here earlier, you could not walk without stepping in the dung of the pigs that were roaming around freely. Then, if you had to go to the toilet, you had to sit with the pigs.'

It happened on several occasions when people were asked about former times that they said: 'Oh, you mean when we were still dirty', or, alternatively, 'Oh, when we were still ignorant …' This was not during conversations about cleanliness or education, but about agriculture and land use one generation ago. These remarks were apparently time markers, a general reference to the 'old days'. Equating the old days with 'dirty times' stems no doubt from decades of missionary teaching during colonial days, followed by American efforts to educate Filipinos that 'Cleanliness is next to Godliness', as can still be read in today's classrooms.[6]

On the other hand, people take pride in their origins as Igorots. In their civic organizations extensive use is made of traditional symbols. They reiterate values attributed to kinship and community solidarity, while ignoring other sides of their cultural heritage, such as headhunting practices. Barth (1969) laid the groundwork in identifying ethnicity as a form of social organization, with the ethnic boundary as a critical focus for investigation. If ethnicity is constructed by drawing boundaries, one might say that in Kayatuan people re-create their ethnicity by drawing a boundary around their past. Both literally and in a symbolic sense, Kayatuans seem eager to 'clean' their past. They are Igorots, but adhere to modern hygiene and selectively celebrate what they consider the 'proper' elements of tradition. This is illustrated by the present-day use of traditional dress. At activities, women don traditionally woven garments. These, however, are bright, new and neat. Although they are of the same fabric as the torn, dirty, stained skirts wrapped around the old women in the fields, the former are a symbol of today's Igorots, while the latter are looked upon with derision. The traditional dresses during celebrations are reminiscent of Igorot traditions, while simultaneously underlining the distance people from Kayatuan have travelled from their past.

Projects in Kayatuan A second concept from which the local meanings of development can be derived is projects. People use the term in three different ways: as community improvement, as instruments of welfare and as personal enrichment. First, government rhetoric bestows upon community members the responsibility of civic duty, which is mainly upheld by women working for the government or being married to politicians. Second, projects are associated with helping people in need. This has continuity with kinship obligations and redistributive social institutions that ordered social community life from time immemorial. Kinship ties remain central even today, and are maintained up to the third degree. A couple belongs to the clans of both parents of both spouses and, due to this bilateral kinship system, family ties have become diffused throughout the community. This results in strong notions that people have of helping each other when they are in need, since they are all family. This value is reinforced through the churches, which are very active in the community. Thus projects that are meant to benefit the 'indigent' people, or, as they are referred to in the local vernacular, the *kakaasi* (literally 'the pitiful'), often have a double ring of kin solidarity and Christian charity about them.

A quite different meaning attached to projects is as venues for personal enrichment. This is clearly related to the practice of 'contracts' explained above. Projects for tendered contracts are not primarily formulated for the development they bring, but for the prospects they contain. The most pressing issue with these projects is not about needs, goals and beneficiaries, but the question of who is going to be the contractor. The desired outcome of projects as 'bringing development' becomes secondary at most, and sometimes outcomes are not even part of the deal at all. Illustrative is the situation in lower Kayatuan, where 70 households share one single water tap. Four projects were initiated to construct additional water tanks, and they all failed. One tank was taken into use by the contractor as his personal fishpond. Another tank remained empty, after the contractor had removed the pipes upon completion of the project inspection. A third tank was never built and a final one was never completed.

Community organizations in Kayatuan There are around 30 community organizations in Kayatuan, some dormant but many active. A large number of these have been formed at the instigation of outside institutions, such as government departments, churches and politicians. There are also independent organizations, like a co-operative and a Ladies' Association. Because of the proliferation of organizations, most people have multiple memberships and there is often overlap in the sets of officers. The organizations are important in the life world of Kayatuan residents. Partly, they are interwoven with kin ties, since organizations become immersed in extended family relations. On the other hand, they also help in ordering social relations in the village. Because of the proliferation of kinship in multiple directions, it is not a very effective way of discriminating relationships. Associational affiliations help to give additional meaning to social relationships, in terms of which are important and which of less significance.

As with progress and project, organization has several meanings. First, it relates to the community itself. It denotes a sense of togetherness and belongingness, as well as a certain competition with other communities that is reminiscent of former village rivalry. People are proud to have an active community and always seek occasions to show off their village in contests and competitions. When a Kayatuan baby wins the provincial 'Healthiest Baby Competition', the news that 'we' won is quickly passed around.

Second, organizations are associated with community politics. Officers use organizations to expand their influence over community affairs. Government employees are not entitled, according to Philippine law, to run for political positions. Government employees, who none the less want to be involved in community affairs, find occasion through the village organizations to promote government programmes. Those people who are not government employees can use the organizations as a springboard for election to political office. Organizations, as described above, are also used to acquire contracts for infrastructure projects. Although the contractors explain their involvement in organizations as an expression of civic responsibility, it is common knowledge that this serves them well. When a teenage girl sighed that she wanted to become rich, and I asked her how she could, she immediately giggled: 'Then I have to become the president of the PTA (Parent–Teacher Association).'

Finally, organizations are identified with community solidarity and mutual support. They place high emphasis on co-operation and on helping those members of the community in any kind of need. These needs can be material, for example, when the community gets together to construct a house for a young couple who want to live in Kayatuan. But they can also be in the sphere of education and values, such as when an organization officer explained: 'These poor women are not even aware of the need for cleanliness, and we have to educate them.'

Three meanings of development From the meanings accorded to progress, projects and community organizations, three definitions of development can be derived: development as 'modernizing and improving the community', development as 'helping those in need' and development as 'getting personal benefits'. As shown in the Table 4.1, all three draw on discourses from within the village and on discourses introduced by intervening agencies. Community improvement is associated with kinship and tradition in the village, but also with public administration. The solidarity language is based on values of redistribution and reciprocity, and is more closely associated with church initiatives and NGOs. Development as personal benefit reflects the entrepreneurial and adventurous character of villagers who migrate, and fits with practices of certain government line agencies and politicians.

These meanings are more than a local dictionary on development. In the first place, they are obviously gendered. Improving the community and helping those in need belong typically, although not exclusively, to the languages of women, whereas development as individual progress is more expressed by men and through masculine activities. The discourses imply different roles and obligations for men and women. In the second place, these different notions are not static. The following section analyses how they are being used in everyday practice to categorize and label village women and to pattern social distance between them.

Table 4.1 Multiple meanings of development

Meanings of 'progress'	Meanings of 'project'	Meanings of 'community organization'	Development as:
'Cleanliness' 'Modernization' (infrastructure)	'Community improvement and beautification'	'Belongingness and village pride' 'A means to regulate smooth social relations' 'Channel for promoting government policies' 'Expression of civic duty'	'improving the village'
	'Instruments to help indigent people or the *kakaasi* (pitiful)' 'Welfare services'	'Extension of kinship solidarity' 'Expression of mutual support, Christian duty'	'helping those in need'
'Adventurous, daring to take opportunities' 'Material advancement'	'A means for personal enrichment'	'A means to gain political power' 'A means to acquire lucrative government contracts'	'bringing personal benefits'

The Kayatuan Ladies' Association, Inc.

The Kayatuan Ladies' Association Inc. (KLAi) was founded in July 1989. It started with 30 members, and grew to 70. KLAi is run by a core group of six people. The central figure is *Manang* Juliet. Originally from the lowlands, she came to the area in 1956 to assume a position as midwife. She is the widow of a former headmaster of the high school and has six adult children. Midwives don't readily come to mind as powerful people, but *Manang* Juliet is one of the most respected authorities in the community. Conditions in the area are harsh, and every baby safely delivered is a major accomplishment, creating lifelong obligations to the person who has assisted in the delivery. Over the years, *Manang* Juliet became co-ordinator of all Rural Health Units in the province. She also became increasingly involved in 'volunteerism', as she calls it, and initiated many organizations and projects, usually with a health angle to them. *Manang* Juliet has many contacts in the provincial capital that she can mobilize and she played a pivotal role in recruiting and consolidating the membership of the organization, using her leverage and social influence as a midwife and the wife of the high school principal. She is the unquestioned authority of the core group.

Two other members of the core group are teachers: Mrs Dulay and Mrs Barlig. Mrs Dulay is married to the vice-mayor. She is in her fifties and appears to be the second-in-command of the KLAi. She takes community affairs very seriously and cannot sleep if work is left undone. She resents every instance of politics entering community organizations, and prays every night that her husband, the vice-mayor, will 'stay clean' as she calls it. Mrs Barlig is tasked to keep records and do the bookkeeping of KLAi. She often reiterates how she owes her job in the school to the late husband of *Manang* Juliet. Adriana Lapadan belongs to one of the old families of Kayatuan and has kinship relations in different degrees with most Kayatuan residents. She is the wife of the *barangay* captain. She is also the largest vegetable trader in the community, has business relations with most members and often uses meetings to make arrangements. On the other hand, her dedication to organizing matters goes far beyond this practical interest. She visibly enjoys applying her skills and learning new ones to be able to handle projects.

Finally, there are two women I came to consider as belonging to the core group, although they were not officers of the KLAi. They were a housewife (and neighbour of *Manang* Juliet) and a farmer (and sister to Mrs Dulay) who made it a habit to hang around when the KLAi officers meet. The two of them are representatives on the *barangay* council. As non-professionals, they could run for political office, which they did with the support of the KLAi. Together with Adriana Lapadan, who attends most council meetings to assist her husband, they were able to secure a monthly stipend for the voluntary work of the *Barangay* Health Workers. The core group, then, is very close-knit, with longstanding friendship and kinship relations. Most of them have multiple positions as officers in other community organizations. They also have close associations with people in local politics and government. *Manang* Juliet, Mrs Dulay and Mrs Barlig are professionals in government service, and through both marriage and activities are linked to the political structures of the village and the province. Adriana Lapadan has high standing in the locality because of her marriage to the *barangay* captain. The two remaining women figure in elected local government positions.

When KLAi was formed there were already several women's organizations in the community and the reason to form yet another was explained as follows: 'We observed the need to get the women together to talk about our problems, to improve our situation, to help one another and to solve our problems. That is why we wanted to have a Non Government Organization.' From the beginning of the process of organizing, then, it was clear that this organization was not just a women's club, but an NGO, a concept associated with projects and external fundraising. Note, for example, the way the organization's name is written, with the 'i' for 'incorporated' always added to the acronym. The 'i' signals that the organization is registered as an NGO with the Security Exchange Committee, which was done even before the first membership meeting. The consistent use of the 'i' stands out as a symbol underscoring the NGO-ness of the organization. Immediately after the organization was formally established, the search for projects started. This was done by asking existing contacts outside the community to approach 'sponsors', and then to apply for whatever a particular sponsor had to offer. The contacts that could be tapped for this purpose were both social (for instance, with people originating from the area) and those established in the course of earlier development interventions, such as some academics who had previously worked in the area. The officers of KLAi were apparently very skilful in this game, and before long projects started to come in. These included two different swine dispersal programmes, a village pharmacy, and two cash prizes[7] used for the construction of an organization office and the purchase of a set of drums for the village youth.

The core group of KLAi is well aware of the value of contacts to obtain projects, and is careful not to jeopardize its good relations. As the graduation party shows, the women apply many strategies in order to maintain positive relations with people they may need for future projects. As mentioned above, the graduation party followed two years of patiently teaching 'no-read-no-write women'. The project started because officers of the KLAi had heard that CWNGO offered possibilities for a literacy scheme. They decided that this was a good idea and *Manang* Juliet mobilized a class of participants. Later, asked about their motivation to join, most of the participants explained they were 'told to do so by the midwife'. As the project evolved, it became a kind of social venue for these elderly women, and a far cry from the objectives given by the supporting NGO and the teacher. Nevertheless, this big party was organized for the women to celebrate their graduation. As the ethnography will make clear, the literacy class attained meaning in relation to wider organizational processes. It became one of the episodes through which development notions were played out, shaping perceptions and altering power relations in the village.

The literacy graduation party It is 8 December 1995, a day long anticipated in Kayatuan. Today is the graduation of the 'no-read-no-write women'. After two years of twice-weekly training, the women finish the equivalent of 'grade one' of the elementary school system. The day before the graduation, five officers of the KLAi gather to prepare for the festivity. They first decorate the school building where the event is to take place, putting up a huge backcloth made of a white sheet with big red letters to announce the occasion. They also type out several copies of the programme. The remainder of the day, until well beyond midnight, they spend cooking. All the graduating women contribute some vegetables and a prescribed amount of rice, equivalent to the volume of two sardine cans, and money is collected to purchase meat. The preparations are carried out smoothly. The women obviously had been through these routines before.

The graduation takes place in the morning. Around seventy people are cramped into a classroom and numerous children play around. Then, at a sign from the *barangay* captain, all rise to share a prayer and sing the national anthem. Most of the audience consists of women, dressed in the uniform of the organization – a traditional wraparound skirt with a blue T-shirt with the name of the KLAi printed on it. All officers of the *barangay* council of Kayatuan are present, and a large number of representatives of the government have travelled to the village for the occasion, including the municipal mayor. Ironically, only the NGO that initiated the literacy class was unable to send staff to the celebration.

The official guests are treated with great reverence. The mayor is frequently referred to in the welcome address and the speeches. He is called 'Apo mayor', a form of address which is normally reserved for 'Apo Dios', God. Another high official among the guests is the District Supervisor of the Department of Education and Sport. During the welcome, the speaker makes a deliberate mistake by referring to him as the Superintendent, one rank higher than his present position. To the delight of the audience, she corrects herself and says: 'No, the Supervisor, Superintendent-to-be.' Other speakers follow her example, and before the morning is finished the 'mistake' will be repeated three more times.

After the welcoming address, the graduating women present themselves. They walk to the front of the classroom; some of them use a cane or are bent double. With one or two exceptions, they are grandmothers and even great-grandmothers. They start with a demonstration of their skills and write down their names on a blackboard. It takes some of them more than five minutes, and several have to erase the name repeatedly before getting it right. When, finally, the list is completed, they form a line in front of the classroom. One of them speaks on behalf of the group and giggles: 'We are the *balasang di kalman*, the girls of yesteryear.' This self-imposed label sets the tone for the entire morning. When the District Supervisor distributes the diplomas, he takes the joke further and addresses the women as *ading*, the address used for younger siblings. Considering his age, he could easily pass for one of their sons, so each time he uses *ading* the audience roars with laughter. Before the distribution of the diplomas, however, the graduates have prepared a little programme. Some of them present a skit that centres around their newly achieved capacity to read the place of destination on public transport vehicles, and one of the women recites a nursery rhyme in the national language (Tagalog), entitled 'I love my dog'.

When all the 'distinguished guests' have finished their congratulation speeches, it is finally the turn of the mayor to take the floor. He says to the graduates:

> I am very happy that you went to school. Even if you didn't know how to take a bath before, now that you have come to the school, you know how to take a bath, how to wash your clothes and how to clean your house.

The graduating grandmothers continue to look up at him, smiling and beaming. None of them protests or seems the least bit upset by the suggestion that until last year they did not know how to keep themselves or their houses clean. The mayor thus continues undisturbed and starts to reiterate a number of municipal policies. He reminds them to go to the mountains and plant trees, to stop using cyanide and electric current in the river to catch fish and to stop burning trees on the mountain slopes.' Everybody should help his neighbours and maintain unity in the village. Finally, and most importantly, 'people should stop the widespread vices of gambling and drinking!'

Then the graduation is over. While the women gather up the lunch utensils, the *barangay* officers and the government representatives quickly disappear. They assemble in the house of the *barangay* captain, where several bottles of *ginebra* (gin) stand waiting with plates of *palutan* (a popular appetizer made of intestines fried in blood). The solemn caution of ten minutes earlier is apparently not meant for the officials themselves, and with pleasure the mayor is the first to start the heavy drinking session. In the meantime, the women and children enjoy their lunch in the school building. Afterwards, they put on a tape with *gangsa* music (brass gongs) and start to perform traditional dances. A photo session concludes the graduation programme and everybody returns home.

Managing the interfaces of development   Through their organizational experience and strategic position in the *barangay* and *vis-à-vis* government structures, the core group members of KLAi have become highly skilled development interface experts. They have the knowledge and the skills to organize development and to manage relations with outside convenors of development. The graduation event clearly displays this. The ease with which they provide a meal for more than seventy people, the invitations, decorations and ceremonial composition of the programme all bear witness to their skills. The same holds true for the way they manage relations with government representatives.

The graduation is meant as a celebration for the literacy class partici-pants, but they are certainly not the central actors. The main purpose of the event is to invite government representatives so as to strengthen ties with them and enrol them for future support. The women know how to do this. They pay ample respect to the officials in their speeches and go to great lengths to flatter them, for example in the deliberate mistake of addressing a representative by a rank higher than his actual position. That the flattery is obvious enough to invite laughter apparently does not diminish its effect. They are well aware that the government officials like to have their lunch separately and preferably added to a drinking session. Through a smooth collaboration of the Lapadan couple, Adriana remains in charge of the lunch at the graduation site, while her husband entertains the officials, no doubt using the occasion to discuss some projects with them.

The KLAi officers are thoroughly familiar with the different practices of development. They master the idiom of community development and projects for the poor (in this case the old women), and are equally familiar with practices that require treating officials well in order to be rewarded with a project. They know everything about the official aspects of projects, such as writing proposals, bookkeeping and recording. But they also know that development has a social component and needs constant enrolment and investing in relations with those in a position to offer development. By using their knowledge, the KLAi officers not only mobilize development but also bend it to a considerable extent. In the case of the literacy training, for example, they managed to change sponsors without much ado. The project was originally sponsored by an NGO. After two years, the KLAi wanted to have the activity adopted by a government agency that could possibly remunerate the volunteer teacher. When the NGO was not able to send a staff member to the graduation activity, the women took the opportunity to ignore the NGO involvement altogether. Not once during the celebration was their support mentioned, instead the government representatives were requested to '*continue* [*sic*] their support'.

Manipulation of projects seems a normal aspect of development in Kayatuan. KLAi can do this successfully because its core group is more knowledgeable about the intervening agencies than the representatives of these agencies are about local dynamics. While seemingly playing along with the rules of these institutions, they are very well able to implement their own 'projects'. The KLAi officers use different development concepts to manage relations with intervening agencies and to appropriate development for their own projects. They do this deliberately; in interviews, they explain what they do and why this is important. In a much less clear-cut way, development concepts are also used to negotiate social order in Kayatuan. People often talk about the social changes that have occurred in the village, but how this happens remains largely unnoticed by the local actors. They may not realize what role they play in these social changes. Yet they have a role, and one way in which they play it is by negotiating development through applying different discourses. One method of making these processes visible is by focusing on moments of conflict, when ongoing negotiations of the social order become apparent.

Dynamics within the KLAi

When members of the KLAi are asked during interviews why they are not officers of the organization, they usually reply: 'Because I don't speak English.' It is a tacit understanding that being a KLAi officer requires knowing English, at least if one wants to be part of the core group. Consider this statement of one of the officers: 'At the start of KLAi we were with Mrs Peñaranda, Mrs Barlig, Mrs Vergara and Joanna Bagaba. Joanna was there, although she hardly understands English, but she was always willing to sit with us.' The participation in the initial core group of a non-English speaker needed explanation. The quote also shows the separate status of Joanna Bagaba. She is not included in the 'us' referred to and her participation is defined in a passive sense. She is, moreover, the only one called by her Christian name, although she is one of the oldest in this group. Joanna is a housewife and farmer; the others mentioned are professionals.

Role and conflicts of professionals The professionals are keener than others to be officers and competition easily arises over the control of the organization. At the start of KLAi, a conflict occurred between the core group and Mrs Balatas. Mrs Balatas is a government employee and married to one of the contractors in the village. Although she had been active in setting up earlier women's organizations in Kayatuan, she was not invited to the founding meeting of the KLAi. The core group maintains this was just a mistake, but she believes, probably correctly, that it was a way of excluding her from taking a position in the new organization. She refuses to be a member and gossips viciously about the organization. It is only when she is given the presidency of yet another new women's organization in the village, for spouses of government officials, that the conflict subsides.

Apparently, then, it is considered rewarding to be an officer. Without denying the genuine desire of these officers to help their fellow villagers, or the obvious pleasure they have in organizing and social interaction, it seems there are other motives for becoming an officer. One could be that the position offers opportunities for material reward. When the first consignment of money arrived for one of the swine-fattening programmes, the core group retained 20 per cent and distributed this among themselves to 'cover their expenses'. The incident fits into the multifaceted conception of development in the village. In a mild version of contracting practices, the core group claimed they 'deserved a reward' for bringing the project to the village. Other members apparently did not agree and six of them resigned from the KLAi.

More important than the material rewards, I believe, is the question of status and a desire to be different from the ordinary members of the KLAi. In some ways, professionals are not very distinct from other people in the village. Their houses do not stand out (expensive houses in the village belong to either the contractors, or to families with several children working overseas); they are embedded in extensive family relations in the village; and are all involved in agriculture. Mrs Dulay can be seen every day collecting sweet potatoes for her pigs, Mrs Barlig often works in the fields, as do the children of *Manang* Juliet. But in other respects they are different from other women, a difference they enjoy. This becomes apparent through a conflict with a teacher, who is not an officer but a member of the KLAi. This particular woman had the bad luck to have the piglet that was handed out to her die in her care. She was convinced that the animal was sick when she received it, but the core group held her responsible and demanded that she pay back her loan. In the end a compromise was reached, but the teacher remained spiteful. When she spoke about the incident several years after it happened, she burst into tears. Her grief, as it turned out, was not about the loan that she had to pay back but about the way she was treated, namely, as one of the ordinary people of the village. In particular, her case had been publicly discussed in front of the entire membership. As she explained:

> When I see her [*Manang* Juliet], I still smile. But she should not have talked in front of other people. If only she had done it individually but not in the meeting. She is the midwife, and I am the teacher. And then she speaks to me in front of the common *tao* [the common people]. That is why it really hurts.

For this teacher, it was a major insult and humiliation to be addressed in front of (and therefore as if she is one of) the common people. The professional, in other words, although she does not have a position as one of the officers, does not want to be treated as just a member. After the incident she felt it her duty to retain her membership of the KLAi, but when its core group becomes active in setting up a local chapter of the nationwide Catholic Women's League, she refuses to become a member of this new organization.[8]

In the project proposals and in the eyes of the sponsors, the KLAi consists of a group of undifferentiated beneficiaries. In practice, however, this is not the case. The KLAi core group receives the same benefits as other members, but with a different rationale. For example, they are among the first to receive a pig as part of the swine-fattening programme. During a discussion on the selection of beneficiaries, one of them explains: 'We look at the members who need it. But of course, we also have a pig ourselves. Why should we not also have a pig? We are even the ones who bring the project to the community.'

In everyday practice, a differentiation is made among the participants of the project. Ordinary members obtain a pig because they are *in need*, but the core group receives a pig *as a reward* for their efforts. Different fragments of development discourses are simultaneously applied to different kinds of participants. By doing so, a distinction is created between those people who receive development (the ordinary beneficiaries) and those who bring development (the core group). This difference contributes considerably to the desired 'status apart' of the professionals in the community. How the distinction works out for those considered the beneficiaries will be explored in the case of *Manang* Esmeralda.

Peasant women as beneficiaries *Manang* Esmeralda came to Kayatuan as a girl, and became a housemaid for one of the teachers. She then
married a local resident and had four children, all of whom had grown
up by the time of my fieldwork. Esmeralda and her husband live in one
of the smallest houses in the village. They have a vegetable garden and
the husband has occasional jobs in construction work. *Manang* Esmeralda
is one of the *Barangay* Health Workers in the community and she is a
member of the KLAi. As she explains, her interest in community organizations is for the material benefits provided. As a *Barangay* Health Worker,
she is entitled to free medical care at the hospital and, through the KLAi,
she has availed herself of several loans to buy pigs.

The position of farmer women such as Esmeralda in the KLAi seems
clear: they are the beneficiaries for whose needs the socioeconomic projects are organized. However, *Manang* Esmeralda obtained more than this.
She became enraptured with the teachings about modern values. *Manang*
Esmeralda always received a lot of special attention from the officers of
the KLAi. During activities of the KLAi and Health Workers, Esmeralda
never says anything but is often herself addressed. In meetings, she is
always singled out to illustrate whatever point an officer wants to make.
She is, for example, the only member of the KLAi to receive an award
for having quickly repaid her loan. One of the teachers remarks: 'When
you see Esmeralda, you don't want to give her a loan. You think she will
never pay it back, she looks so poor. But she is a member, so she also got
her loan. And she paid it back.'

When Esmeralda paid back the loan, she was given a piece of paper
acknowledging her good credit status. Since she was the only person given
such an award, the implicit message was that if even Esmeralda had paid
back, everybody could. Several times in every meeting, *Manang* Esmeralda
serves as an example. When an officer announces a municipal activity, for
example, she says: 'When we go to that day, of course we want to make
a good impression. So, Esmeralda, that means that we have to take a bath
and put on a clean dress.'

Reference to *Manang* Esmeralda's behaviour also happens outside of
meetings. The core group interferes with her appearance and personal
habits in everyday life. *Manang* Esmeralda is thought to be dirty, and is
repeatedly told to take a bath and change clothes. One officer told me that
she went to see Esmeralda to talk with her: 'I told her that she has to take
a bath every day and that she especially has to take care to wash her
vagina. I told her she should do that every night, so that when her husband
wants to sleep with her she is fresh for him.' From this meddling in *Manang*
Esmeralda's very personal life, a picture emerges of the core group turning
the women's organization into a vehicle aimed at modernizing peasant

women in the village. The core group seems as much engaged in the actual projects as in their own project to transform the 'girls of yesteryear' into their version of 'modern Igorots'.

The question remains of how peasant women felt about this. Never during my fieldwork did I encounter a woman who openly challenged the teachings of the core group, nor the loss of status they experienced. If these women had developed a counter-discourse, it remained a carefully 'hidden transcript' (Scott 1990).[9] This does not mean that women simply subjected themselves to the education of the core group. From observation, they occasionally avoided or ignored it, kept silent and withdrew. After the graduation, for example, I asked several participants if they had taken note of the mayor's praise for the graduates – who had been housekeepers for decades – that they had finally learned to clean themselves and their houses. It turned out they had noticed, but had not taken offence. They had simply not felt addressed. As one of them said: 'Of course, we know how to clean our houses but maybe some others don't.'

Manang Esmeralda had her own way of challenging the ideas of the core group. She was the only person who withdrew from the literacy class. Like the other participants, Esmeralda had been 'told by the midwife [*Manang* Juliet] to join the class'. After some time, however, Esmeralda began to complain. Like her classmates, she was not able to retain what she learnt, but, while the others enjoyed the classes, Esmeralda considered them a waste of time. She started to absent herself from the lessons. Esmeralda's absence soon caught the attention of the core group and for some reason this annoyed them. I witnessed three occasions in which they spoke to her about it. First, one of the officers went to her house and told her to resume the classes. Second, another officer stopped her one day on the road and, in the presence of several other people, asked her why she had stopped coming to the classes. Third, it was made an issue at the KLAi meeting. When reporting about the class, one of the officers said there was a problem with attendance and that one of the women had dropped out. At that point everybody looked at Esmeralda. On all these occasions, Esmeralda did not mention the fact that she found the class a waste of time. Once she replied that she had no pen to write. On other occasions, she kept silent. The insistence of the core group that Esmeralda resume the literacy class does not tally with the idea that the class was a mere service to these women or even a social pastime. Apparently, they perceived her withdrawal as a challenge to their initiative and thus implicitly to them. They reacted by trying to make her resume her place in the class. The incident emphasizes the social change that has occurred for women in the village. Until very recently, Esmeralda, as an older woman, would command respect and authority. Today, the authority of the educated women in the core group has to remain undisputed. Trespassing against this unwritten rule by women like Esmeralda is not acceptable any more.

Development Discourse and Social Change

What can be said in conclusion about the question of how discursive notions alter local social realities? As it turns out, local development actors master multiple development notions, and use these for their own ends and to categorize different groups of actors. In particular, those actors through whom development enters a locality find in this way room for manoeuvre to manipulate development for their own 'projects'. These village experts are living illustrations of the saying that 'knowledge is power'. At the same time, one has to realize that other forms of power are at work in village development that are more fluid and remain largely unnoticed. This relates to what I have called the 'duality of discourse': the use of particular notions may partly be strategic, but has unintended repercussions for confirming, accelerating or altering social change. In Kayatuan, an NGO aimed to empower women by giving them access to the written word. Local actors transformed the project on the way, turning it into a space where elderly women enjoyed getting together, playing at being schoolgirls and remembering the past. By defining the women as lacking something – namely the ability to read and write – and by turning the project into a vehicle for education about modern values, the project contributed to an erosion of the status of older women and underlined a widening gap between educated professionals and peasant women. Chapter 5 will further elaborate on the gaps in understanding development and projects between NGOs and their clients.

There are multiple meanings of development in a community. These are not imposed by outsiders like NGOs, but draw on fragments both of modernity and tradition. The everyday allocation and use of these discourses is one of the constituent elements of social change in the village. Language expresses diversity and social distance in everyday life (Ouden 1979), and differential uses of development discourse can shape hierarchies and pattern relations. By variously labelling people as instigators, catalysts or subjects of development, they are socially positioned (Wood 1985). In the pig dispersal programme all members of the women's organization availed themselves of project benefits, but the concomitant rationale differed. The core group that managed projects applied to themselves a discourse of 'development as reward for personal effort', whereas for others they used a discourse of 'development to help those in need'. In doing so, they categorized themselves as the bringers of development and the ordinary members as undergoing development. The peasant members enjoyed a project that they considered was responding to poor people's needs. However, they obtained more than they 'bargained' for. They were enrolled in a discourse to live up to modern standards, which increasingly locked them into a position of social inferiority.

Hence, women's use of development discourses played into processes of social ordering. In the course of a lifetime, the status of older women had changed considerably. Previously, the sturdy and strong peasant represented the ideal type of Igorot woman (McKay 1993). Elder women enjoyed a status of seniority on the basis of increased wisdom with age. Nowadays, the status of peasant women is eroded in favour of educated professionals. Peasants are mainly associated with dark skins and dirty bodies; professionals, on the other hand, are clean. Notions that distinguish between development as solidarity for those in need, as reward for personal effort, and as a project for community modernization, contribute to these changing realities. Discourse matters. It is through actors' use of multiple discourses that social patterns are negotiated, power distributed and development shaped.

Notes

1. This chapter was published in *Human Organization*, see Hilhorst 2001.

2. Names of people and places have been changed.

3. Saudi is a generic term, used in Kayatuan to denote all the Gulf states.

4. See the volume of Ong and Peletz (1995: 10) for transformations in masculinity in South-east Asia, marked among others things by the label of man as 'deficient provider'.

5. This present conception of their own 'dirty' past coincides with earlier lowland perceptions of Igorots as 'dirty'. Around 1900, if a lowland child was dirty, his mother would say: 'You Igorot, go to the well and take a bath' (quoted in Scott 1993: 55).

6. 'Cleanliness' in the highlands seems mainly introduced by outsiders. According to the old people in the village, their parents hardly ever took a bath. This is not the case in the entire Philippines. According to William Henry Scott, lowland Philippine societies used to have strong norms about cleanliness prior to colonial times (Scott 1997: 116–17).

7. The cash prizes were obtained from a German-sponsored nationwide health programme, called HAMIS (HAMIS 1995).

8. Note the way the multiplicity of community organizations plays a role in the handling of conflict. On the one hand, the organizations provide ways to smooth conflict, as in the case of Mrs Balatas, who was offered the presidency of a new organization to placate her. On the other, a person's membership may be used manipulatively, as an expression of subtle protest, as in the case of this

teacher. In a society where open conflicts are avoided if possible, the signal of withholding membership is meant and received as a statement of protest.

9. Women among themselves spoke Kankanaey, their local language, which I unfortunately could not understand. I thus missed possible references in everyday conversations. However, never once during interviews (in Ilokano and in English) was this referred to.

FIVE

Modelling Development: NGO
Room for Manoeuvre

In order to bring about development for poor or marginalized target groups, NGOs work with intervention models that they can implement with their clients. In this chapter I examine how one such model works in practice, where NGO officers and villagers shape the organizing processes of local People's Organizations. It provides some sobering evidence on the lack of room for manoeuvre that NGOs have in making local development happen. My main purpose, however, is to consider what intervention models look like, and why agencies continue to adhere to them even though they know that these models do not do what they are meant to do, namely, ordering development interventions. As I try to unravel intervention, it is not enough simply to measure performance against some kind of proclaimed target. We have to come to grips with the dynamics of intervention, use this knowledge to revisit the targets or models on which intervention was based, bring out their built-in assumptions and then ask what they do if they are not ordering development.

I set out to do this for the organizing model of the NGOs in the Philippine Cordillera region that is central to this book. The NGOs do not want to implement a particular programme, but instead to *facilitate an organizing process* of People's Organizations (POs). The step-by-step model stipulates that organizing needs to be done in a certain order: People's Organizations are not supposed to proceed to the next step until they are 'ready'. Like most development plans, structural adjustment policies, or policies of funding agencies, we will see that this model leans on notions of modern organizations and the linearity of planned intervention. It aims to empower people by making them self-reliant, but to make this happen the NGO first requires a lot of power to have the model implemented without too much interference from the people in the locality. Villagers, however, have their own projects and understandings that interfere with the NGO-desired organizing process. How villagers imagine the identity and role of NGOs seems to be more decisive for these organizing processes than the envisaged NGO model.

As a result, intervention processes in the villages do not happen in a linear fashion, but have all kinds of directions, ruptures, closures and 'fanning out'. The step-by-step organizing model has little to do with actual organizing in the villages. However, I try to discover why in fact NGOs none the less adhere to this model. I am interested, in other words, in the meaning of NGO intervention models for the organization itself. Even though these models are created with the purpose of steering local intervention, we cannot assume that that is what they do. They may do quite different things in practice. As I shall argue, such models may be more important for processes of sense-making within NGOs and for regulating relations between them than for steering local organizing processes.

Taking It Step-by-step

NGOs in the Cordillera are not interested in implementing a particular programme, but want to facilitate an 'organizing *process*'. The organizing process has a specific meaning for the NGOs. Whereas I defined processes descriptively as discontinuous, emerging and open-ended, the NGOs use the concept in a goal-oriented manner. They want to realize self-reliant People's Organizations, and have developed a step-by-step organizing model to achieve this end. According to the model, the organizing process for People's Organizations is supposed to follow a certain trajectory. It projects a road towards a moment of arrival. The point of completion is when the NGO can phase out, and People's Organizations can continue to organize activities and projects without assistance and as part of the National Democratic political movement.

The model, referred to in Table 5.1, identifies a number of steps for organization building, education and socioeconomic activities. Steps for organization building include entry into the community, initial social investigation and contact-building, formation of a core group, formulation of a constitution and by-laws, expansion of membership and formation of committees. The education programme involves training in leadership skills (basic and advanced), a range of orientations and 'situationers' on the political economy of the region and the country, and, for the case of CWNGO, situationers on the position of women. Socioeconomic activities include skills training to handle projects, such as training in basic book-keeping and in the implementation of projects. The basic principle of organizing is not to proceed to a next step until 'ready'. For example, the NGO staff members (called the organizers) should first have confidence in the abilities and commitment of the core group before proceeding to the formation of an organization, and activities should not be planned until the organization's constitution and by-laws have been implemented. Special caution in the organizing trajectory is given to socioeconomic projects. The NGO Consortium aims to address the 'basic problems' in society instead of simply reforming some of their effects (see Chapter 3). The NGOs acknowledge the need for socioeconomic projects, but are convinced these should not be taken on unless the organization has built up the capacity to manage them. Socioeconomic projects must contribute

Table 5.1 Steps in organizing

1 *Introduction of organization*

    1.1 Social investigation
    1.2 Establishing contacts in the different communities
    1.3 Initial propaganda work
    1.4 Introducing the organization
    1.5 Giving initial education
    1.6 Mobilizing for alliance, propaganda and data gathering

2 *Initial organizing*

    2.1 Recruitment and formation of group members
    2.2 Deepening of social investigation and class analysis
    2.3 Giving education on basic peasant course and situationer
    2.4 Mobilizations: encouraging participation of members in organizational activities for continuous propaganda and recruitment, for further social investigation and for technical needs

3 *Formal formation of organization*

    3.1 Preparation for the formation of organization
    3.1a Expansion of membership
    3.1b Class analyse and consolidate members
    3.1c Giving higher levels of education to more or less consolidated members and continue giving basic education to new members
    3.1d Formation of committees in preparation for the assembly or congress
    3.2 *Things to be prepared by the committee*
    3.2a Constitution and by-laws
    3.2b Particular programme based on the class analysis and the general programme
    3.2c Tactical programme of action
    3.2d Guidelines in choosing a leader
        i. Congress proper
        i.a Unification on the constitution and by-laws and other documents
        i.b Election

4 *Preparation of the things needed for the congress*

to the overall organizing process. If they become a goal in themselves, this is considered 'reformist'.

The model for organizing is designed for situations where no formal organizations exist. There is a variation of the model for situations where organizations have already been formed, for instance by churches or government agencies. The mode of operation in such cases is to build on these existing structures and to reorient them to political and gender issues. Once an organization is brought on track in terms of the envisaged organizing process, it will follow the subsequent steps.

When we look at the step-by-step model, three features stand out. First, the model aims to build organizations according to a *modern* rationale. It wants organizations to follow formal procedures, with laws and by-laws that stipulate the organizational set-up, a set of officers with prescribed responsibilities and authority and a transparent accountability structure. Second, the model is based on a notion of *linear* development. Although the projections for the organizing process are not boxed into time-bound projects, it assumes that progress towards the projected goal is possible. This progress is not exactly conceived of as a straight line from A to B. It is often recognized that the organizing process is composed of progress and regress, steps forward, at times undone by steps backwards. The NGO actors have the view that, with a lot of patience, one can muddle through the setbacks so that the process can crawl towards completion, which none the less contains an idea of long-term 'progress'.

Third, a model of planned intervention is linked to notions of *control*. Drawing a plan assumes that one has the capacity to implement it. In this case the situation is paradoxical, because the model is geared towards stimulating people to organize themselves. On the other hand, the step-by-step approach requires organizers proactively to steer the process in the direction set by the organization's 'vision'. The resulting compromise is referred to as *facipulation*, a combination of facilitating and manipulating (Ibana 1994: 26). Hence, people are supposed to organize themselves, but NGOs require room for manoeuvre to make this happen in the way they desire.

Room for Manoeuvre

The concept of room for manoeuvre is apt for understanding the dynamics of development intervention. It refers to the social space actors have, or lack, to enable their ideas and projects. The idea of room for manoeuvre allows us to analyse the confinements of the social space available to actors. The room for manoeuvre of actors to fulfil their projects is restricted by circumstantial, material and institutional limitations. How these confine actors depends partly on how actors perceive and act upon them. An actor orientation emphasizes that, regardless of the nature of the constraints, actors socially construct their room for manoeuvre through their responses to constraints. At this point it should be added, however, that agency does not necessarily mean that actors in all circumstances stretch their room for manoeuvre to the widest limits. On the contrary, actors continually imagine constraints that are made effective only because actors devise patterns of practice according to them.

How actors expand their room for manoeuvre largely depends on their effectiveness in enrolling others in their projects (Latour 1986). This is effective agency (Long and van der Ploeg 1994: 66). It 'depends crucially upon the emergence of a network of actors who become partially, though hardly ever completely, enrolled in the project and practices of some other person or persons' (ibid.). Exploring the room for manoeuvre of NGOs to complete the organizing process in the villages requires seeing how far NGO staff members can muster the effective agency to get villagers to internalize their ideas and follow the proposed action (or better formulate for themselves the desired actions in line with these ideas), thereby effectively delegating power to the NGO to control the organizing process.

Probing NGOs' capacity to facilitate the development they envisage takes us invariably away from the ethnographic 'here and now' of interaction at the interface of intervention. Actors' strategies draw on historically grown patterns of action, and on wider social processes, institutions and discourses. Although there are numerous ways in which this happens, I found two such elements particularly relevant: the ensemble of development interventions and associational patterns of NGO–state–PO relations.

The ensemble of development interventions   In Chapter 4 I postulated that actors' responses to an NGO intervention can be understood only by looking at the *ensemble* of development interventions in the locality. I now want to reiterate the importance of this idea for understanding NGOs' 'room for manoeuvre' in development. First, the presence of several players in development confines the room for manoeuvre for each of the interveners. The availability of several players provides local actors with alternatives and exit options, and brings competing symbols, resources and networks into the area. This undermines the possibilities for NGOs to implement their organizing model, which implicitly assumes that an NGO and a PO have an exclusive relationship. However, this condition is seldom, if ever, met. Local organizations normally have ties with several intervening agencies. All these agencies offer activities and work according to their own models of intervention, interfering with the trajectory envisaged by the

NGOs. Thus, for example, when an NGO withholds projects that the village organization is considered not ready for, this may be thwarted because the villagers turn to other agencies to acquire a project nevertheless.

Second, the *memory* that people have of previous interventions tends to shape the way they imagine development relations, and to shape their present demands accordingly. In one village, for example, I was struck by the modest requests of villagers in comparison to the problems they experienced in organizing their livelihoods. Instead of asking NGOs to help them, for instance, to cope with rising prices for agricultural inputs or a badly needed reconstruction of the irrigation system, they requested a set of little wooden chairs for the day-care centre. What happened was that the requests were not based on real perceived needs, but instead reflected their assessment of the kind of assistance NGOs could provide. In this area, several small infrastructural projects had been offered in the past by other NGOs, as well as by government line agencies and politicians at election times. The *memory* people had of this history of development interventions had shaped the ambitions of the People's Organization or what they thought they could ask for (see also Olivier de Sardan 1988). They boxed their demands to NGOs according to their practical knowledge about development organizations.

Associational patterns   The room for manoeuvre that an NGO can marshal is affected by the relations between NGOs, the state and People's Organizations, or, more precisely, by how actors perceive and respond to these relations. In this respect, Jenny Pearce speaks of *associational cultures*, or 'patterns of interactions between organizations and the state which vary widely across societies and change over time' (Pearce 1997: 261). The historical development of the relations between the state and organizations of civil society makes a difference to how an NGO operates and how local people respond to NGO initiatives (van der Borgh 1999: 22).

Although I agree that NGO–state–society relations are constitutive of NGO interventions, we should be careful not to generalize about them as if the state were a unitary phenomenon. At the very least, we have to distinguish within the state between political representatives, the bureaucracy of line agencies, and the military. In the Cordillera region, the relations between the NGOs and each of these parts of the state have evolved differently through time. With the line agencies relations of co-operation have been possible even in the most troublesome periods in history. The relation with the political administration of the government changes with different presidencies. The relation with the military has generally been antagonistic, but has varied in intensity throughout the region and through time. Until the early 1990s, military action and propaganda against NGOs played a major role in the region. This was followed by a period of relative laxity until 1996, when the military again expanded their involvement in the Cordillera.

Furthermore, it is not enough to fine-grain the understanding of associational cultures by incorporating state segmentation into the analysis. It should further take into account the different ways in which these relations evolve locally, even within one country or region. This can be explained by portraying a locality (like a village) as at the centre of a set of concentric circles, representing political arenas in the village, region, province, country and finally the globalized world of international development. How the relation between states and NGOs becomes shaped in a village draws upon these relations in the other arenas, but is not a simple translation. It derives its *couleur locale* from local political history, the allocation and use of local resources and the personalities and performance of local office-bearers. For this reason, I do not want to adhere to the concept of associational culture, which denotes a regularity in historically grown associations applicable to a whole country. Instead, I prefer to speak of *associational patterns*. These are differentially shaped in localities: they are not autonomous from associational patterns in other arenas, but get transformed according to local contingencies. If we want to establish how, against the backdrop of regional developments, NGO–state relations evolve in different provinces, we have to establish how these evolve in the localities.

The staff of NGOs often originates from the province where they work, and their tribal affiliation and family standing may cut across political differences in shaping relations with the state. In most provinces of the Cordillera, NGO staff members have been in and out of the state bureaucracy. Several hold elected positions at *barangay*,[1] municipal or provincial level, at the same time as their position in the NGO. Some even have relatives in the military, and can make use of certain facilities such as their telephone equipment in the field. The room for manoeuvre of the provincial NGO actors is therefore situational. The situations in Mountain province and Kalinga may illustrate the variety in state–NGO relations and the clout NGOs have in shaping intervention. The NGO Consortium in Kalinga is headed by a medical doctor, who is married into a wealthy business and whose family has produced several politicians of regional importance. This lends the NGOs a certain status and respect in the province. In contrast, Mountain province is governed by a politician with a strong hold over the provincial government and bureaucracy and an equally strong dislike of the NGO Consortium. His wife has established a couple of NGOs and actively campaigns against the Consortium. The

NGO staff in the province, not from influential families, are hardly a match for her and the relation remains openly antagonistic. Even within one region, associational patterns thus evolve quite differently.

With these elements of the ensemble of development interventions and associational patterns in mind, I will elaborate on NGO room for manoeuvre in shaping intervention processes by discussing some case studies.

Luaya:[2] Constituting NGO–PO Relations

Luaya is a *sitio*[3] of 23 families in the province of Kalinga. NGO involvement in Luaya dates back to the 1970s, and there have been an extensive number of NGO activities. Hence, in this village, if anywhere, one expects NGOs to be effective in steering the organizing process. However, it becomes evident that the same closeness that provides NGOs with ample room for intervention also gives rise to alternative narratives that constitute the organizing process. Here we can use the work of Alberto Arce, who speaks of the 'social life' of a project, to denote that projects are 'constituted of a complex set of relationships, interests and ideas that are socially defined by the different actors involved' (Arce 1993: 147). According to him, during the implementation of a project a number of social, situational, cultural and institutional conditions are locally translated and transformed. Subsequently, 'these constitute the social life of a project which penetrates the political and administrative contexts of the project' (ibid.: 147–8). In the village of Luaya, the NGO intervention process was dominated by overriding interpretations of kinship relations and local concerns.

Luaya, with 23 families, is situated on the off-road shore of the Chico river in the province of Kalinga, a 30-minute hike from the adjacent *sitio* of Paregatan, with 20 families. In comparison to the village of Kayatuan in Chapter 4, Luaya constitutes a small life world. None of the adult residents has a history of migration beyond the provincial capital, and many have never been to Baguio City. Apart from some battery-operated radios, news from the outside world reaches the village only through word of mouth. Nobody has a salaried job, everybody lives from subsistence cultivation. There are wet rice fields, fruit trees and slash-and-burn swidden fields for dry rice and vegetables. The latter have increasingly turned into permanent gardens. Pigs and chicken provide occasional meat, fish is obtained from the Chico river. Coffee and vegetables are sold to generate cash for medical expenses and school fees.

Luaya's history of state, people and NGOs The history of the NGOs in Luaya is rooted in the struggle against dams in the Chico river in the 1970s. Once constructed, the dams would inundate the entire area of Luaya, the adjacent *sitio* of Paregatan and several other areas. The local protest of villagers was reinforced by the support of the churches and, some time later, the armed support of the New People's Army (NPA) (see Chapter 2). The struggle against the dams occupied the residents of the river *sitios* for a period of more than ten years. They were involved in all kinds of legal action, and for years people cooked food for the NPA and found ways to get it to them, involving practically everybody in the villages. In return, the NPA provided education and helped the villagers to govern their local affairs.

In 1986, the struggle against the dams ended, when President Aquino first froze and finally abolished the project. A few months later, however, the military stepped up actions against the NPA and their local supporters. A period of military raids followed, in which the military sealed off the entire area of Luaya. No one was allowed to visit without official permission, and people were cut off from their fields because of extremely restrictive curfew hours. Food shortage was the result, exacerbated by the fact that even close relatives had a hard time obtaining a visitor's pass. In 1990, this culminated in an evacuation. All residents had to abandon the village so that the military could carry out air raids, including bombings. This lasted several weeks, and it took several months more before food production had effectively resumed. This period is still often referred to in the village, and one woman who became permanently psychologically disturbed in the wake of the evacuation is a constant reminder, feeding people's ongoing resentment against the military.

Luaya has a long history of People's Organizations. Since 1957, there has been an organization simply called the 'Community', that generated money from within the village to install a sugar mill and construct waterworks. The organization had a credit fund until 1987, when the treasurer left the area and the 'Community' came to a standstill. In 1985, an organization was formed for the youth. It was affiliated to the Cordillera People's Alliance (CPA), which had spearheaded the regional social movement. Soon, however, its active members were under the constant scrutiny of the military for being NPA sympathizers, and subsequently had to leave the area.

In 1990, the women of Luaya and another four riverside *sitios* formed a Women's Organization, which two years later started to develop projects with the support of the Cordillera Women's NGO (CWNGO). Soon after, staff of the CPA and other NGOs of the Consortium began to visit the area again, in order to revive the organizing process. This was not easy. At the start, every meeting was dominated by arguments over the controversy surrounding the credit fund of the former organization, the 'Community'. When this old organization stopped functioning in 1987, 30,000 pesos (equivalent to approximately US$400) had simply disappeared from the credit fund, and the remaining outstanding funds had stayed with the credit takers. Accusations continued over the money that disappeared, as well as discussions over the question of whether the credit takers should still pay the outstanding interest on their loans (at a rate set at 30 per cent per month, this amounted to considerable sums of money). Despite this unresolved conflict, a new People's Organization was formed in 1993 with members of all 23 families, again in affiliation with the Cordillera People's Alliance. Since then, the Luaya People's Organization (LUPPO) has developed a range of activities, including several projects supported by NGOs of the Consortium.

The relation between the Consortium of development NGOs, including the CPA and CWNGO, and the 23 families of Luaya (plus the 20 families of Paregatan), remains closely linked to local political history and continues to be a potent ingredient in the organizing processes in the riverside *sitios*. Everybody in Luaya closely identifies with the NGOs. They insist that 'the government does nothing for us, we get everything from the NGOs'. This statement tells us more about people's perceptions than about the history of project implementation in this area. When I made a list of the services and projects in the *sitios* during interviews, it turned out there were quite a lot of state-sponsored projects. However, due to the Chico dams episode and subsequent militarization, people remain convinced that the state is anti-people and cannot be trusted. In contrast, the NGOs that entered the area after the Chico dams struggle was over are considered allies of the people. These NGOs belong to the same National Democratic movement as the former NPA comrades, and the more politicized villagers appreciate that although they look different and have projects, the present NGOs 'still have the *principio*'.

People's memories stretch farther back than organizational histories. Many of the former activists and NPA cadres have moved into NGO work, and villagers are aware of this past of the older NGO staff. They will always be 'old comrades', regardless of their present employment. In addition, quite a few of the younger staff of NGOs originate from the riverside *sitios* that were at the heart of the anti-dams struggle. Politicized as children, they find employment with NGOs as adults. No fewer than six staff members of the NGO Consortium in Kalinga originate from the 43 families of Luaya and Paregatan. Their parents are core officers of the People's Organizations in the *sitios*. Two brothers from Paregatan have found employment in an NGO. One of them married a third NGO staff member, who is a daughter of a Paregatan family. Three NGO staff members are from Luaya, two of them are brothers. These staff members are related through kinship to practically everybody in the *sitios*. As we will see, the multiple ties between staff members and villagers have some particular consequences for the organizing process in the area.

The Luaya organizing process: the official history When I started my fieldwork in Luaya in 1996, both People's Organizations and the Women's Organizations had developed a large number of projects and activities. The Luaya People's Organization was implementing a food and nutrition programme with one of the Consortium NGOs. They handed out *carabaos* (water buffalos) for animal traction, distributed seeds and rented out farm implements. In addition, the organization constructed water pipes and taps to bring water to the *sitios*. The Women's Organization had obtained two loans from CWNGO, which they used for setting up an emergency fund and a rice loan fund. They had been able to repay both loans, and continued to operate an emergency fund with the money they had earned by raising interest on loans. They also had a pig dispersal project. Apart from these socioeconomic projects, there had been numerous training activities, political situationers, and education on health and skills training to operate the organization and the projects. The village had hosted a Congress of the CPA, and received a large number of national and international visitors interested in hearing about local history with the anti-dam struggle and their present organizational activities.

Despite the impressive record of activities, the organizational process in 1996 had become problematic. Before I went to the field, I was given a briefing by one of the co-ordinators of the NGO network, who was called Butch. Butch came from Paregatan, and was one of the NGO staff originating from the area. Having been engaged in the Chico dams struggles as a youngster, and after having spent years in Manila, he had come back to the area to work with the NGOs. Butch's briefing lasted for two hours, in which he told me in great detail about the concerns of the NGO co-ordinators regarding Luaya. According to him, activities had gone down, and there was little interest in attending meetings. People had developed, as he expressed it, a 'project mentality', meaning that they were more interested in the socioeconomic activities and not so much in issues concerning the community or the region. Moreover, the Women's Organization had problems, since a number of women, not from Luaya but from more off-shore *sitios*, had announced that they wanted to leave the Riverside Women's Organization to revive their Rural Improvement Club with the Department of Agriculture.

The co-ordinators of the NGO Consortium ascribed the current problems to two factors. First, they blamed the two NGOs that implemented socioeconomic projects. They said that both CWNGO and the NGO responsible for the food and nutrition programme had not properly co-ordinated with the Consortium. They also implied that the NGOs had been implementing projects without sufficiently taking into account the intervention model of step-by-step organizing. In particular, they had allowed the socioeconomic work to outrun a solid organizational and political build-up in the organizing process. Second, Butch blamed the difficulties on a number of conflicts internal to the community. The matter of the community credit fund of the 1980s continued to play in organizational meetings, and quarrels came about over several other issues. In particular, there were problems between two women, both of whom were influential in village affairs. These women were Lorena and Francesca. Lorena had been married to Francesca's brother, and when her husband died there was a conflict about the distribution of land. It so happened that Lorena and Francesca were also the two women whose sons work with the NGOs. The view of the NGO Consortium co-ordinators was that the organizing process had been hampered because the NGOs had not played according to the rules and because of distractions caused by intra-village conflicts. Before continuing the official NGO narrative on how this problematic situation was to be solved, I will elaborate on the organizing process viewed from within the village.

The social life of the organizing process During my fieldwork in 1996, it became clear indeed that there were tensions in Luaya. Gossip and quarrels abounded, and some conversations could not be held unless in the fields or at other places where nothing could be overheard. On the other hand, looking at the organizations, the situation was not as 'bad' as I had anticipated on the basis of the introductory talk with Butch. There was a lot of project activity, meetings were regularly held and were well attended. What became most remarkable for me about the gossip and quarrels was the everyday nature of the issues involved, and how they were intertwined with the close social ties to the NGO staff.

The quarrels were about local and detailed issues. As mentioned above, the life world, the 'lived-in and largely taken-for-granted world of social actors' (Schutz and Luckmann 1973) in Luaya is mainly confined to village and family affairs. The villagers became involved in a political movement of the region, at a time when their land and resources were immediately threatened by the prospect of dams in the Chico river. Although they continue to be part of this movement, they are at the same time rather indifferent to what happens beyond the village. One of our neighbours in the village put it quite pointedly: 'As long as we have three meals a day, we have nothing to do with those people in Manila.' They enjoy listening to NGO education on 'wider issues', but many people say they easily forget the content. The education of NPA organizers in the 1980s is remembered less for its alternative political orientation than for initiatives to confine pigs to pig-pens, and to take measures against the use of alcohol and marihuana.

Given the everyday interests of people, where the matter of a stray pig can capture the attention of the whole village for days, it is not surprising that the disappearance of a substantial amount of money of the old community organization still enrages people ten years after the fact. Added to this old conflict are questions about the use of NGO-generated resources. One evening I was invited into the house of a man who – whispering – enumerated a list of items that allegedly had been appropriated by co-villagers after the Congress of the CPP in the village, one year before. The list included a sack of rice, a box of batteries for radios and flashlights and one can of gasoline. This man, and other people who talked to me about this, did not blame the NGOs for this problem. NGO staff members were generally admired. In the eyes of the villagers, these people had forfeited a career in the city after their college education, to devote themselves instead to ameliorate life in the villages they had come from. Not the NGO staff members, but their relatives, were implicated in the complaints. Missing items were claimed to have been confiscated by close family members of the NGO staff. Although people only wanted to talk about these issues in secret, it turned out that the NGO Consortium was well aware of the allegations. According to it, they were ungrounded: the CPA had deliberately brought back everything after the Congress to avoid these kinds of problems. Unfortunately, people in the village had not believed this.

Relatives of NGO staff members were not just suspected of abusing their close relationship to the NGOs, they were also looked upon with more moral scrutiny than others. In particular, the behaviour of Lorena and Francesca towards each other and towards village matters was secretly criticized. Invariably, critical comments would be topped with a remark such as: 'They should know better, they even have their children in the NGOs.' This is well illustrated by one event that happened during my fieldwork. Ever since I arrived in the village, people talked a lot about stray pigs. There were pig-pens, but several people allowed their pigs to roam around in search of food, which inevitably led them to trespass into vegetable gardens. One morning, we were woken up by loud screams. It turned out that an elderly neighbour had lost his temper when he found one of Lorena's pigs in his garden. He shouted with anger and kept hitting the galvanized iron sheet of a pig-pen with a big stick, waking up the whole village. The fact that the pig was Lorena's seemed to evoke the old man's anger more than the damage the animal had done. He kept on repeating: 'It is even she, whose child is with the NGO, who does not follow the rules. She is always nicely talking to the NGOs, but she does not even implement what we agreed.'

Conflicts among their relatives also affected the NGO staff members. One CWNGO staff member felt ashamed that her parents were involved in these conflicts. She considered herself a bad organizer because 'I cannot even organize my own family.' Another NGO staff member from Luaya seemed to feel personally offended when things went wrong. One evening, for example, the gong, which is used to call people to a meeting, suddenly sounded. This was at 11 o'clock at night! It turned out that the organizer had become angry, because to his mind too few people had attended the meeting held earlier in the evening. When somebody had commented: 'you should not be mad with us, because we attended in the first place', he clanged the gong to wake people up for a middle-of-the-night meeting. A third staff member, the same Butch who had given me the briefing, was also enmeshed in local village politics. He was a *barangay* councillor, and acted like a political rival to the *barangay* captain. Not only was NGO staff members' performance affected by their social and political entanglement in the village, this also had repercussions on how they reported on the Luaya organizing process in regional meetings. Their reports about the everyday quarrels and 'problems' contributed to an image of the Luaya People's Organization as a problematic case, notwithstanding its good record of project implementation, which continued irrespective of the quarrels.

Alternative Narratives in Luaya: Analysis

The story of the organizing process in Luaya can be told in terms of NGO politics. This is a narrative of how an initially successful and politicized organization process was eroded by a lack of co-ordination and a penchant for socioeconomic projects. However, this is at most a partial story. It is challenged, or at least complemented by, an alternative narrative that focuses on everyday languages of kinship, family feuds and local history. The organizing initiatives of the NGOs cannot be viewed separately from the centrality of kinship and of the social ties between NGOs and villages that are created by local political history.

Interlocking projects The case of Luaya reveals that even in a village where NGOs are the major development interveners, and have become accepted and respected as such, the organizing process does not follow the rationale of a step-by step choreography directed by NGOs. Organizing processes are constructed by multiple actors and an amalgam of different discourses and practices. Rather than viewing interventions as linear processes, they can be seen as composed of interlocking projects of different actors with diverging life worlds, ideas and aims (Long and van der Ploeg 1989).

Over time, NGO staff members and local villagers developed complex multiple ties and multiple accountabilities. They act on the basis of their own translations of policy, discourses and ambitions. Villagers, on the other hand, are strategizing actors who naturally want to appropriate resources coming into the village for their own projects, be these material, social or symbolic resources (see Elwert and Bierschenk 1988). However, the responses of staff members, as well as villagers, are not just reflections of strategic considerations. Staff members are not the implementing arm of NGO policies, but invest their own meanings and ambitions into the process, inspired as much by their personal involvement with the village as by their NGO orientation. Villagers, on the other hand, base their expectations and responses as much on the social ties with NGO staff members as on their historically grown affinity with the NGO Consortium. Hence, there is no such thing as a step-by-step organizing model that is *interrupted* by adverse effects of kinship relations. Instead, the organizing process is *constituted* by these social ties. In the case of Luaya, the relation between state, people and NGOs, as it grew through history, through personal relations in the village, through contingencies such as stray pigs and the confinements of people's life worlds, all join into shaping actors' responses and negotiations at the social interface of intervention.

Transforming modern organization The relationships that evolved through time between NGOs and villagers have locally altered the way meetings are held, projects organized and activities conducted. This becomes clear when we examine the meaning of the People's Organization in the village. In Luaya, the PO has developed pretty much according to the modern ideal of formal organizations incorporated in the step-by-step organizing model of the Consortium NGOs. The organization had its laws and by-laws (in English) and there were no fewer than six separate committees responsible for aspects of the organization's activities and projects. Meetings were held according to modern organizational standards. There was an agenda, people took turns in speaking, and discussions were followed by the adoption of resolutions and the distribution of tasks. That does not automatically mean that these meetings did what they were supposed to do, namely, to regulate everyday organizational activities.

Villagers have their own historically grown organizing practices and patterns (Nuijten 1998: 217–26). Nuijten observed, for example, how meetings in a Mexican *ejido* did nothing one might expect from meetings: they appeared as a chaotic 'arena for bickering and indecisive confrontation' (ibid.: 208–13). These meetings, however, turned out to have different symbolic meanings that could be understood only within the context of local organizational patterns. In similar vein, we cannot assume that organizational features that have been adopted by villagers actually acquire the discursive meaning and functionality foreseen by the NGOs that introduced these features.[4]

In the case of Luaya, I concluded that the ordered way of holding meetings reflected, on the one hand, the desire of people living in a very small community to contain conflict to a tolerable proportion, which also characterized their wheeling and dealing outside of organizational matters. On the other, it seemed that people played along with the game of these meetings in order to pay respect to the well-appreciated NGOs. How seriously they played this game was apparent when one man commented after a meeting that they should have had name tags, even though the meeting consisted only of people from the 23 houses of Luaya. After this meeting, another person complained about the fact that one NGO staff member had presented a lecture wearing shorts. He felt that this person should have replicated the respect shown by the villagers attending the meeting, by dressing properly.

Respect and a sense of moral obligation seemed informative of other aspects of the organization as well. Participating in NGO education was not just interesting, but also an expression of respect and gratitude. Likewise, the villagers politely followed the NGOs' suggestion to form separate committees for different activities. In practice, however, committees don't meet or, when they do, everybody attends their meetings so that they can keep an eye on what happens in the organization. The formal mode of organizing, then, becomes transformed in the localities of the villages. In Chapter 4 we saw a Women's Organization that had taken on board a full set of officers, not with the purpose of expanding organizational activity, but in order to divert conflict and competition among women professionals. In the case of Luaya, villagers embraced this form of organization in homage to the NGOs and as a strategy to confirm the social ties and obligations between NGO staff members and themselves.

Attributing Identity to Intervening Agencies

From the above, it appears that villagers have more impact in shaping NGO interventions in the area than the NGOs themselves. One more aspect of this strikes me as important for the question of what is an NGO. It is that their clients largely dictate the identity of NGOs in the localities.

Development interveners have often been accused of creating their subjects by the labelling practices that are inherent to policy making (Wood 1985; Escobar 1995). Interestingly, in the cases I studied, villagers are much more effective in creating the NGOs than the other way round. By fostering a certain representation of the NGO, and responding accordingly, they reshape the NGO and its interventions in correspondence with this client-constructed image. In the case of Luaya, the NGO was not able to overcome the kinship-centred expectations and practices of the villagers. In other cases, the identity accorded to the NGOs was different, but the mechanisms remained the same.

For example, in Aritonin, another *sitio* in Kalinga, I found the organizing process largely dictated by the rivalry between two factions in the village. The two factions roughly coincided with social networks differentiated by migration background, kinship, history and language. They had become two factions in *barangay* politics, competing over elections, projects and other resources.

NGOs were fitted into these local politics. It turned out that relations with the government were concentrated in one cluster, while relations with the NGOs were mainly in the other. Between the two, mutual accusations went on regarding the monopolization and mishandling of projects. While the NGO cluster considered the *barangay* officials of the other cluster as corrupt, the *barangay* officials called the NGO cluster 'Communist'. Aritonin seemed an ideal-typical Philippine village organized around two factions, where leaders' competition for power is strongly shaped by their dyadic political relations beyond the village (see Wolters 1983; Kerkvliet 1991: 8, n.9; Sidel 1999). However, while the ideal-typical case portrays ongoing village feuds as related to competing government-linked political factions, here we see that NGOs have been accorded a place in this game, providing a 'new' channel to resources and contacts outside the village. In this case, the relations between NGOs and People's Organizations gets shaped through the dynamics of two factions in the village. Whether they like it or not, NGOs were left no choice but to enter this game and act as an alternative to the government in providing competing projects.

Another example was a poor urban community where the NGOs had an ongoing functional literacy programme and assisted a rice-lending co-operative. It was a squatter community, which, despite several years of legal and political efforts with the help of some NGOs, had not been able to obtain permission to stay on the lot where their houses were built, and thus to get access to basic services like electricity and water. It turned out the people were very angry about the perceived failure of the NGOs to achieve this for them. While the NGOs defined their role as facilitating the squatters' organizing, the squatters had put their hopes in the NGOs, whom they considered as *political leaders* who had steered them into the squatter adventure and now failed to solve their problems. They felt misguided, to the extent that they did not trust other NGO activities any longer. In this case, local perceptions of NGO–PO relations was one of trust, evolving into a relation of broken trust. This determined the way in which these poor urban squatters responded to new NGO activities.

These examples all testify to the overwhelming influence that local actors have in shaping NGO intervention. Because of the different ensembles of development interventions and associational patterns that have grown in localities, people anticipate and expect certain behaviour and contributions from intervening agencies. The 'imagined' agency that people attribute to NGOs was so forceful in these cases that the NGOs, contrary to their own ambitions, started to live up to these images.

For many reasons, then, organizing processes do not often happen according to the step-by-step organizing model. Furthermore, in cases where they do, this may not at all be the result of NGOs' effective agency. There are many villages where organizing happens more or less in the NGO-desired direction, and where the relationship between the NGOs and their clients in the communities is mutually considered positive and beneficial. In these cases, we can nevertheless not assume that the NGO has mustered the room for manoeuvre to control this process. Rather, it may be a (temporary) coincidence, a matter of interlocking projects. We may thus safely conclude that NGOs in most cases lack the room for manoeuvre to implement the step-by-step organizing model. This leaves one more question to be asked, namely: if not organize, what does the model do and why do the NGOs adhere to it?

The Social Life of Policy Models

At the start of this chapter I elaborated the step-by-step organizing model as a policy projecting a linear road towards a given objective. The cases subsequently brought out how NGOs generally lack the room for manoeuvre to realize their goal. We should not jump to the conclusion from this observation that these policy models are therefore not worth considering for analysis. It remains important to look critically at the model, if only because development practices without policies are unthinkable and should therefore continue to be an important focus for analysis (van Dusseldorp 1995: 5). However, instead of looking at the models for what they claim to be, I think we should keep our minds open as to what they mean in practice. Just as one can speak of the social life of interventions, we may have to search for the social life of policy models to complete the exploration of the dynamics of the development intervention.

When a policy model doesn't do what it is supposed to do, we cannot simply conclude that it is a mistake, or a brainchild of leaders who are alienated from the field of implementation. Let us instead ask what it does *in practice* (see Hilhorst and van Leeuwen 2000). As Colebatch notes, the perception 'that policy consists of the pursuit of known goals is deeply rooted in the "common-sense" understanding of the world, and tends to be assumed rather than analysed' (Colebatch 1998: 54). This author contends that policy may be for very different things, for example, to establish routine, to make sense of action or to create order in policy fields. These 'other' meanings of policy are unstated.

Who believes in the model? When NGO actors explained their work to me in general terms, they often referred to the step-by-step organizing model. However, as soon as the conversation turned to actual cases this model disappeared completely out of view. Then, the organizing appeared as highly personalized and constituted by social relations and everyday politicking, and the same conclusion can be drawn from the cases of Luaya and Aritonin. Interestingly, even management actors who themselves hardly ever went to the field, displayed this difference between theory and practical knowledge of local dynamics. In the offices of NGOs, everyday stories regarding organizing often centre around the whereabouts of local peoples (see also Chapter 7). As a result, even the Baguio-based management of the CWNGO knows many details of the lives of the women involved: the life events of birth, marriage, migration, disease and death, as well as the latest intrigues from the villages. Bits and pieces of information could be as everyday as the following conversation:

> CWNGO manager: Have you seen *Manang* Tess (a woman living in a tiny Mountain province village), I heard she has new teeth?
> Local organizer: Yes, they look good, her daughter bought them for her, she works in Taiwan.

This conversation also included a matter-of-fact understanding of the arena of development interventions. One of the managers could, for example, comment about an incident involving a women's PO leader: 'That is to be expected, she is after all related to the provincial governor's wife.' The interest in personal information and local politicking was raised in relevance to the organizing, but it also contains an element of sheer pleasure in juicy or funny details. Some local people or situations are subject to continuing stories as if they are soap operas. The contrast between the intimate knowledge of actual village organizing processes and the idealistic or normative way in which NGO actors talked about the step-by-step organizing model amazed me. At some point, I had the idea that the model had only a formal life. In meetings of the NGO it was used to report on organizing processes, even though all the cases were always presented as exceptions. I wondered if there was anyone who seriously believed in the possibility that the model could be achieved in practice. I slowly came to realize, however, that most people in the NGO did.

Only once did I encounter a staff member in the NGOs who doggedly tried to implement the model in practice, and he met with scorn from colleagues for being 'mechanistic'. On the other hand, only a few staff members distanced themselves from the model, and would in private admit that they did not believe it helped them in their work. The majority, however, were well capable of accommodating to both realities. The management of the NGO, when asked, immediately agreed that the 'step-by-step' organizing did not work as such in practice. Nevertheless, it continued to provide guidelines on how to do this, and expected staff to report according to this model. The status of the model was reinforced when an evaluation was held of the NGOs in the mid-1990s. The evaluation brought out that the step-by-step approach had not worked, and that the NGOs had little control over the People's Organizations (see Chapter 3). Curiously, this observation did not lead to a reconsideration of the model in accordance with the observed dynamics in the localities. Instead, it was concluded that the approach had not been properly implemented. The step-by-step organizing model was reinvigorated, and the deployment of staff and co-ordination of NGOs with a more limited number of villages were adjusted towards improving the step-by-step organizing approach. This raises the question of what the meaning of this model is for the NGOs.

The step-by-step organizing model revisited In the *villages*, the step-by-step organizing does not often happen as foreseen by NGOs, but it is none the less not without effects. In particular, the model provides the NGO organizers with an anchor that they can fall back on when faced with decisions or dilemmas in organizing practice (see also Hilhorst and Schmiemann 2002). Even though the model may not adequately project their actions for the future, it helps them to establish certain routines and standard operation procedures to facilitate everyday practice. As Colebatch (1998: 46) says: 'organization is about routinization – developing known and predictable ways of dealing with events'. NGO staff members working in the field face many unexpected ambiguities and they are alone when they have to respond to them. In these cases, the model provides them with a guideline to act upon. In those villages where NGOs have substantial room for manoeuvre, this can have important implications.

In the *NGO offices*, I found that the step-by-step organizing model performs three main functions: discursive, political and symbolic. First, the organizing model provides a common official NGO language for making sense of organizing practices. In everyday exchanges, staff members mainly talked about their work through storytelling and anecdotes. In meetings where the staff had to give a concise overall report, the model provided a language of accountability for the organizing. It also provided a basis for comparison and compilation. During a meeting, a provincial organizer would report, for example, that she was working with: '18 Women's Organizations, 10 of which are at the stage of core-group formation, 5 have completed their basic leadership training and 2 have formed their committees'. As soon as organizers provided details on a case, these always turned out to be exceptional when compared with the model. However, even if every single case turns out to be exceptional, the model still provides the language in which they can be expressed.

Second, the model serves the purpose of an implicit contract, as 'terms of reference' between NGOs of the Consortium. In cases where two NGOs work in the same community, and disagree on the implementation of a project, the argument that 'the organization is not yet ready' can decide discussions and legitimize decisions like no other. As we will see in Chapter 6, this plays an important role in accountability processes. Finally, and perhaps most importantly, the model has a symbolic meaning in providing a basis for the belief of NGO actors in their final goal. The National Democratic NGO Consortium aims to build a regional social movement, and eventually to accomplish a social revolution. This implies a future moment of completion. Such a distinct project cannot be imagined without the belief that it is possible to work systematically towards this goal. If I am right, this means that the seemingly highly rational and systematic planning model turns out to have a primarily symbolic function for the NGO actors themselves.

This chapter started with elaborating some assumptions built into NGO intervention models. It then explored the room for manoeuvre of NGOs in organizing processes in the villages and, finally, set out to discover the 'other' meanings of such models for the case of the Cordillera NGOs. In conclusion, I want to underline that analysing the model, which is officially meant to guide organizing in the villages, takes us away from these localities into the organizations of the NGOs. The organizing model turns out to be of limited significance in the villages. It is important in guiding NGO actors in day-to-day decisions, but has little bearing on the long-term prospects of organizing. At the same time, the model turns out to be of utmost importance for the NGOs. It provides a language that is evoked in their meetings, is a political device in regulating relations between NGOs, and has a symbolic meaning in underpinning the belief in the possibilities of a social revolution. Hence, the step-by-step organizing model may be more significant for processes within NGOs than for the local interventions it was designed for. This points to an interesting phenomenon, namely, that NGO actors manage particular domains of operation through strategies and practices that are seemingly directed to one of their other fields of action. This phenomenon, as will be seen in the remaining chapters of this book, is typical of everyday politics in NGOs.

Notes

1. *Barangay* is the smallest political administrative unit in the Philippine government system, governed by an elected *barangay* council, headed by a *barangay* captain, also elected.

2. I spent a total of three months in the village in the first half of 1996, divided between four periods of fieldwork.

3. A *sitio* is a subdivision of a *barangay*, which is the smallest political administrative unit in the Philippine government system. Luaya belongs to the *barangay* of Luaya, which consists of eight *sitios*, four of them onshore and four offshore. They are separated by distances of a more-or-less 20-minute hike.

4. More likely than not, villages have already been touched by modern ways of organizing introduced by other development interveners by the time an NGO arrives in the area.

SIX

Whose Reality Counts? Issues of NGO Accountability

One of the hottest topics for discussion among NGO practitioners and observers today concerns the issue of accountability. As intermediary organizations that provide development for poor and otherwise marginalized people, NGOs must answer for the quality and impact of their work in a range of different arenas. To whom NGOs are accountable is one of the major questions raised. As the debate goes, governments are (in principle) accountable to their voters, private companies to their shareholders and the market, but NGOs risk operating in an accountability void. The concerns are that, in practice, NGOs are either not accountable or accountable only to their funding agencies.[1] The problem with these discussions is that they often focus on a rather narrow view of accountability and are far from clear as to what constitutes accountability in practice.

This chapter seeks to unravel the notion of accountability and to explore NGO practices. Edwards and Hulme (1996: 8) define the concept as 'the means by which individuals and organizations report to a recognized authority (or authorities) and are held responsible for their actions'. Although this definition will be closely scrutinized later, I introduce it here because it clearly brings out three elements of accountability. First, accountability is *relational*, since one party (the NGO) is accountable to another party (the stakeholders or authorities). Second, there is an element of control and *legitimation*. As Brett (1993) points out, accountability can be effective only if the stakeholder has an exit option and/or a voice to influence the NGO. Third, there is the account: the report, story, calculation or compilation that presents the performance to be accounted for. Remarkably, discussions on NGO accountability have concentrated mainly on the first two elements, that is, on the questions of the nature and influence of the stakeholders that NGOs have to answer to. Little, in contrast, has been said about the accounts that form the substance of the accountability process. This may be an important omission. During accountability processes, the project that needs to be accounted for never lies on the table as such, but is represented by a particular account. NGO projects have, so to speak, multiple lives. They acquire additional realities, beyond the locale where they are implemented, as *representations* in areas of accountability. In these areas, accounts become devices to make sense of the project. Accountability is therefore not just a process of legitimating action, but also one of *attributing meaning* to NGOs. Accountability can then be defined as a process in which different actors negotiate the meaning and legitimacy of NGO activities.

Although we normally associate accountability with rational and formal processes of making development practice transparent, the first part of the chapter discusses other ways in which accountability can operate, which I shall call moral accountability. The rational mode of accountability starts with Max Weber, the other with Emile Durkheim, and more recent proponents of these lines of thought are Foucault and Garfinkel. After analytically separating the two modes of accountability, I will argue that they are empirically intertwined in many different ways.

The second part of the chapter consists of a case study of an accountability process in the NGO Consortium of the Cordillera. It concerns a weaving project for women that involved two NGOs, both of which are affiliated and accountable to this Consortium. When conflict occurred, the case was brought to a gathering of this NGO network for judgement. As I will show, the way the NGO accounts were composed and sustained tells us more about discursive practices and power processes in the arenas of accountability than at the locus of implementation. What actually happened in the village had little bearing on the accountability process.

Rational and Moral Modes of Accountability

The term accountability is associated with rational organizations. It is reminiscent of Max Weber's characterization of Western bureaucracies as structures in which responsibilities and authorities are clearly defined and ordered, and practices and decisions accurately reflected in written documentation. The definition of accountability as the means by which individuals and organizations report to a recognized authority and are held responsible for their actions is in line with this rational approach. It presupposes a clear division between the authorities and the accountable actor, and assumes that accountability takes place through formal reporting mechanisms. People and organizations work according to certain procedures and are allotted particular tasks to which they have to respond. As Morgan (1986) points out, from this line of thinking organizations appear as machines. Accountability may be considered as the device to ensure that different parts of the machine function properly.

However, there are also modes of accountability that can be traced back to another of the 'founding fathers' of sociology, Emile Durkheim. Durkheim conceived of modern societies, characterized by advanced divisions of labour, as bound together through organic solidarity. In his view, in order to function well (and not to fall into a state of anomie) societies force individuals to surrender to shared norms and values and to fulfil their part in the division of labour on the basis of a 'moral contract'. Individuals breaching this moral contract are sanctioned in different ways, some of them institutionalized in law, others operating through social mechanisms of exclusion and correction. I suggest labelling this idea of being responsive on the basis of moral obligations as moral accountability. Alternatively, it may be called everyday accountability, since it permeates and operates through everyday social life.

Moral accountability contrasts with rational accountability on different points. It can be both horizontal, within social groups, and hierarchical. However, it is not so much associated with the higher authorities in unequal social relations, as with the accountability of 'little people' – those in subordinate positions. It concerns the informal means by which leaders are forced to be responsive to their followers or patrons to their clients. Jonathan Fox, for example, directs our gaze to informal practices of accountability in regional peasant organizations in Mexico (Fox 1992). He points out that followers find parallel channels to make their leaders responsive, outside of the formal mechanisms of representation. Anthropological literature abounds with cases where people get rid of unwanted leaders or patrons by creative informal practices, ranging from plain violence and ingenuous conspiracies, to evoking the assistance of supernatural powers.

Moral accountability, in the heritage of Durkheim, can be highly formalized and institutionalized in rituals or common law practices, through which social groups deal with offending group members. However, in organizations it is more associated with informal ways of accounting. What the report and the statistical record are to rational accountability, stories, ironic remarks and gossip are to moral accountability. Unlike rational accountability, processes of moral accountability are integrated into everyday life and embedded in organizational culture. In a more obvious way than with rational accountability, it is an extension of everyday power games. Moral accountability is not transparent, but neither can its non-transparency be captured by one single concept. Instead of transparent, moral accountability processes can be radiating, prismatic or obscure. This form of accountability can be portrayed as exemplary, a shining phenomenon of respectable individuals or organizations that respond to their moral obligations. In other cases, it can be considered prismatic: distorting incoming insights by cultural biases. Finally, it is associated with opaqueness, with the muddy workings of rumours, slander and vengeful acts. This association has little to do with the noble idea of pressuring people to fulfil their moral obligations, but with competition and dirty politics. Moral or everyday accountability thus has many faces.

Accountability as a Sense-making Exercise

In the introduction I mentioned three elements of accountability: as a relation between the authority and the accountable organization, as an activity to attribute meaning and as a device for legitimation. By discussing two recent proponents of rational and moral accountability, Michel Foucault and Harold Garfinkel, it becomes clear that the linkages between these elements vary in the different modes of accountability.

Rational accountability is considered an exercise for making everyday organizational performance visible, in order to control it from a distance. The parallel with practices of surveillance and discipline, as analysed by Michel Foucault, is apparent. Surveillance in his work is symbolized by the Panopticon of Bentham, an annular institution built around a tower, so designed that subjects are separated from each other by partition walls but are visible to the superviser in the tower. Because those in the cells of the Panopticon can never tell when the supervisor (who is invisible to them) looks at them, they are forced to discipline their actions throughout the day (Foucault 1995/1975: 200–09). Rational accountability works as such a Panopticon: it concentrates information about segregated parts of organizational performance in the hands of an authority. As in the Panopticon, discipline, in the eyes of Foucault, is not effected only by surveillance. It is the result of a double bind. On the one hand, authority and discretion is generated by the visibility of surveillance. On the other, the individualized objects of visibility assume responsibility for the constraints of power and make them play upon themselves. 'This is a "capillary form" of power, a power which "reaches into the very grain of individuals", a "regime that is exercised *within* the social body rather than *from above* it"' (Foucault 1980; cited in Clegg 1998: 31). It is discursive practice in which people, by acting upon this absorbed 'knowledge', make it become true.

An alternative line of thinking more associated with everyday informal forms of accountability is found in Garfinkel's ethnomethodology. Garfinkel was concerned with the question of how social relations are constituted in groups, through creating identities, sanctioning processes and, ultimately, by delineating who belongs and who does not, who is included or excluded from membership. What is interesting about his approach is the emphasis he places on the importance of sense-making in everyday accountability. The term ethnomethodology refers to the human capacity to give accounts, in the sense of stories, explanations and reasons for conduct. It is the kind of accountability that is embedded in everyday activities and is an 'endless, ongoing, contingent accomplishment' (Garfinkel 1967: 1). Garfinkel claims that any setting

> organizes its activities to make its properties as an organized environment of practical activities detectable, countable, recordable, reportable, tell-a-story-aboutable, analyzable – in short accountable. (ibid.: 33)

According to ethnomethodology, the relationship between account and the substance it evokes is contingent. The contingency of accounts often remains hidden, because a close correspondence to the substance is assumed, and because they tend to be legitimized by appealing either to reason, as a universal value, or to nature (see Douglas 1987). However, at most there is a loose connection, shaped in a particular context, so that accounts are in a sense 'indifferent' to what they describe (Heritage 1984). In ethnomethodology, the creation of accounts is a group endeavour and members of the same group have methods by which they sanction other members' conduct. In the work of Garfinkel, people, in order to belong, have to comply with understandings prevalent in their social setting.

Both these approaches point to the importance of sense-making for accountability, but in two different ways. For Foucault, sense-making happens as a result of discursive disciplining, whereas for Garfinkel it stems from group socializing. John Roberts argues that both processes work simultaneously in organizations:

> Those whom an individual works alongside or encounters elsewhere in the organization become the network through which an individual shares and builds a common understanding of organizational experience. The unsurveilled spaces of organizational life – corridors and toilets, chats before and after meetings, lunchbreaks and outings – all become the contexts for an alternative form of accountability *in which the sense of events is negotiated* [italics added]. (Roberts 1996: 49)

Roberts stipulates that in accountability processes, socializing and disciplining forms of accountability are interwoven and mutually dependent upon each other. What I find problematic in his analysis, however, is that he locates sanctions only in formal and hierarchical forms of accountability, and juxtaposes these with lateral forms of accountability that are based on solidarity and the construction of a sense of self in organizations. Instead, I would argue that both rational and moral accountability combine elements of disciplining and sense-making. To elaborate this point, let me discuss the process of rational accountability, in particular the premise that it is transparent and stands apart from everyday organizational practice.

Shattering the Dream of Transparency

Rational accountability is based on the idea that accountability produces transparency. In order to make organizational practice visible, the means of accountability have to remain invisible, in the sense that they stand apart from everyday organizational practice. The accountability process itself should not distort the accounts. As Michael Power has stated for audits, the purpose of accountability is to produce trust out of mistrust. In order to succeed in this operation, the credibility of the audit has to be taken for granted. 'By the same token that the audit has to visibilize in order to produce trust, the audit and auditor themselves thus have to remain invisible' (Power 1994: 304–6). Accountability means to be *impersonal*, it eliminates the personal by insulating the accountability process from everyday politics and cultural practices. Not only is there an assumption that reports and other paraphernalia of accountability can be accurate reflections of the activities reported on, there is a twin assumption that the requirements and act of accountability do not interfere with the practices under scrutiny. Producing accounts is supposed to be a neutral, technical job. Several authors have challenged this ideal notion. They have demonstrated that accountability processes invade and constitute everyday organizational life, and, in turn, everyday practices invade and constitute accountability processes. This notion shatters the dream of transparency.

The means of accounting, such as formats for reporting, shape *organizational relations* because they open up spaces of discretion and allow evaluation and comparison of individuals and organizations. One could go as far as to say that authority gets constituted through the possibility of control: because of the means of accountability, the person in authority can avail him/herself of the discretion, insights and proactive attitudes inscribed in him/her (Law 1996). The introduction of computer formats and the use of e-mail for reporting can serve as an illustration of the point. The availability of electronic communication has brought funding agencies much closer in time and space to NGOs. This has led to a range of new accountability demands, and leaves NGOs with fewer excuses for untimely or incomplete reporting. E-mail and the use of e-mail forms for project applications, planning and monitoring have provided such illusions of control that representatives of funding agencies may even start to take on the identity of 'proximate managers', instead of the distant suppliers of funds they used to be.

The idea that the technological means of accountability constitute *organizational practice* is also no stranger to development practitioners. Accountability requirements and formats elicit particular accounts and invite a certain ordering of activities within development NGOs. Intrinsic to accounting mechanisms are particular rationales. Those aspects that are or can be measured, such as particular forms of efficiency, acquire priority over aspects that fall outside the scope of accounting, such as localized standards of effectiveness (Gasper 1998). Consequently, people will start to act towards the requirements embedded in the means of accounting. The application of particular accountability models or techniques not only generates standards, but also 'enhances certain ways of perceiving and assessing economic or organizational life' (Miller 1994: 2–5). Socializing processes of sense-making are thus permeated by these formal procedures: they suggest a certain reading of the organization's practice.

Conversely, everyday organizational relations, practices and discourses also constitute formal accountability procedures. Reports, statistics and other accounts are based on information provided by social actors that already reflects their interpretation. At the other end of the accountability process, actors read, interpret and make sense of the accounts within their own life world and rationalities. Far from being impersonal, the accountability procedure is thus filled in with social organizational life. This renders the accountability process essentially social. As Munro says: 'Modes of accounting are always interdependent. Conversation can never be separated, and delimited from other accounting media. Each technology or media draws on and sustains the other' (Munro 1996: 9).

Before presenting a case study that substantiates the notion of accountability as a social process, let me emphasize that this notion is geographically neutral. I do not want to condone the unpleasant position that portrays rational organizations as the Western norm, with cultural and informal organizations as its deviant non-Western counterpart. We should not derive, from the forceful way in which the idea of Western rationality is advocated in development discussions, the expectation that organizations in 'the West' (whatever that may be) actually operate according to this image in real life. Michael Herzfeld unmasks modern bureaucracies as no more rational and no less symbolic than non-Western organizations. Accountability in Western bureaucracy, he finds, is 'a socially produced, culturally saturated amalgam of ideas about person, presence, and polity. Despite its claims to a universal rationality, its meanings are culturally specific, and its operation is constrained by the ways in which its operators and clients interpret its actions' (Herzfeld 1992: 47). Exit transparency.

The Case of the BPO Women's Weaving Project

This example aims to demonstrate how accounts are constructed and find legitimation in accountability processes. It is most clear in cases where conflicts occur and the composition of accounts becomes a controversy, as happened in a weaving project of 19 women in the agricultural village of Binasan, in Mountain province. The village has around ninety households. The participants of the project have a loom in their houses. They weave blankets and fine cloth, which is made into objects like blankets, backpacks, hats and wallets. These are sold through the offices of supportive NGOs. The participants form the Women's Committee of the Binasan People's Organization. This is supported by two NGOs, both belonging to the NGO Consortium in the Cordillera. One of them is the Cordillera Women's NGO (CWNGO), the other the Mountainous Development NGO (MOUNT), which specializes in programmes for sustainable agriculture. Unlike CWNGO, which is a region-wide organization, MOUNT mainly works in Mountain province. Its office is just one hour away from the village of Binasan. The case centres around a conflict over matters of interpretation and co-ordination, which built up between these two NGOs in the course of the project and reached a climax in 1994.

The NGO Consortium to which CWNGO and MOUNT belong consists of twelve organizations. The network is organized in a hierarchical fashion, which means that the Consortium prevails over member NGOs. The NGOs, in other words, are accountable to the co-ordinators of the Consortium. As discussed in Chapter 5, the Consortium works according to the step-by-step organizing model, which stipulates that People's Organizations should follow a trajectory of organization building, training, and socioeconomic activities. They are not supposed to proceed to a next step until 'ready' in the eyes of the NGO staff members. The principle of step-by-step organizing is both an ideological cornerstone of the Consortium as well as a tool for the management, planning and evaluation of NGO activities. The weaving project started at a time when the model had been watered down considerably in everyday NGO practice. However, at the time that the conflict between MOUNT and CWNGO erupted, it had just been revived as part of a political campaign that wanted to bring NGOs back to their 'basics' (see Chapter 3). As we shall see, this is an important detail for understanding the dynamics of the accountability process around the conflict. A history of the events of the project and of the People's Organizations and the NGOs is given below, and two accountability interfaces analysed: the interface between the NGOs and their clients in the village, and that between the various NGOs in the Consortium.

History of the Binasan People's Organization and the NGOs The Binasan People's Organization (BPO) was formed in 1989. It was the initiative of one of the villagers, *Manong* Roy. *Manong* Roy used to work for an NGO, so he knew what he was doing. He went through the formation steps of drafting a constitution and forming organizational committees. One of the committees of the BPO was the women's committee. The women already had an Episcopal Church Women's Organization that pre-dated BPO. Once the BPO was formed, this organization was not abolished, but assumed a second identity as the BPO Women's Committee. The leader of the committee was *Manang* Mary. The BPO was then launched with a big event. A large number of government and non-government organizations were invited for the launching, which made BPO from the very start a well-known People's Organization in Mountain province. As it turned out, this considerably facilitated the accessing of funds and other resources of different organizations.

After the BPO had been underway for more than a year, *Manong* Roy requested the assistance of MOUNT. MOUNT did some consultation with the members, after which it was decided that the women's committee should have an income-generating project. A social analysis done with the BPO had shown that lack of cash was a major problem in the livelihoods of people, and was especially felt by the women. An evaluation report of MOUNT looking back on this period cites an additional reason why the BPO embarked on such an income-generating project. There had been rumours sparked by the military, that the BPO had connections to the New People's Army (NPA). The military started to monitor the organization and harass its active members. According to the report:

> In 1991, the gravity of the red scare had succeeded in isolating BPO members from the mainstream of the community. Such experiences gave the PO the lesson that a strong community solidarity has to be built up for them to be able to pursue their goals and for their tribe not to be divided again. Based on this insight they made a strong resolution to strengthen their organization through membership expansion at every opportunity – through education, organizing work and project implementation. (Unpublished MOUNT document)

This means that the project had two objectives: it was meant to generate income for the members of the women's committee, but at the same time MOUNT wanted it to be instrumental for the organizing process of the BPO as a whole.

The women's committee initially consisted of seven women, under the leadership of *Manang* Mary. They decided to have a weaving project. For the patterns and colours the women could rely on generations of experience, since Mountain province has a long and famous tradition of backstrap weaving. Present-day weaving, however, is done on looms. *Manang* Mary was familiar with this technique, because she had been an industrial weaver for several years. Following her specifications, a carpenter was able to construct a loom that the husbands of the other participating women could use as a model to reproduce. The women thus had the technical expertise required for the project, and what they needed was money for the materials to make the looms and to buy thread. In consultation with MOUNT, the women decided to approach CWNGO for support.

The project takes off In April 1992, during the regional indigenous celebration of Cordillera Day (see Chapter 1), *Manang* Mary talked to Minda, who was the project co-ordinator of CWNGO. Minda was interested and invited them to submit a proposal. One month later, Minda and another CWNGO staff member came to Mountain province. They first discussed the project with MOUNT and then proceeded to the village to talk with the women. The discussions were apparently satisfactory and without further ado the project was approved. *Manang* Mary and some other women travelled to Baguio to receive the first payment of funds and, with the help of a CWNGO staff member, went to buy assorted threads and other project items.

This release of money by CWNGO was the beginning of a controversy between the two NGOs. MOUNT wrote a letter to protest against the way CWNGO had handled the project. Their objections were threefold. First, MOUNT regretted not having been consulted before the approval of the project. CWNGO apologized for this and assured MOUNT in a letter that 'this will definitely be a joint project since this is basically your area and the women belong to the bigger organization'. Second, MOUNT insisted that a feasibility study should have been undertaken prior to the project. According to the director of MOUNT, a woman named Fay, such a study was necessary to 'build up their [the women's] critical thinking and analysing ability.' Minda, on the other hand, claimed that CWNGO had approved the project on the assumption that the BPO was sufficiently 'empowered to be capable of handling its own affairs'. It was agreed that a feasibility study was still to be conducted as part of an interim evaluation. Finally, MOUNT told CWNGO that they should have consulted with the executive committee of the BPO, instead of dealing directly with the women's committee. This point revealed a difference in attitude of the two NGOs regarding this project that was not going to be resolved. According to MOUNT, the project belonged to the executive committee of the BPO, on which only one of the women was represented.

On the other hand, CWNGO saw the need to co-ordinate, but considered the project primarily an activity of the women. During the research, it turned out that this difference was reproduced in the village. The women weavers obviously considered the project theirs. They thought of the BPO executive committee as a group to consult with. The executive committee, however, held on to the idea that the project ultimately fell under their jurisdiction. The differences were clear from the way the two groups referred to the project and from the different issues they raised. The executive committee, for example, complained that the women did not submit regular (written!) reports on the project. The women, on the other hand, assumed they did not need to report, and normally would only seek consultation when problems arose.

In the meantime, the project went ahead with the seven women participants. Soon after they started, a Canadian visitor of the NGO Consortium came to the area and was able to place some orders to be sent to Canada. This was a boost for the project. It expanded their marketing, which mainly depended on outlets in the NGO offices. Because of the project's high initial costs, money soon ran out. In October, some of the BPO women presented themselves at Baguio's CWNGO office with a new shopping list. They put Minda in a difficult position. She realized she had to co-ordinate with MOUNT, but could not contact their office, because Mountain province has no telephone system. Yet the women were right there in the office and it was obvious that the items they requested were needed to proceed with their activity. Minda decided to let the interest of the women prevail. She gave the money, and purchases were made so that the women could continue their weaving. As a result, the second release of money was again done without prior consultation with MOUNT.

The project expands and inter-agency problems escalate This time, Fay, the MOUNT director, was furious. Again CWNGO had not consulted her, and besides, had released money before the agreed-on feasibility study was conducted. She wrote an angry letter to CWNGO's director. The letter hinted at problems with the project: 'misunderstanding among women and questions raised relating to the project', and reminded CWNGO that the BPO is MOUNT's concern: 'Whatever problems and gains in the weaving project of the women will have a bearing on the organization which will definitely affect the development work of our programme in the area.'

The conflict was not resolved. For reasons that are not clear, the organizations did not get around to meeting and sorting out their problems. Instead, they stopped communicating about the project and continued to deal with the project separately. Both agencies helped in the marketing by selling weaving products from their offices. The regional staff of CWNGO came occasionally to check the audits of the project. The Mountain province-based staff members of CWNGO also regularly visited the area. They gave the women training (a basic women's situationer and leadership training) and involved them in their provincial activities. MOUNT continued to relate to the project as part of their organizing work with the Binasan People's Organization.

Six months after the project had started, MOUNT noticed some tension as a result. The income the project provided raised *imon*, jealousy, in the community and this was exacerbated by the fact that there were only seven participants. This was discussed with the women, who agreed to expand. In the course of one year the project grew from seven to 19 participants. Around the time that this problem came up, another group of international visitors came to the area. They offered to bring in additional funding and marketing channels for the project. At this point, MOUNT intervened. They advised the executive committee of the BPO to decline the opportunity, and so they did. In an evaluation report of August 1993 MOUNT legitimated this as follows: 'Had it not been for the intervention of the BPO-EC as a body (one of whom was a member of the weaving group), the women's group would not have resolved their problem, disregarded all existing issues about their project and attended to getting the promised funds.'

The conflict is brought to the Consortium   In mid-1994, the Binasan weaving project was brought up in an important assessment meeting of the NGO Consortium concerned with socioeconomic work. Just before this meeting, an evaluation was conducted by staff members of the two NGOs and myself. The study revealed that the impact, from the point of view of the 19 participants, was overwhelmingly positive. The project had brought the women a substantial income and had increased their room for manoeuvre to manage many tasks. If, for example, a child was ill, and the mother had to stay in the house to take care of it, she could use the time to weave, and the money generated could pay somebody else to take care of her garden in the meantime. The management of the project seemed to run smoothly. The problems of the previous year were overcome, according to both the participants and the members of the executive committee of the Binasan People's Organization. Although the project went well, the villagers made it clear they needed continuing support from the NGOs, especially with the marketing of their products. This had become problematic. Most products were left in consignment with NGO offices and sales lagged considerably behind production. They needed the NGOs to help them devise and implement strategies to improve this situation. Unfortunately, however, the NGOs were occupied with their own problems.

Soon after the impact study, the project was discussed in the NGO Consortium. At this meeting, Fay charged that CWNGO had mishandled the project. Although MOUNT shared the opinion that the project was presently doing well, it insisted that the involvement of CWNGO had created problems that would have ruined the project but for the intervention of MOUNT. Her account emphasized the problems the project had encountered in the community. She stressed that these problems would have been avoided if CWNGO had done a feasibility study and had followed the arrangement of the co-ordination by consulting both MOUNT and the executive committee of the Binasan People's Organization. After the whole history of the project was spelled out during the Consortium meeting, the participants agreed that CWNGO was to blame for the problems. The Consortium adopted the position that the project was problematic. This meant that the project from then on was always labelled as a problem case. It was considered that this project was an example *par excellence* of bad co-ordination between NGOs and, moreover, that this situation was due to CWNGO. The project co-ordinator of CWNGO, who was present at the meeting, told me later that the criticism was so harsh that she had not seen a chance to defend CWNGO. She had simply taken on the blame and apologized.

NGO Accountability

The local village organization that implements a project is accountable to the supporting NGO, at least in financial terms. In the course of the project, CWNGO had trained the women in bookkeeping and went several times to the village in order to check the financial accounts of the weavers' group. But how about the accountability of the NGOs with regard to the villagers? NGOs obtain funding in order to provide services to People's Organizations, and should therefore be accountable to their clients. In the weaving project, there were no formal accountability procedures in which the two NGOs had to legitimate their activities *vis-à-vis* the villagers. Does that mean there was no accountability? Of course not. Villagers had their own ways of influencing NGO performance and certainly had both voice and exit (Brett 1993, based on Hirschmann 1970).

When the BPO was formed, *Manong* Roy was well aware of the requirements and practices of NGOs. After all, he had been an NGO staff member himself. He took the organization through the necessary steps of setting up regulations and committees to make it eligible for NGO support. In addition, under his guidance the BPO was launched with a big event.

Thanks to *Manong* Roy, the BPO managed to convey the image of a strong organization that was worthy of having a project. Indeed, Minda later defended her fast-track support of the project by stating that she acted on the presumption that she was dealing with a well-established organization, an impression she had derived from the enthusiastic stories going around the region after the launching event. The influence of local people was also apparent from the way *Manang* Mary and her companions managed to get a second tranche of funding from CWNGO simply by presenting themselves at the office. Instead of putting their request in a letter or passing it through the nearby office of MOUNT, they undertook the arduous trip to Baguio to give *acte de presence* in the office. The social pressure they thus put on Minda to respond to their needs was so strong that Minda felt she had no choice but to give the money, even though this was against the co-ordination agreement she had with MOUNT. As she said: 'What could I do, they were just standing in the office with their shopping list.'

In Chapters 4 and 5 I dealt with the issue of room for manoeuvre of NGOs and People's Organizations respectively in shaping development in the villages. In all the cases presented, it was clear that villagers largely manage to appropriate NGO-supported development programmes. They invest their own meaning in projects, develop their own organizing patterns and practices and manage to reshape the relation with NGOs, partly by acting upon identities they ascribe to these organizations and partly by playing on the multiple ties between villagers and NGO actors. In such a context it hardly makes sense to speak of accountability. The development relations, the meaning and practices of interventions, all reflect the manifold ways in which the different actors enrol or pressure each other for their respective projects. In many cases, the question of whether NGOs are accountable to their clients may be far less to the point than the question of whether NGOs have the necessary room for manoeuvre to exert some control over their intervention. But how about the accountability interfaces beyond the locality?

NGO accounts under construction Even though MOUNT and CWNGO were involved in the same project, their accounts on the process differed substantially. MOUNT found the process problematic, due to what they called CWNGO's mishandling of the project, whereas CWNGO itself thought the project was quite successful. Although there had been problems, these had been solved without leading to major conflicts. The narratives of both NGOs were largely informed by their own approaches to development and by their positions in the conflict. Both were from the same Consortium and therefore abided by the same policies, but their approaches in practice were quite different. In the first place, MOUNT put much more emphasis on inter-agency co-ordination, whereas CWNGO, in this case, let their relation with the women in the village prevail.

At the time the project started, in the early 1990s, CWNGO's management had developed a certain fatigue from the co-ordination involved in their programmes, especially since the organization usually worked in areas where other NGOs were present. MOUNT, on the other hand, clearly had different ideas about co-ordination and wanted CWNGO to abide by the correct procedures.

In the second place, MOUNT did not share CWNGO's approach to gender. CWNGO dealt directly with the women, relying implicitly on their own problem-solving capacity, and trusting that what was good for the women would also contribute to the community. MOUNT, on the other hand, was primarily concerned with the project in relation to the overall organizing process of the mixed People's Organization. It feared the project could turn into an isolated economic 'business' venture. MOUNT wanted the project to fall under the general People's Organization. Fay had a clear preference for 'mixed'-gender organizations. As she contended: 'Women are an integral part of the community. Maybe in other provinces separate women's organizations are necessary, but here in Mountain province women are more outspoken and can assert themselves in "mixed" organizations.'

She felt that CWNGO divided the communities by 'promoting' separate Women's Organizations. The CWNGO management, on the other hand, claimed that they did not promote separate Women's Organizations, but simply followed existing practices. In Binasan, as in practically all villages, there had been Women's Organizations operating in connection with churches or government agencies prior to the development of the NGO-related People's Organizations.

Besides these different approaches, other more everyday considerations played a role in the conflict. As one of the staff members of MOUNT said, the controversy could be viewed as 'simply a clash of the personalities involved', believing that it resulted from an individual problem between Minda and Fay. Another narrative about the conflict circulating among staff members explained it as a matter of *turfing*. Turfing is the expression used by NGO staff to denote conflicts of competition over territories or People's Organizations. Competition among NGOs easily sparks frustration among the staff. In the case of the BPO, a MOUNT staff member said that the problems with CWNGO were felt strongly because 'we were just establishing ourselves in the area'. Another said that, due to these problems, they lost their enthusiasm and developed instead a 'wait-and-see-attitude'.

These different principles and everyday competition seemed to inform each other. Perhaps MOUNT's insistence on procedure was also meant to safeguard its position in the village. Perhaps CWNGO's confidence in women was partly informed by its need to defend its disregard for the co-ordination procedure. This intertwining of principles and organizational interests is, of course, not openly stated. Anyway, the idea that people try to enhance their interest by evoking principles is not new. What I find more interesting is to see how both NGOs build their narrative on what happened in the localities, and the role of local villagers in this. Both NGOs thicken their narrative by referring to events in the village in order to make it more plausible. MOUNT claims to have had a better approach, and that CWNGO was responsible for quarrels and jealousy in the village. On the other hand, CWNGO focuses on the way problems were solved. In order to make their case convincing, both NGOs enrol villagers for support.

The NGOs bring the villagers to the accountability interfaces in the NGO Consortium, but not as social actors. Both agencies incorporate the villagers as supporters in the conflict. In the social construction of ac-counts by the NGOs, the local villagers, lumped together as 'the people', appear as the anonymous supernumeraries of a power play. Fay explained her exclusion of CWNGO in the evaluation by claiming that 'this was between me and the people'. In similar vein, Minda defended herself by saying that 'the women themselves asked for it'.

What we see, then, is that NGOs legitimate their role in the village by narrating selected issues and events of the project. In order to close the narrative, they sustain it with fragments of different discourses. MOUNT stresses the step-by-step organizing model and co-ordination procedures that prevail in the Consortium. CWNGO emphasizes the capacities of indigenous women, and justifies its decisions by prioritizing agreements and obligations with the women rather than with the other NGO involved. Both NGOs use a language of participation and claim to have acted in response to people's requests. I argued that local people appropriate NGO projects in the villages. However, as this case shows, once the project enters a 'second life' beyond the locality at accountability interfaces, the NGOs appropriate it right back. The accounts they construct reflect more the NGOs' attitudes and interests than their accomplishments in the project or the ideas of their clients. Even though they express their narratives in accepted discourses of organizing and participation, these conceal a range of organizational matters from within the NGOs that inform and invade these accounts. The result is that the two NGOs, despite the fact that they largely share the same discursive repertoire, arrive at quite different nar-ratives of the project in question. This leaves the question of why, in this case of two competing narratives, the members of the NGO Consortium favoured the MOUNT version of the story.

Accountability interface in the Consortium At the meeting of the NGOs' co-ordinating body, where the Binasan project was discussed, it was agreed that the project was problematic because CWNGO had mishandled it. The reason that the MOUNT account found legitimation was to do with discourses in the network. In Chapter 3, I described the discursive changes in the NGO Consortium. This Consortium, which started primarily as a political movement, expanded in the late 1980s, when it became hinged around several discourses: political, indigenous and developmental. The role of local people differs in each of these discourses. The political discourse centres on the notion that social change has to be initiated by an educated vanguard, which implies an emphasis on top-down approaches in local interventions that need to be well co-ordinated and systematic. The indigenous discourse centres on indigenous knowledge and traditional institutions for regulating conflict, which implies confidence in local villagers, from whom outsiders could learn. The development discourse centres on participation and consultation with villagers. In 1994, the Consortium underwent a rectification campaign in which the political discourse regained its dominance.

The accounts of MOUNT and CWNGO surf between all three discourses of the network, but with different emphases. The political discourse is much more pronounced in the account of MOUNT, while the indigenous and participatory discourses are more central in the account of CWNGO. When the project started, the hierarchy between the discourses in the Consortium was not very clear. However, by the time the conflict was brought before the Consortium meeting, the political discourse had been reinvigorated. Following the right procedures, adhering to a step-by-step organizing method without moving too fast into socioeconomic projects, and integrated organizing rather than focusing on particular groups such as women, had all become the priorities of the time. The MOUNT story seamlessly fitted into this line of thinking.

This was exacerbated by elements of power. It was also the period when the mood in the NGO Consortium had turned against CWNGO. CWNGO had recently had several other co-ordination problems with agencies from the network, and had become a kind of 'lame duck' that constituted an easy target. Also, the general director, who had always strongly promoted and defended the approach of CWNGO, had left the organization, creating a certain void in the 'negotiations' over the meaning of projects. At this moment, it was not difficult for MOUNT to enrol the members of the NGO network in their version of the story. Perhaps people felt that CWNGO needed a lesson, or perhaps the organization had simply become an easy target for scapegoating, but the result was that the BPO episode now became known as an 'inter-agency mess created by CWNGO'. In the case of the BPO, then, the way in which accounts regarding the project were constructed had little to do with what happened locally, or with the narratives of the participants involved in the village. What mattered more were the values and priorities of the NGOs and, in the end, discourse and power at the accountability interface of the NGOs.

An Actor-oriented Perspective on Accountability

At the start of this chapter I outlined two modes of accountability: rational and moral. Each has its own pedigree and they are often treated as having little in common. However, as I suggested, in practice these two modes of accountability inform each other. The case of the Binasan People's Organization underscores this point. Moral or everyday accountability and rational accountability are intertwined in practice, leading to possibly endless constellations of the three elements of accountability: actor relations, sense-making and legitimacy. Instead of assuming that accountability brings these elements together in a particular way, one is faced with three open-ended questions, namely: how are accountability relations shaped, how are accounts constructed, and how do some accounts become more convincing than others? I shall briefly discuss each of these from an actor-oriented perspective.

Proponents of rational and moral accountability alike assume that *accountability relations* are clear: one has to respond either to an authority in a particular chain of command or to the society or group one belongs to. In previous chapters, I presented NGOs as constituted by networks of actors that cut across organizational boundaries, making inter-organizational relations more ambiguous than the official ties between them suggest. Moreover, the cases presented point to multiple ties between NGO actors and their clients and other stakeholders. As a result, what appears as an instrumental accountability relation may evolve into a social arrangement of mutual obligations, where the ties that bind are both contractual and moral. Accountability relations between NGOs and their stakeholders appear, then, as negotiated properties: actors negotiate the nature of their obligations in accountability processes. The outcome is unpredictable. It has, for example, been observed that certain NGOs are capable of manipulating seemingly stringent accountability demands to their own ends (Biggs and Neame 1996; see also Chapter 8).

The *accounts* that are the substance of accountability processes – both formal and informal, technical and social – are representations. The material presented here illustrates that the connection between accounts and what actually happens in a locality is loose. One implication of this insight is that we have to bring the 'accounter' more explicitly into the analysis, that is, the person or organization composing and presenting the accounts. As the above case demonstrated, explanations why certain accounts are constructed, and not others, may be more telling of the discursive frames and the everyday politics of the accounter than of the phenomena accounted for.

The question of how certain accounts become more *convincing* than others bears little relation to their 'accurateness' or 'truthfulness'. Entirely different accounts can be constructed on the substance of the same project. The case presented also points to the fallacy of judging the nature of accounts by their appearance. Seemingly factual accounts of a project may hide underlying power dynamics and conceal implicit appeals to the moral responsiveness of the authorities receiving the account, in order to avoid harsh judgements. Actors make their accounts convincing by drawing on particular discourses and by enrolling other actors in accepting their interpretation of events (Latour 1987). An account becomes convincing, in other words, because its accounter is more successful than others in enrolling support and negotiating standards at interfaces of accountability.

I propose, then, to look at accountability processes from the angle of negotiating actors at accountability interfaces. In Chapter 5 I argued that an NGO intervention model meant to steer local development was, in fact, more meaningful as a tool for sense-making and ordering relations within NGO offices. Likewise, the above discussion of accountability leads me to conclude that local events and processes have relatively little bearing on accountability. What matter far more are the dynamics within accounting NGOs, and how NGOs negotiate their reading of events at the social interfaces with their stakeholders.

Finding accountability in unexpected corners Accountability is becoming increasingly important in development. In the 1980s, the term was rarely used. NGOs were the 'good gals' of development. Their responsiveness as value-driven intermediate organizations was taken for granted. We could say that NGOs 'radiated' moral accountability. Responsive by nature, their accountability did not have to be checked by formal means (van Dusseldorp 1992). Then, in the 1990s, formal accountability assumed importance. This can be understood as a response to the fact that impact studies revealed discrepancies between what NGOs claimed and how they performed. However, it can also be understood as part of changes taking place in dominant development discourses in the wider development 'community', and especially among donors.

The assumption of accountability seems to be the pillar on which the entire edifice of development by NGOs is built. First, the growing support for NGOs in development has been understood in the context of what Robinson (1993) calls a New Policy Agenda. Notwithstanding detailed variations in policies, it is argued that post-Cold War development policy is generally driven by 'beliefs organized around the twin poles of neo-liberal economics and Liberal Democratic theory' (Hulme and Edwards 1997: 5). In this agenda, NGOs have a double advantage. They are seen as the preferred channel for service provision in deliberate substitution for the state, and act as vehicles for 'democratization' and essential components of a thriving 'civil society' (ibid.: 6). I want to point out how inextricably interwoven this is with expectations of formal accountability. Delegating service provision requires a notion that it is possible to control it from a distance. Investing trust in the democratizing capacities of NGOs carries with it the expectation that NGOs will be transparent. This has led to a development in which accountability is stretched to cover ever larger domains of development. Originally largely restricted to financial accountability, it now becomes increasingly common to speak of impact, private, efficiency, fiscal, client and legal accountability (Smith-Sreen 1995: 36). The increased focus on NGO accountability may thus be viewed as an offspring of neoliberal and liberal democratic development discourses.

What are the implications for this discussion on NGOs and development of viewing accountability as a social process? It means that we have to abandon the idea of a correspondence between accounts and the projects accounted for. This implies that the accountability process cannot be separated from the social constellations and processes that it is intended to reveal. The accountability process itself is as vulnerable to power, hierarchy, conflicting interests and interpretations, and as much informed by culture, as the 'real' situation it aims to provide an account of. This is the case as much for classical accountability as for the newer varieties, such as the stakeholder approach (Fowler 1997) and social auditing (Zadek and Gatward 1996). Transparency turns out to be a myth. The idea of transparency has the connotation of making the wrappings of the message as well as the messenger invisible. Transparency is meant to reveal the 'real stuff'. However, as this chapter argues, there is no real stuff outside of actors' accounts and the practices of making these accounts workable and legitimate (Law 1994: 26).

Although accountability will not lead to transparency, this does not mean that it is impossible. We may just have to step away from our ideal notions, and ask instead how it operates in practice. Students of rational accountability tend to limit their view to the formal mechanisms of accountability, apparently without reference to the cultural embeddedness and everyday practices of NGOs. As a result of this normative approach, investigators researching NGO accountability may have no eye for localized forms of checks and balances. They assume that accountability does not exist where they do not find their preconceived mechanisms in place. Rather than asking what makes the NGO operate, and how a certain degree of coherence is achieved despite the absence of particular forms of accountability, they risk concluding that the NGOs operate arbitrarily, without any form of control.

In practice, however, accountability relations evolve (Brown and Fox 1998). They are based on a much wider range of accountability practices, that appeal to moral responsiveness and different sanction mechanisms, than are provided in rational accountability. They operate partly through formal accountability, altering its working in the process. They also operate outside of it, in the grey areas of social interaction, chatting, gossiping and rumour-mongering. Although this happens in a less controlled manner than rational accountability, it may none the less be workable. The major asset of NGOs is their reputation as organizations-that-do-good. They are, therefore, susceptible to accountability processes, even if they do not concur with rational accounting procedures. Actors' accounts regarding NGO performance can obviously be mistakenly or maliciously wrong, but they do have a large impact on how NGOs 'survive' accountability processes. This may be effective in forcing NGOs to live up to their own standards as much as they can.

Notes

1. See Lehmann 1990: 201–4; Smillie 1995: 149–51; Edwards and Hulme (eds) 1996; Zadek 1996.

SEVEN

Making Sense of NGOs: in Everyday Office Life

This chapter looks at questions of how NGO actors give meaning to their organization. Organizations, as I have emphasized, are characterized by multiple realities: they hinge around various and often conflicting discourses, and interweave different modes of operation. In everyday practice, NGOs are many things at the same time, which can be expressed metaphorically (see Morgan 1986). The Cordillera Women's NGO (CWNGO) can simultaneously be understood as a giver of services, a family, an ideological bastion, a source of livelihood, a space for women, a cultural statement of 'unity in diversity', a project bureaucracy and an indigenous institution. NGO actors, as a result, do not have a single notion of what their organization is, does and wants. My interest is in knowing how these varying meanings interact, conflict or converge, and how NGO people define which is the more appropriate for particular times and spaces. This is not often subject to explicit reflection. Implicitly, however, questions of meaning underlie many of the minutiae of everyday life, the dealing with endless seemingly insignificant decisions. NGO actors negotiate the meaning of the organization, for example, in facing questions like: Should I compliment or criticize a staff member for a particular action? Shall I go to a political rally or use the time to finish a report? How should I respond to a request from a visitor? Whom shall I join at the table for lunch? How should I deal with a staff member who is not productive, but has been a friend since high school? Hence, questions of meaning are implicit in virtually everything NGO actors face and do.

Several authors consider the issue of meaning so central to organization that they practically equate the two. Stewart Clegg (1998: 43) says that 'the analysis of organizations concerns the endowment of the material forms of institutional life, be it economic, religious, or whatever, with significance'. Likewise, Susan Wright conceptualizes organizations as 'continuous processes of organizing and negotiating meaning' (Wright 1994: 20). The NGO literature, however, is virtually silent about meaning-making within organizations. Several authors, for example, are concerned with how boards govern NGOs (Tandon 1996 and Baig 1999), but not how staff members themselves give meaning to these organizations. Similarly, there is a lot of attention given to the relation between NGOs and their stakeholders, but very little to relations within the NGO. Given the importance of processes of negotiating meaning for understanding organizations, this seems a major gap.

This chapter, then, is concerned with social processes of meaning in NGOs. It explores how different ideas are generated and how NGO actors manage to live with and work in these situations of multiplicity. Even in the most coherent organization, there are always multiple readings of what the organization is and alternative modes of action to choose from. This leads me to wonder how the staff alternate between them, how they accommodate the discontinuities in organization, and how they none the less arrive at a certain level of coherence and continuity in their work.

Which actors are involved in shaping the meaning of an organization? NGO literature usually focuses on management actors. Implicitly, it is assumed that management gives a face to the organization, provides its brain and directs the practices of the staff. This view of management is also found in organization theories that consider management the centre of decision-making. Leadership may then be defined as 'the management of meaning and the shaping of interpretations' (Smircich 1983: 351). I take a different perspective. It should not be taken for granted that management has a dominant influence in organizational processes. When a management effectively imposes meaning, this needs explanation, just as much as when their influence is challenged. When management turns out to be powerful in shaping the organization, we should ask how this power is effected. Taking their influence for granted implies a belief that they have influence simply because they happen to be the management.

Other approaches that have a more inclusive interest in organization actors assume that differentially positioned categories of actors each carry their own perspective. Numerous studies analyse organization processes by distinguishing management from the rest, sometimes with further distinctions among the rest such as administration versus fieldworker perspectives (for NGOs, see, for instance, Suzuki 1998). This strand of approach assumes that people have perspectives according to their position in organizations. Again, I take a different perspective. As I found, *all* NGO actors are engaged in interpreting events and reflecting on their work. Their interpretations do not simply differ on the basis of their position, but are informed by a number of things. Alberto Arce identifies the latter as a combination of institutional knowledge, type of life world and experience with clients (Arce 1993: 97).

The chapter is divided into three sections that focus on meaning-making and ordering in the Cordillera Women's NGO. The first starts with a tour around the office of the NGO. It gives a picture of the organization and introduces some everyday practices. It concentrates on the use of *locales* in the office, which are domains for sense-making that help staff to traverse different modes of organizing and to manage relations in the office. The second section is about the backgrounds of NGO actors and social networks in the organization. It discusses five elements around which social networks are organized. The focus on social networks turns out to be very powerful for understanding how diverse meanings attributed to the NGOs cross-cut hierarchical and horizontal relations, and how NGO actors create a workable situation without necessarily having a shared understanding of the organization. The third section looks at certain organizational practices, in particular those that are considered to be 'typically Pinoy' (Filipino). This gives me the opportunity to discuss the concept of culture, which, after all, is very much associated with the production of social meaning. As I argue, cultural institutions from the wider society are important in ordering the everyday practices of NGOs. However, they do not impose themselves on NGOs, but are invoked by actors in some cases and not others.

Although each of the three sections of this chapter presents an angle of its own, they all add up to the same story. They all point to the idea that organizational meaning emerges through the everyday practices of actors, who have agency. Meanings are not a product of culture, policy or a group of powerful actors. The construction of meanings is not located in one particular centre, but emerges from organizing processes. These processes are of a decentred nature, which means that 'there is no single centre of control and that there is no single group or organizational body which controls this process' (Nuijten 1998: 316).

Tour d'Office

CWNGO's office is a brightly white two-storey house, surrounded by a wall. It is located in a relatively quiet neighbourhood of Baguio City. The immediate impression it conveys to visitors familiar with NGOs in the Philippines is of a well-to-do organization that has secured stable funding. The iron gate of the office opens on to a courtyard with a garden. It is planted with flowers and with vegetables that are used to cook lunch in the office. The garden is the responsibility of *Manang* Jenny, an elderly woman who is the office cook and factotum. Other staff members occasionally like to work with her in the garden. Many of them know gardening from the farms or gardens of their families and like the physical endeavour as a break from office work. They also like chatting with *Manang* Jenny. She seems the ideal representation of an indigenous woman of the Cordillera. She knows about things such as the use of medicinal plants. She also knows everything about everybody and never misses a wedding, funeral or baptism. With her traditional outlook and ideas, she is often the centre of jokes, but, on the other hand, everybody is obviously very fond of her.

The courtyard with its old three-piece suite is a favourite place for staff to sit during breaks and lunch. When a staff member returns from a field trip, people usually gather in the yard to listen to stories of the trip. The stories are a mixture of anecdotal field experiences, such as how a staff member lost her way, and accounts of the actual work undertaken: the response of women in the villages, work relations with the provincial staff, and problems encountered in the locality. Every staff member is required to write detailed reports about trips. In practice, these reports are not always read and the informal reports given in the yard are often the primary means by which both staff and management remain updated on developments in the field.

In the yard is a blackboard, on which issues are written that require immediate attention. They announce activities in the city, such as a lecture to be given at a local university, a wake for a deceased person from the extensive NGO network, or a call to all staff members to attend the hearing of a sexual harassment case that will be held in court. Such activities are usually attended by the administrative staff and organizers. They enjoy doing things outside the office and, unlike the management, can arrange this within their workload. The yard is further used as a waiting room for the many people who visit the office. Visitors range from members of a CWNGO-sponsored weaving co-operative, who bring their bags of finished blankets to be sold at the office, to staff of other NGOs or occasionally government offices, a host of visitors from Manila or abroad, and people who come to see a particular staff member on a personal matter. Visits are both scheduled and unscheduled, and the latter in particular take place in the informal setting of the yard. Finally, the yard is regularly used for spontaneous gatherings at the end of the day, when husbands pick up their wives and visitors from other NGOs drop by. Occasionally, the relaxed chatting, gossiping and joking that belong to this time of day are extended to a restaurant where participants enjoy beer and food.

From the courtyard, a carved wooden door forms the entry into the office, a large glass sliding-door gives direct access to the library, and iron-wrought winding stairs lead to the second floor. The library is extensive and up-to-date, due mainly to the director's many travels abroad and her passion for collecting books. Like so many other NGOs, CWNGO maintains its own clippings service, a vast file of newspaper clippings on a range of topics that is maintained by the librarian. The clipping takes many hours, and staff members who have nothing particular to do will sometimes sit down and help out. The task is considered arduous and of little fulfilment, since it never ends and because the file is not often consulted. The library table with all the newspapers, however, has its own attraction as a favourite locale for chatting. More than any other place, this is the domain of staff at the lower end of the NGO's hierarchy, and it is here that they exchange their views on the management of the office. I related above how informal storytelling in the yard after returning from a field trip often has more meaning than a written report on the same trip. However, despite the apparent spontaneity, these oral reports are also edited. That is, they are shaped in a way considered to be acceptable to the management. Frequently, another kind of reporting takes place later, in more secluded settings with a few staff friends, where the 'report' is retold without reservations, so that personal opinions find an outlet and events are positioned and given meaning within a general assessment of the NGO and its work. The library is a suitable place for these kinds of discussions.

Apart from the library, the ground floor of the office consists of a spacious kitchen, a bathroom and two other rooms. The larger of these two rooms serves many purposes. It contains a number of corners with desks and filing cabinets. During meetings, the furniture is reorganized to form a large conference table, with a number of blackboards and easels for flap-overs on which staff members can present their reports. The smaller room is almost empty of furniture and has built-in cabinets along the wall. It is used to store materials for the field, such as cartons of books and clothes donated by international support groups. It also stores an enormous quantity of sleeping mats and blankets used during meetings, when the entire provincial staff comes to Baguio and many sleep overnight in the office. The small room is also ideally suited for after-lunch naps.

Upstairs, there are another five rooms positioned around a landing. On the landing stands a television set, which is normally left switched on, mainly for the sake of the children. There are always children at the office. Some come with their mothers daily, others only when their daycare centre is closed or the babysitter is not available. When one of them starts to cry, whoever is nearby comforts it, without bothering to call for the mother. The children are used to playing by themselves and, when bored, one of the staff will play with them, or a younger staff member is told to take care of them.

The smallest room, across the landing, is the director's office. It is the only room that is normally kept locked. The lock is not so much a token of the status of the director, but rather a means of security, because this room houses the vault containing the records of the NGO as well as correspondence and financial files. As in other NGOs, details on finances are firmly locked away, concerning both income and expenditure. Project proposals, for example, can easily be borrowed by other NGOs to help them formulate their own, but not without first removing the accompanying budget. One of the rationales for this practice is that, once people know how much money a proposal has brought to the office, other NGOs may want to borrow money for their own programmes. The director is the only one who has a separate room and her own computer. All the others share. The cabinets and desks in the rooms are placed to create different corners for staff members, although one can easily overhear what happens in other corners. Those staff members who do not want to be overheard leave the office or lower their voice to a whisper. Sometimes it suffices to shift into one of the local languages, when staff from the same area of origin wish to talk in private. The four computers available to staff members are placed in one of the office rooms. This room is mainly the domain of Liwaya, a young, Tagalog-speaking woman, and a pronounced lesbian. On the wall near her desk are several cartoons about female sexuality, one of them displaying a woman drowning in the bathtub after giving herself an orgasm while taking a bath.

The walls in the office are decorated with posters and weavings that are a reminder of past and present NGO campaigns, globalized indigenous and women's causes, and past international visitors. In between the decorations, notice boards are scattered with announcements of activities and newspaper clippings. A remarkable element in the use of the walls are the numerous computer-printed instructions of office rules. Some of them are funny reminders, such as the one in the toilet that reads: 'If you don't flush, we shall flush you; signed: the spirits of the peach tiles (look around, we're here).' Most are made up as official instructions. Another paper in the same toilet, for example, gives a list of instructions on how to use the facility, such as 'flush after using', and 'refill the pails when near empty'. This list is signed, the 'management committee CWNGO Inc'.

The number of desks occupied during working days varies considerably, except for the bi-monthly paydays when practically all the staff reports to the office. In the morning, staff members trickle in. It is not unusual for them to report late. An explanation for being late is normally given, but practically any excuse is acceptable, even if one occasionally admits to having been too 'lazy' to come in early. Usually, however, being late is related to family responsibilities, which, as everybody knows, are inevitable and often need priority. During the day, staff come and go.

Because of close collaboration with other NGOs, there are many meetings and training sessions outside as well as many other things to attend to in the city. Although staff do not always adhere to the standard office working day, they frequently extend their working time beyond office hours. On most evenings, there are people working at the computers or preparing a training session or field trip. There are always some who sleep in the office. They finish work too late to go home, or they simply enjoy staying together, preparing snacks in the kitchen and watching rented videotapes. Thus the large room is transformed into a cosy space for social gatherings.

Locales for Sense-making

What does this tour around the different spaces of the office tell us about negotiating the meaning of NGO relations and activities? In the first place, it shows how 'locales provide a variety of arenas in which current issues and problems are interpreted and re-interpreted' (de Vries 1992: 59). The locales are the domains of different groups in the office. While the management gathers in the room of the director, the lower staff chat in the library to arrive at an understanding of ongoing issues. It is here that they discuss whether certain statements or decisions of management actors are right or wrong in their eyes. It is also in these locales that values are negotiated and practical consciousness tested, such as those regarding gender and sexuality. Stories about marital life and other aspects of life experiences are shared in office corners and discussed from different angles, including feminist perspectives versus notions of family obligations. It is in the kitchen that staff members playfully engage in discussions where *Manang* Jenny teaches the staff how to accommodate to gender expectations. In their turn, Liwaya and another lesbian provoke *Manang* Jenny – to the great enjoyment of the other staff members present – with statements that lesbian women actually engage in sex with each other. *Manang* Jenny always replies with open revulsion, asking incredible questions about the details of how they do it. It is a two-way teasing with lots of laughter, yet with serious undercurrents providing room to explain and negotiate norms of sexuality.

In the second place, the locales provide space to accommodate the different styles of organization that interplay in the NGOs, for instance, to help NGO actors to regulate formal and informal aspects of organizational life. The courtyard is the place for informal reporting, but when the big room on the ground floor is transformed into a conference room, staff members will switch to a style of reporting that befits the formal language of NGO organizing models. The spatial separation helps staff to bridge different modes of NGO work that are all inherent parts of the organization. In the court they 'think' informal, and in the conference room they automatically 'think' formal. This is also apparent in bodily practices: in the courtyard one can literally relax by sinking into the cushions of the sofa, but before re-entering the office a staff member must straighten her skirt.

Third, the different locales help NGO actors to organize and negotiate their relations. NGO actors in the office are bound by multiple ties and have developed multifaceted relations. As we see below, in the office, the social networks of family, friendship, political comradeship and formal relations are all intertwined. Using the symbolism of different locales is one way in which NGO actors manoeuvre these multiple relations. When a management actor calls a staff member to her office, the staff member instantly knows that it is likely that there is a problem and that she may be reprimanded. If it were an ordinary matter, the management actor would simply walk over to the staff member's corner to discuss it casually, half-sitting on the desk. Conversely, when a staff member has a problem to discuss with the management, she carefully deliberates whether to address the manager in her office, or wait for an opportunity to discuss it more informally and thereby call upon the social ties that bind.

Locales are thus domains of sense-making, and help NGO actors to order and organize office life. Although the different locales have a symbolic connotation linked to particular aspects of organization, it is important to realize that this symbolic meaning is not a property of the locales themselves that structure people's behaviour; instead, such meaning is achieved only when invoked by an actor. The meaning of these locales must be invested in and interpreted by people. To paraphrase Henrietta Moore (1994: 96), one might say that it is only by actually falling down on the sofa and sighing that you are tired, that the informal meaning of the courtyard is invoked. As Moore points out: 'Actors are continually involved in the strategic interpretation and reinterpretation of the cultural meanings that inform the organization of their world as a consequence of their day-to-day activities in that world' (ibid.: 76). Even though these actors may not always be discursively aware of the symbolic use of different locales, they use them strategically through a practical knowledge of their meaning. They use the different spaces to facilitate some of the complexities of organization and to manoeuvre their social relations in the office.

The Importance of Social Networks

Whatever an NGO is depends on how NGO actors perceive and act upon the organization. Everything has to be made sense of in order to be valued, judged or acted upon. How actors interpret the policy and practices of the

NGO depends on their life worlds, institutional histories, experiences with NGO clients and other elements that differentiate actors. These may be individual, but considering that sense-making is largely a social process, networks are an important focus for analysis. It is in social networks that actors shape and play out the meaning of their organization. In CWNGO, an initial differentiation in networks appears to separate management both from middle cadres and from organizers or field workers. However, as I gradually found out, social networks are formed around a number of elements, resulting in shifting constellations in the office that cannot be reduced to two or three separate social networks whose members share a particular organizational perspective. Before discussing some of the elements of social networking in the office, I will recount the stories of two staff members: Aster and Susan. They are both college graduates in their early thirties, working as middle-level staff members in the Baguio office of CWNGO. Yet their stories differ.

Aster Aster grew up in a city adjacent to Baguio, where her family has some land. She attended college in the 1980s in one of the lowland towns, at a time when the National Democratic Student Movement was very strong in Philippine universities, and she was quickly turned into a political activist. As a city girl, Aster never experienced herself as indigenous until her college years in the lowlands, when she became conscious of her indigenous background because of occasional questions of her college mates about whether Igorots had tails, or lived in trees. After graduation, Aster engaged in the National Democratic movement in the Cordillera. She briefly joined a guerrilla group of the New People's Army, but soon decided to work above ground instead. She then became a programme co-ordinator of an NGO belonging to the Cordillera NGO Consortium. After a year, Aster quit that job for a combination of political and personal reasons. She lost political confidence in the movement's leadership when, during an internal crisis, some of her personal friends were forced to resign from the movement, without receiving, in her mind, a fair treatment. The other reason was that she could not combine NGO work with her family obligations. Her husband went to study in Australia when she was pregnant. When the baby came, she had to stay home to take care of him. For several years she lived in a house owned by her in-laws and lived on an allowance sent by her husband. During one of the visits of her husband she became pregnant again, so she soon had two children to take care of.

At the end of 1992, the director of CWNGO met Aster and asked her to help organize a conference. Although Aster was aware that CWNGO belonged to the political movement that she had come to dislike, she was motivated to work for the organization as long as she was not to be politically involved again. She started to work at the socioeconomic desk of the office and was involved in research. I came to know Aster better when we made several field trips together for research. She turned out to have a keen interest in village ways of life, especially those aspects of village life that were reminiscent of 'tradition'. After a day of interviewing professionals attached to modern institutions like the school, she would suggest that we walk to the higher part of the village where the old men were seated in the *dap-ay*, a sacred circle of stones. We then chatted about their lives, while young boys were busy scratching the soles of the old men's feet with sticks. Although Aster grew up in Baguio City, her family originated from a village which, according to Aster, was one of the oldest and most traditional in the province, with people practising many of their indigenous institutions. She was obviously proud of this background.

Her interest in the indigenous lifestyle was complemented by a special concern for women. This was directly related to her own experiences. When her husband returned from Australia the marriage became problematic, and she commented:

> There are many things I would like to do, but I don't have the time. I have to be at home because of the children. I actually have three now, because the other one came home [i.e. her husband]. You see, it was easier when he was not around because I only had to worry about the two. *That is how you can see women's lives in the communities, how you can feel the problems of motherhood.*

The identification of Aster with local village women's lives did not mean that she herself fitted into this life. Her own lifestyle was quite different from the way Cordillera women behaved, and this was not lost on the women of the village. They started to comment on the way Aster spoke and some of the things she said. One day she dropped by a village on her way to a meeting in the provincial town, in the company of a male friend. I was not present on this occasion, but several of the women told me later that they did not like Aster any more. '*Madi ni Aster*', one of them said, 'Aster is a bad woman'. Apparently, they felt Aster's behaviour had not been appropriate: 'She behaved towards the man as a wife, not as an acquaintance.'

In the meantime, Aster grew increasingly critical of CWNGO and began to consider searching for another job. Eventually she resigned. Her objections against the organization were several. First, she was critical of the way that work was organized. There were the ordinary irritations that seem to be an inevitable part of hectic NGO life. The head of her desk was often out of the office for meetings, and there was no clear communication about activities and the arrangement of tasks. Aster felt especially irritated when such things affected the local women, and expectations were not met. She did not see these incidents as isolated events, but interpreted them in connection with her own past disappointment with the political movement. When a management actor forgot something, Aster would assert 'you see, they do not live up to their own principles', or, 'the movement for social change does not care about its own people'.

Second, it seems Aster was disappointed with the way her position evolved in the organization. When she entered CWNGO she already had a history, albeit briefly, as an NGO programme co-ordinator. In comparison to other staff members, she did not feel much distance between herself and the management. This was apparent in the way she reported and fed back information to the management. The management actors initially seemed to treat her as an experienced NGO person. When a new position was created of co-ordinator of the organizers, Aster applied for the position, along with another staff member who had been working with CWNGO for the past four years. It turned out that the position was given to the other person. Initially, Aster stated that she did not mind, but she kept referring back to it, until I concluded that she had in fact felt very insulted.

Despite her critique, Aster continued working for CWNGO, if only because her salary was the sole source of income for the family. In the course of months, however, the misgivings between Aster and CWNGO became increasingly two-way, especially when Aster linked up with a new NGO that worked with the government. When CWNGO found out she was working simultaneously for another organization, she was given an ultimatum to choose between her two commitments. Although the new NGO was not successful in getting funds and in providing her with a salary (in fact it collapsed within a few months), Aster decided to leave CWNGO.

Susan Susan is one of the single women in the office and a few years younger than Aster. After obtaining her college degree in education in a Baguio-based university, she wanted to have a job as soon as she could and therefore applied to a wide range of organizations. She knew of the NGO Consortium through her brother, who worked for another of the NGOs, so she applied to CWNGO. She became a day-care teacher for several years, until funding stopped and the day-care centre closed. Then Susan became responsible for literacy training. She started to provide this in a poor urban area, conducted a region-wide survey on literacy, trained village volunteers and took the initiative to work out a programme with one of the government offices in the region.

Susan originates from and grew up in a provincial town of the Cordillera. She feels, in her words, 'indigenous by blood, by birth, by genes and by everything. Ever since I was a kid I have known I am part of the indigenous group and that I belong to a clan and a tribe.' What seemed to matter in her everyday life were her specific Bontok origins. Local indigenous politics affected her relations in the office. This was particularly clear when one of Susan's cousins was killed in the streets of Baguio. It was a random killing, and the perpetrator was taken to prison. Over some snacks in one of Baguio's many American-style hamburger parlours, she explained to me what the killing meant to her family. Immaculately dressed as usual, a soft-voiced city girl, she told me that some of the elders of her family clan had come to Baguio. She said she was tired after night-long rituals and deliberations on how to deal with the killing:

> We had a long discussion with our cousins. The killer will probably get a life long sentence but for them this is not enough: revenge is revenge and blood is blood. They are considering killing him, but they are still looking for the right person for revenge. The actual killer wouldn't suffice, because he is nothing. Our cousin was a working professional, so it would also have to be a working professional.

While these deliberations went on for several weeks, she never mentioned anything about them in the office. She explained: 'Most of our staff are from Sagada and Besao, and the killer is partly from Sagada and partly from a place near Besao. There are actually some who know his family, that's why I can never talk about this in the office.'

Susan's origin from Bontok has further implications for her work in an NGO. When her brother started to work for an NGO, word went around in Bontok that he had become a Communist. When Susan started her job with CWNGO she decided not to tell her folks since she was afraid it would further affect the position in the community of her mother, who was already criticized for her son's involvement. Some of her siblings, however, knew of her position and tried continually to convince her to find another job. Apart from the political considerations, they felt that as the youngest daughter she had to take financial responsibility for her parents and thus needed to look for a better-paid job. As a result, Susan often considered the possibility of changing to a government office.

Like most staff members of CWNGO, Susan was familiar with and dedicated to the political standpoint of the NGO movement, or 'the principle', as she called it. In her everyday practices, however, she found more direction in her identification with women from the point of view of a daughter-cum-educator in the Cordillera. Susan firmly believed in the merits of adult literacy training. Her students remind her of her mother. 'My mother is also "no-read no-write". I can see that every time she comes to Baguio, she always needs assistance. When crossing the street, when buying, everything.' Susan also identifies with the feminist ideas of CWNGO, but she is not so sure if gender equality is feasible in the Cordillera. To her mind, it will need years of patient training to achieve changes in this respect. According to her:

> The idea of equality is a very nice one, but it only works when your husband goes along with the idea. As for now, in our family, it seems it is not applicable. I see all my brothers are very patriarchal. And especially when your parents agree with their ideas, you cannot quarrel about it.

Unlike Aster, Susan felt a large distance between herself and the management committee. She said: 'It seems that you must practise every word, before you can utter it to them.' In meetings, she would not say much unless it directly concerned the literacy programme. In 1995, the workload changed. In an assessment of NGO work, it was decided that NGOs should concentrate on basic organizing. A specialized programme such as the literacy training was given low priority. As a result, Susan would have to shift her work towards organizing and maintain the literacy programme on the side. She did not oppose the decision.

Several months after the management of CWNGO had reorganized her work, Susan took a job with a government office in Bontok. As with Aster, the considerations and experiences leading to the job transfer were multilayered. One layer was made up of mounting pressure from her relatives. For this particular job, her sister had simply made an appointment for her with the head of the government office. Another layer was formed by the erosion in her motivation to continue working with CWNGO. She was very disappointed that her literacy programme had been abandoned. In addition, she had grown impatient with the long political reorganization process in the NGO (see Chapter 3), and especially by the fact that this was dealt with only at management level. She became frustrated that she was never informed what happened and was just told to be patient, but, as she said: 'When was this process going to be finished and when would they start to listen to us?'

Although Susan had increasingly been playing with the idea of moving jobs, the decision was activated by a particular incident in the office. She had written an application letter that was printed by mistake under the eyes of one of the managers. In her presence, this person proclaimed: 'Look, here is an application letter.' Susan recalled the moment:

> She then called everybody and showed them the letter. I was just watching them. When I said it was not true that I was leaving, she said in a high-

pitched voice: 'So, why do you apply, is it to show you are overqualified?' I did not expect that. *I thought that they would sit with me and talk and ask me how I see things and try to keep me in the organization.*

Susan felt the response of this manager to be deeply humiliating, especially because it was done in public. This settled her decision to resign. When she resigned, the only motivation she reported to the management was family considerations. She never mentioned the other layers, such as her disappointment about the literacy programme, her qualms about the political reorganization and the sense of humiliation she had felt. Through the way she formulated her motivation to resign, she avoided conflict with the management of CWNGO. That did not mean she had kept silent. She had discussed her motivation more completely with other members of staff, during lunches and in the library, where ideas about the management of the office and the reorganization in the NGOs were aired. Rather than bringing their ideas into the meetings, staff members defined their options as carrying on or resigning. Their experiences and ideas were channelled into endless deliberations on whether, how and when to resign and where to create alternative livelihood options.

Of Backgrounds and Social Networks

From the stories, it appears that Aster and Susan have a lot in common. They were both highly motivated to work with indigenous women and both were confronted with competing loyalties. While Susan felt the pull of family obligations, Aster had to accommodate her commitment to the NGO with the responsibility for her children and loyalty to her old friends. In both cases, an important factor eroding their identification with the NGO consisted of the sense of not being appreciated by the management. There are, however, also differences in the stories. Because of their backgrounds and organizational experiences they had arrived at different interpretations of the meaning of NGO activities, a different construction of their clients and different ways of behaving with local women. They also differed in how they defined and used their room for manoeuvre within the NGO organization. In the following section I discuss five elements that account for some of these differences.

Political involvement   In Chapter 1, I asserted that politics is considered a highly important aspect differentiating NGOs in the Philippines. The CWNGO staff consists of three political categories. A handful is deeply involved in the National Democratic political movement. This group includes the management committee and deals almost exclusively with external relations, including funding agencies, co-ordination with other NGOs in the network, planning, staff meetings, etc. Group members form a close social network in many respects. They carry out many activities together, have lots of issues to co-ordinate and go back together a long time.

The second group is composed of staff who have insight into and affinity with the National Democratic body of thought. It consists of lower staff in the Baguio office and a number of provincial staff members. They do not assume a position in the political movement, except that those in Baguio usually belong to a group that meets sporadically for education purposes. They form a social network, but not so close as the first mentioned core group. They derive much of their motivation for their work and loyalty to the organization from their political ideas and sense of belonging to the movement. They often talk among themselves about the political meaning of their work. As exemplified by Susan, they may feel excluded from discussions on which they nevertheless have opinions.

A third category of staff members is not familiar with the political aspects of the NGO. They are staff hired for particular jobs, as well as some of the provincial staff. They have only a vague conception of the wider movement in which the NGO is situated. They do not have a particular loyalty to the network, and may easily move on when other job opportunities arise. They are not a social group in the sense of relating on the basis of a shared understanding of the work they carry out. Almost by default, they have some influence in the organization simply on account of not knowing when to shut up and not being aware of certain taboos. This means that they occasionally raise questions in meetings that would be unthinkable from others. Such questions may none the less resonate for some time in office discussions.

Family background and place of origin One thing that all staff members of CWNGO share is their enthusiasm for going to the field and interacting with indigenous women. As Susan once expressed:

> I praise the vendors and that kind of women more than those in the offices. Because they are the women who are not ashamed of what their life really is. With those women you see the real 'them'. When I am with peasant indigenous women, I feel more open and my real 'me'. No plastic smiles, no plastic actions.

Every single member of staff I talked to found their primary motivation for the work in their commitment to indigenous women. They did not mean just any indigenous woman, but those who were poor and had little education. These were the 'real' women. Although all staff members shared this commitment, the cases of Aster and Susan are exemplary in revealing the difference between women born or educated in the lowlands and women who spent most of their lives in the Cordillera.

A number of staff members were born or raised in the lowlands and only got to know indigenous women when they started to work for CWNGO. They had their own stories to tell of how they had moved from prejudice to an appreciation of indigenous culture. These lowland and urban-raised staff members tended to view indigenousness in terms of properties. Aster's interest, for example, in the indigenous way of life was selectively focused on the traditional aspects that she considered 'truly' indigenous. One of the lowland staff explained her admiration for 'grass-roots' indigenous women as follows:

> Staying with the women in the Cordillera really humbled me. As a low-lander, I had those attitudes on what clothes to wear, and the things I wanted to have. But when I was integrated with these women, I noticed they have one-room houses, they really don't have so many material things and they are satisfied with what they eat, even if they have *camote* all the time. Me, I was not like that. I didn't even eat vegetables before. It really humbled me.

Staff members who had grown up in the provinces, like Susan, did not often refer to generalized indigenous properties, but to more local origins. To them, being indigenous implied, in the first place, that they had to respect certain practices and obligations, in the villages as well as in the office. This difference had several implications for social networking and sense-making in the office, as well as for client constructions,[1] styles of intervention and room for manoeuvre of organizers.

To start with the office, place of origin combined with place of education made a difference in the language used, and therefore the social networks one belonged to and the influence one could have. Staff educated in the lowlands were fluent in English and Tagalog, which gave them a definite advantage in dealing with policy matters, paperwork and external relations. They often spoke English or Tagalog among themselves. Staff raised in the provinces were more at ease with their local vernaculars. Among them, those speaking Kankanaey were a majority. This was also the native language of two out of the three managers of CWNGO. Although at times clan or village membership would set Kankanaey people apart, as happened when Susan's cousin was killed, those speaking Kankanaey often had news to exchange and enjoyed talking together. Those speaking other indigenous languages were minorities within the office. The only two Ifugao-speaking junior staff members were very close friends, but had little to say in the office.

The two groups of staff – lowland, educated, city-raised staff, and provincial staff – differed in the way in which they constructed their images of the women they worked with. The lowland, educated staff had a general admiration for indigenous women, but at the same time often viewed them as 'in need of learning', almost with the endearment adults display towards children. Those from the provinces were raised with a firm respect for older women. They saw their clients in the first place as women to be respected, in whose service they worked. This resulted in different styles of intervention. Those staff members who were not so closely embedded in the localities tended to assume the role of organizer and educator, and entered the villages with a certain aura of authority. Although they could be very effective, their attitude could also put their women clients off, as happened with Aster. Provincially raised staff, on the other hand, had the tendency to assume the modest role of a young woman in the village. They were soft-spoken, and prepared to help the women they visited, among other things with household chores. This made them well-liked and accepted. On the other hand, they found it difficult to influence the organizing process in the village, because they might feel too shy to speak when the elder women were present.

Kinship Real and symbolic family relations are pervasive of everyday life in the NGO. In the first place, the space staff members had in which to manoeuvre their positioning in social networks in the office differed according to the involvement of their family in the NGO Consortium and the wider National Democratic movement. At the time I conducted a survey among the staff of CWNGO, 13 staff members were married, and eight of their husbands worked as staff or volunteers in the network. In addition, several staff members had siblings or cousins working with organizations of the movement. Having a husband in the same field of work mattered for the involvement of staff members in the organization. This can be exemplified by the difference between Minda and Violet. Both of them belonged to the management committee. However, while Violet was married to a man within the NGO Consortium, Minda's husband wanted nothing to do with the NGOs. Violet could stay late in the office and work during weekends, and her husband took his share in picking up the children from their day-care. Minda, on the other hand, always had to rush home and to negotiate every trip she wanted to make to the field. At the end of the afternoon husbands often dropped by the office, and quite regularly this resulted in suppers in one of the downtown restaurants. Because Minda could not join these gatherings, she missed the social occasions that often followed the working day, where the latest information was passed on and social bonds were glued together.

In the second place, NGO organizations take on many of the aspects of family relations. The longer staff members are involved, the denser their relationships with colleagues. Bonds of symbolic kinship are forged through godparenthood on the occasions of childbirth and marriage. Children normally have at least four godparents and twelve is not exceptional. Often when a child is born within the NGO, a majority of its godparents will be drawn from the office or NGO Consortium. Some management actors in the Consortium have as many as 20 or 30 godchildren. The sense of family in NGOs goes beyond mere interpersonal relationships. The Consortium NGOs make the personal life of staff members a cause of their concern if necessary. When a staff member had a fight with her husband, this became an agenda item in a management meeting, resulting in an attempt to reconcile the couple.

Motherhood, marriage and sexuality Social networks in the office partly coincide with motherhood. The mothers usually get along well together, and share many concerns. They take care of one another's children, help each other with practical things like passing on baby clothes and maternity dresses and attending birthday parties. Among them, married women spend a lot of time discussing sexual matters and jokes, which they refrain from when the single 'girls' are present. The singles, on the other hand, discuss things like boyfriends, matchmaking and movies, and often plan things to do together in their spare time. Their time allocation leaves more room for leisure, and they occasionally take their lunch in town, and go shopping or watch a movie on Saturday afternoons.

Motherhood had a great bearing on everyday office life. Usually, mothers with small children refrain from fieldwork and have to be given deskwork. At some point in time, it was generally acknowledged that there were too many staff undertaking administrative jobs, but this was considered the inevitable result of a 'baby-boom' in the office. Once the children were a bit older, so that mothers could engage in fieldwork again, they found it easier to be accepted as figures of authority in the communities and to identify with women clients in the villages.[2] Motherhood is more constitutive of NGO work than fatherhood. Young children interfere only minimally in the availability of their fathers for work and travelling. Since CWNGO is an all-woman organization, parenthood plays a major role in office life compared to so-called mixed NGOs. This is not just the result of a particular staff composition, but stems also from the feminist ideology of the organization. While some of the mixed NGOs maintain policies to restrict their (female) staff from bringing in children, the CWNGO management stipulated that their office should be child and mother friendly. In the course of time, this resulted in the unintended consequence that all staff started to bring in small children, including the unmarried women, who brought nephews and nieces. They were either asked by relatives to baby-sit, knowing the opportunities in the CWNGO office, or they just wanted to join the ongoing 'baby show', if only with a borrowed child. When the number of children in the office continued to expand, the policy changed and children's access became restricted to staff children alone.

Finally, I should mention the two lesbians in the office. They were both active in a lesbian organization demanding a lot of their time and absorbing much of their interest. In the office, they found space to discuss their sexuality and relations, and apart from the never-ending jokes they organized several discussion activities on lesbianism. Since many foreign visitors were interested to learn about lesbian experiences and activism, they found it easy to network with visitors in the office (one of them even had a love relationship with a foreign visitor). The lesbians seemed to be the token of feminist identity of the NGO. These two women found part of their motivation to work with indigenous women in their fascination with lesbian indigenous experiences. The women of the regional lesbian organization were convinced that indigenous women, not being tainted by Hispanic colonial history, were more likely to be lesbian than lowland Philippine women. This belief had taken mythical proportions, with stories roaming around about a lesbian utopia in an unknown place in the Cordillera.

Economic differentiation and livelihood Finally, economic differentiation accounts for some of the networking activities of staff members in CWNGO. The salary and allowances of staff members differed to the extent that the director earned more or less twice as much as the lowest salary. The differentiation was based on a rating of job description, education, age, years of service and family composition. In practice, most staff members earned much the same. Although differentiation on the basis of salaries was thus reasonable, staff members' economic positions were stratified, due to other sources of income and their family composition. When we compare Violet and Minda, the difference becomes clear. Violet had a salaried husband and a number of relatives in the USA who supported them and their two children. Minda's husband was unemployed and the family of four children relied on her income.

The economic situation of staff members interfered with office life, since those who were hard up financially were always looking for sidelines to supplement their income. Economic concerns formed a major topic of conversation for them, and they often sat together to scheme ways of obtaining a little extra money. Staff brought clothes or other items to the office to sell, including sweets or pastry during office meetings, and spent part of their working days arranging their additional activities. These activities also entered the office administration. Transactions among staff could be settled through the administration of salary payments. One day, for example, Aster returned from the province with ten kilos of oranges that she had purchased at a bargain price in a local market. She resold the oranges at a modest profit to the other staff members. Payment was administered through the salaries. As a result, salary calculations every month became very complicated because of the small loans and payments occurring throughout the month.

The importance of management in social networks The analysis of social networks shows that the influence of management actors is not based only on the authority and discretion they command on the basis of their position. It is multiplied because they are situated at the nodal points of many of the social networks in the office. Because of their political backgrounds, they are well prepared for developing policies. They are the oldest members of the organization, which demands respect from the younger staff members. They have the longest involvement in the NGO and, over time, have developed multiple ties with staff members. This starts at the moment of hiring new staff. All staff members enter the office through one of the management committee members. As a result, they feel a moral obligation, or *utang na loob*, to respect them throughout the years. Most staff members are Kankanaey-speaking and the management often knows their family in the province. All these elements substantiate the importance of the influence of the management in the office.

However, the discussion at the same time points to the limitation of management to *monopolize* the meaning of the organization. First, non-management actors are also engaged in networking and continuously redefine their identification with the organization, their motivation, and the legitimation of programmes and practices. Since these staff members are most responsible for the everyday wheeling and dealing with NGO clients and the implementation of programmes and campaigns, their interpretations have a large imprint on the outcome of what the NGO is and does. Second, the members of the management committee do not always appear as a unit, because of their different involvement in organizational life. The director of the NGO, Amanda, had individual ties with all staff members, but was not much involved in everyday networking activities outside of the management committee due to her many commitments in Manila and abroad. This significantly limited her control of the day-to-day activities in the office. Violet and Minda were both part of the management committee, but their positioning in the social networks in the office was quite different. In many respects, Minda had more in common with middle-level staff members, with whom she discussed family affairs and her economic hardships, than with Violet. Violet was more involved in political networks, partly because of her husband, and had more space to engage with the single women because a nanny often took care of her children. As a result, the management did not act as a unitary actor with a clear vision, capable of imposing itself on other staff. The ambiguities of managers' partly contradictory perceptions left substantial room for other staff members to negotiate the meaning of the organization.

The social networks in the office were organized around different dimensions, leading both to overlap and segmentation. As a result, there were no marked cleavages between groups within the office. This provides a clue as to how the organization arrives at a certain cohesion. Because of the interweaving of many networks, the NGO actors arrived at a certain shared understanding of the organization. They did not develop the same perspective, but, due to these entwinements, they arrived at an intimate knowledge about each other's backgrounds and perceptions that allowed them to have at least a workable relation, in which they could read each other's meanings and respond accordingly. Although management actors were more influential than others, they were certainly not the manufacturers of the organization's meaning. The everyday practices of the organization were beyond anybody's making.

Questions of Philippine Culture in the Office

After having analysed processes of multiple realities and ordering in locales and social networks, I wish to discuss the issue of how cultural institutions order everyday NGO practices. Linda Smircich has given an overview of theoretical strands regarding culture in organizations (Smircich 1983). She notes that an extensive body of literature in the field of comparative management (popular among multinational companies) considers culture as an independent variable invading organizations. According to this structuralist perspective, culture in society shapes the character of organizations. It is a system of meaning that provides the infrastructure for social relations and interaction. A second position looks at culture *within* organizations and is interested in questions of how organizations produce culture. These studies conceive of culture as shared key values and beliefs, a 'glue that holds an organization together' (ibid.: 344). This is where we find ideas on how to mould and shape internal culture in particular ways consistent with managerial purposes. Culture in organizations appears as highly 'makeable', as a system of meaning that can and should be directed by management. A third line of thinking 'leaves behind the view that culture is something an organization *has*, in favour of the view that culture is something an organization *is*' (ibid.: 347). In this line, 'the researcher's attention shifts from concerns about what organizations accomplish and how they may accomplish it more efficiently, to how organization is accomplished and what does it mean to be organized?' (ibid.: 353). Instead of searching for a property of organizations, the question of culture then becomes a quest for understanding how things, events and interactions come to be meaningful. In this constructivist view, modern organization, with its meetings and reliance on statistics, is as cultural as the former headhunting practices of the Cordillera. As Morgan (1986) says: 'it directs attention to the symbolic or even "magical" significance of even the most rational aspect of organizational life' (Morgan 1986: 135).

Adhering to this perspective, I am none the less interested to know how certain Philippine cultural institutions play a role in office life. It indubitably makes a difference that the NGO I concentrate on is a *Filipino* NGO (leaving aside, for the moment, regional variations in the country). After spending some time in the Philippines, I started to notice and become accustomed to certain recurring patterns in the way staff members in the office behaved. Let me elaborate on two of them. The first one is *pakiramdam*, a Tagalog term that means 'feeling the other'. It denotes the tendency to act according to what one thinks is the desire of the higher-ups or those in authority (Andres 1988: 90). The second is *pakikisama*, which refers to 'the tendency to conform or give concession to the wishes of the group to maintain smooth interpersonal relations with them' (ibid.: 28). *Pakikisama* denotes belonging to and sharing loyalty to a group, but it also involves sanctioning those who do not conform.

The notion of *pakiramdam* obviously ordered discussions during meetings, when in most cases staff members refrained from speaking unless they had a prior idea of the position of the management on the issue. It was also constitutive of how staff members viewed the organization and even each other. One of the aspects of office life that initially amazed me was how fast particular staff could rise and fall in what seemed like an office-wide appreciation. One case in point was Maribel. Maribel was the young, skilful editor of the NGO's magazine. One day, a problem occurred when she wrote a feature containing some critical notes about the NGO Consortium. The office management decided to return the entire edition to the print shop and have it removed. They were very angry with Maribel. One of them suggested she had purposely tried to damage the organization's reputation. In a matter of days, the atmosphere turned against Maribel. Different staff members uttered comments that she was *makulit* (stubborn) and that they did not like her manners. When, some time later, Maribel announced she was going back to college, nobody seemed to regret her departure. During the period of my research, several other staff members, just like Maribel, fell into rapid disgrace. This happened after management actors signalled their dislike of these staff members, thereby apparently generating organization-wide critique, or at least legitimating the overt expression of reservations already held by lower staff members.

Pakikisama was also easy to recognize in numerous office practices. A strong forging of groups was apparent in 'pacts' either to stay together or to resign. Staff members could feel 'betrayed' when a colleague resigned. On one occasion, a staff member who had resigned later withdrew her resignation because, as she explained: 'Cora [her colleague/friend] wants to stay until the end of the year, so I decided to stay with her.' The other aspect of *pakikisama*, namely, that of enforcing group conformation, was enacted when staff members treated each other very harshly, even outside the knowledge or consent of the management. One day, for example, a staff member cancelled a field trip because she had been held up at home by the incessant rain, and did not have dry clothes to bring along. Even though the management did not know about this, when she came to the office, a group of three staff members was waiting to reprimand her and give her a strong sermon about her obligations and general attitude.

Ambiguities Although practices like *pakiramdam* and *pakikisama* were constitutive of everyday relations in the office, they did not operate like 'rules' of the game. There were just too many exceptions to make this true. While, for example, lower staff members enacted the disapproval of management actors with regard to certain staff members, they refrained from doing so with others. Some staff members subject to management criticism were openly defended, some issues evoked heavy discussion without regard for smooth relations, and diversity among staff members often accounted for conflicting values. There were always, in other words, alternative possibilities for response. Organization practices were therefore not *invaded* by Philippine culture, but NGO actors *drew on* (dominant) Philippine culture, among other things.

To begin with, the NGOs provided a conscious alternative to government bureaucracies. They rejected, for instance, the dress code and the many status symbols associated with rank in bureaucracies. Belonging to the National Democratic movement reinforced hierarchical tendencies in the office, but altered them in the process. The National Democratic movement was organized in the top-down style deemed typical of Communist organizations. This was especially the case for the underground movement, where it was exacerbated by strong security concerns. NGOs had taken over some of this style by organizing themselves into a

Consortium, whose authority was higher than that of the management of any one individual NGO.

The tendency towards hierarchy was counterbalanced by ideas prevailing in the office that were drawn from feminist, participatory and indigenous discourses, as well as discourses on management. Organizing work, especially in the villages, required initiative and creativity, and management actors often said they needed staff who could work independently and use their own discretion. They often lamented about the Philippine educational system, which, according to one of them, 'does not teach students to think but only to obey'. Feminist, participatory discourses resulted in notions of equality and the need for sharing experiences and opinions. During staff meetings, management actors always invited staff to speak out and give their opinions. Indigenous discourse found interpretation in notions of talking until consensus was reached, and was thus used as an alternative for management by decree.

This amalgam of discourses led to ambiguity. This was perhaps frustrating, for example when staff members like Susan found their expectation of being included in policy discussions unfulfilled. It also gave room for manoeuvre, and provided a repertoire of alternatives that management and staff alike used to negotiate organizational meaning. Since there were always alternatives, this implied that staff members acting according to cultural institutions, for example, 'feeling the other', or 'maintaining smooth relations', were not merely following rules but were *enacting* these practices.

The importance of jokes and viewing culture as a verb In every situation, NGO actors made use of alternative options to respond. Following certain cultural practices was therefore not automatic, but an expression of human agency. Actors invoked these practices in certain situations and not others, although not always consciously so. In many instances, they habitually resorted to patterns based on particular familiar practices they had grown up with. Without claiming that all responses were necessarily rational, I must add that these practices were largely effective in facilitating everyday organizational life. Because they referred to shared notions, others could easily read the meaning of certain behaviour, and they brought about a certain ordering in the complexities of the organization. The notion that both the following and the not following of cultural practices signals agency was particularly clear in the use of jokes. Jokes were a culturally grey area. They had different faces. At times, they were used to blow off steam in a mild way, while maintaining smooth relations and confirming hierarchies. However, there were also jokes that overstepped boundaries and implicitly criticized particular practices, in such a way that staff members just got away with it and those addressed just saved face. In the latter cases, jokes could lead to having particular issues put on the 'agenda' for change. Making jokes could be both the enactment of and a challenge to dominant understandings of the organization. Those listening to the jokes used their agency to make out the difference between the two.

The resulting image is a view of culture as a process. Basing herself on Street (1993), Susan Wright takes the position that culture must be seen as a verb instead of a noun, an active process of meaning-making and contestation over definition (Wright 1994: 27). Contestation over the meaning of things and interaction draws on a repertoire of alternative discourses, including (dominant) cultural institutions, and is mediated by agency. No single actor (such as the management) has the prerogative in making culture. Culture as a process is continuously emerging, and therefore appears to be self-generating. We have to be careful, however, not to misunderstand the term 'self-generating' as something that happens outside the agency of the actors involved. The outcomes of these processes were emergent, in the sense that nobody could predict or control them.

Negotiating Order in NGOs

I started this chapter with the notion that all NGO actors are engaged in reflecting on their work and interpreting events related to it. Because of different backgrounds, life worlds, institutional histories and experiences with clients, diversity among staff members defies a simple categorization of management versus the rest. NGOs are more complex than that, which makes the question of how ordering happens a highly relevant one. In the idea of modern rational organizations, ordering is effected by policies, organizational structure, regulations, minutes of meetings and other paraphernalia. Although these act as points of reference for actors in the organization, previous chapters have amply shown that these are only effective through the meaning they are endowed with by actors.

In this chapter I looked at additional ordering processes through locales, social networks and cultural practices. In all these domains, ordering processes do not just happen. NGO actors invoke, negotiate and manipulate the meaning of these in their everyday practices. Although there is ordering, there is never order; 'systems' of meaning never attain coherence and closure. NGOs are continuously reconstituted, but not through orchestrated processes. They emerge through the negotiation of meaning in the minutiae of everyday life, and all NGO actors are involved in these negotiations.

Notes

1. For a review of discussions on how bureaucrats construct their clients, see Wright 1994: 161–8; for discussions on how field workers arrive at differentiated client constructions, see de Vries 1992 and Arce 1993.

2. Note that being single does not automatically preclude caring responsibilities. Several singles had nieces, nephews or ailing parents to take care of. There were, however, other restrictions they had to take into account. It was more difficult to escape the confined roles and expectations related to girls in the villages, and they were more vulnerable to sexual harassment. Single women could more easily be deployed in the field.

EIGHT

NGO Leaders: A Social Analysis of 'Fairly Unusual Human Beings'

NGO personalities and leaders are considered very important for their organization. On the basis of research and a lot of mainly anecdotal references, it seems that the typical image of NGO leaders has undergone some changes (Hailey 1999). Throughout these changing images, their importance has never been questioned. Initially, NGO leaders were uncritically admired as visionary, inspirational leaders providing alternative notions of development. As Ekins puts it:

> This 'new type of activist' is a *fairly unusual human being*: someone with a clear intellectual grasp of social trends and forces, an understanding of commercial and local and national bureaucratic processes, an empathy with and sensitivity to the poor and, usually, a willingness to live on a low income. (Ekins 1992: 201, italics added)

This image of the visionary leader has been dented by notions of NGO leaders as 'charismatic autocrats', or what is called the 'guru syndrome'. As John Hailey summarizes the notion:

> on the one hand such leaders have demonstrated a drive and commitment, and a remarkable ability to mobilize people and resources. On the other they are criticized for dominating organizations, being unaccountable, and failing to adapt to changing circumstances. (Hailey 1999: 3)

Recently, research on NGO leadership has deconstructed the notion of charismatic autocrat. On the basis of research into successful South Asian NGO founders, John Hailey identifies their leadership style as 'value-driven, knowledge-based, and responsive' (ibid.: 9). He concludes that these people are 'genuine development leaders'. Leaders are characterized by 'their strong personal values; their willingness to experiment and apply new technologies or learning; and their ability to actively engage in the external environment and respond to change' (ibid.: 9).

Clearly, NGO managers who inspire writing about leadership have remarkable personalities. Yet I think we have to be careful not to focus too much on personalities, skills and leadership styles and thus fail to take into account a social analysis of leadership. Reflection on leadership should be grounded in an analysis of the meaning and working of NGOs. This chapter first presents some of the discussions on leadership in recent organizational sociology and development literature, and then focuses on one particular NGO leader, whom I call Amanda. She was the director of the Cordillera Women's NGO (CWNGO) at the time of my field-work. The chapter explores what the story of Amanda means for the conceptualization of NGO leadership. Rather than adopting such a catch-phrase as 'development leaders', I prefer the term 'brokers of meaning'.

Leadership in Organization Studies

In a review of leadership studies, Alan Bryman (1996) identifies four stages in leadership theory and research, in which certain aspects gained prominence in the field. Until the 1950s, leadership studies predominantly focused on 'traits' of (male) leaders. The idea was that leaders were born and had certain physical traits, particular abilities and personality characteristics. Leaders, for example, were intelligent, masculine and dominant. Although this kind of trait research continues to some extent in the present, it has been overshadowed since the 1950s by the 'style' approach. Accordingly, leaders are considered to be nurtured and can be trained to adopt an appropriate leadership style. By the end of the 1960s, style research was likewise overtaken by 'contingency' models of leadership that placed situational factors at the centre of any understanding of leadership. The idea behind this kind of research is to specify those situational variables that moderate the effectiveness of different leadership approaches. Finally, in the 1980s several new approaches emerged that can together be labelled as the 'New Leadership Approach'. This approach implied a whole new definition of leadership.

Until then, leadership was conceived of as a capacity to *influence group activity*. A typical definition of earlier approaches was that leadership 'may be considered as the process (act) of influencing the activities of an organized group in its efforts toward goal setting and goal achievement' (Stogdill 1950, quoted in Bryman, 1996: 276). In the 1980s, the conception of leadership changed towards the capacity to *manage meaning*. Concepts emerged such as 'transformational' leadership 'charismatic' leadership, and 'visionary' leadership. These labels conveyed a conception of the leader as 'someone who defines organizational reality through the articulation of a vision' (Bryman 1996: 281). The new leadership approaches direct attention to the importance of meaning and thus to the social construction of organization. However, they are still based on a unitary, leader-centred image of organization. That is, they assume that in order to be effective, organizations require leaders to introduce and manage a shared understanding of the meaning of the organization. However, in the 1990s this perspective on organization was eroded by various researchers. Increasingly, studies pointed to the decentred nature of organizations: the importance of individual leaders appears to be far less important than assumed by new leadership proponents

Indeed, in the previous chapter I discussed processes of meaning-making in an NGO. The role of management was substantial, but not decisive, in ordering processes in CWNGO. The perspective of leadership as managing the meaning of organization was sobered and replaced by the idea of organizational meanings as never closing and never entirely orchestrated. This was related to the fact that *all* NGO actors reflect about the nature of the NGO, the existence of the multitiered networks and relationships in the organization, and the ambiguities resulting from a multiplicity of discourses and cultural repertoires upon which NGO actors draw. The question is how to conceive of leadership in this decentred view of organizations? What about the importance attached to NGO leaders? It is received wisdom to recognize that NGOs stand or fall by virtue of their leaders. Surely, this must be more than a myth? The point is, that if there is substance to the general claim that NGO leaders are decisive for their organization, this cannot be a starting point for analysis; it has to be explained.

In this chapter, an NGO leader is followed at different interfaces where she represents her organization. At these interfaces, she presents and enacts particular images of the NGO and negotiates its meaning with different stakeholders. As I suggest, the strength of NGO leaders may not primarily lie in managing values *within* the NGO, but in presenting a believable and coherent organization to observers and stakeholders.

Composing a Life

As this section will show, Amanda is a perfect illustration of the 'unusual human beings' identified by Paul Ekins (1992) as the new NGO leaders. She has set up several successful NGOs and has rapidly gained prominence in those international venues where NGO activists negotiate new world orders. Amanda was the manager of CWNGO during most of my three years of fieldwork with this organization. I had met her several years previously through a mutual friend, and she invited me to come and work with the NGO. During my fieldwork, Amanda was mostly on the move, but there were several periods in which we worked closely together and developed a strong bond of friendship. I admire her. She has a quick intelligence, a great sense of humour and is amazingly optimistic and confident that seemingly insurmountable obstacles can be overcome.

I will first introduce Amanda by giving some excerpts from her life story. Life histories give us a window through which to unravel how people are constituted as social actors. Although the genetic make-up of people certainly contributes to their abilities and personality, these are further shaped throughout their lives. Life histories also give insight into the importance of social networks in constituting a person's life path, they 'make it possible to look at actual decisions and actions, and to perceive behind these practices the network of social relations which allowed them to take place' (Bertaux-Wiame 1981: 264). Finally, life histories give ideas about the discursive repertoires that actors develop, through which they come to consider what they find important and what they can do to achieve it.

Mary Bateson looks at life histories to see how people *compose* their lives. This author examines how actors 'build' their lives by responding to the variegated demands of life. Life appears in her work as an 'improvisatory art, as the ways we combine familiar and unfamiliar components in response to new situations' (Bateson 1990: 3). As she points out, the need to compose life is increasingly common. Fewer and fewer people in present-day societies can rely on a life path that is carved out for them by following the footsteps of their parents, or by hooking up to a single career perspective. However, this is even more apparent with women who combine work and caring, and it is characteristic of those societies where discontinuities and insecurities are the order of the day and where education and career opportunities are not readily generated. The way Amanda composes her life, as many NGO leaders bred from these kinds of conditions do, tells us a lot about what she thinks about the world around her and how she improvises encounters at NGO interfaces.

Growing up Amanda was born in Baguio City, the daughter of an Anglican priest and a nurse. Both her parents came from a town in Mountain province and belong to the first generation of educated Igorots. Amanda is the fourth of nine children. Her father, as a priest, was regularly transferred, so that Amanda lived in different parts of the Cordillera. The family places a high value on education, and Amanda explains her later urge to collect books, and to endorse projects to supply village schools with books, as stemming from her youth, 'when we always had plenty of books in the house'. Thanks to this intellectual upbringing, one after another of the children, including Amanda, gained scholarships to an outstanding high school in Manila, which brought her to the capital in

1966. One of her friends from Besao moved at the same time, and the two of them had a great time enjoying Manila life. Later, this friend, Minda, worked with Amanda in several of the NGOs that she helped to found.

Apart from an education, attending the Philippine Science High School brought Amanda three things. The school educates the country's elite, and this provided her with a social network that later in life gave her access to a range of highly positioned people in the country. More important, that time was the emerging movement for nationalism. The school was one of the first places in the country where lectures were organized about 'what was really happening to Philippine society' and many students turned activist. Her interest in the movement was endorsed by her elder sister who had become a 'first-day activist'. Practically all her siblings later became active in the National Democratic movement. Finally, she experienced discrimination and began to realize that Igorots were considered a cultural minority in the Philippines. One of the incidents she remembers is of a history teacher explaining that Igorots lived in trees. 'So I thought, my God, no wonder my classmates think like this, when the teacher is already so ignorant.'

By the time Amanda finished high school, the student movement of the 1960s was at its height. Although she had set her mind on studying anthropology, she decided to become a nurse instead. Nursing schools provided students with free board and lodging. Anticipating that she might not finish the course, like so many of her friends who had already turned full-time activists, she did not want to rely economically on her parents and feel a sense of obligation to complete her entire studies. Besides, nursing fitted well into her revolutionary ideas. Both in her college years and during the period she undertook practical nursing training in urban poor areas, she was an active political organizer. She focused on the mobilization of other Igorots for the nationalist movement, finding them mainly among seminarian student priests. This resulted in setting up a first organization, the Cordillera youth organization. This youth organization held its first congress in the Cordillera in 1972, when it began addressing the specific problems faced by indigenous people, then referred to as national minorities.

Becoming an NGO activist The final part of a nurse's training consists of a six-month practical period spent in a rural area, for which she moved to a remote place in Mountain province. On arriving in this place she found she was pregnant. Her boyfriend, Joey, was a union organizer in Manila and after her practical work she joined him. They married and she had her baby. She lived with her mother-in-law but found it too difficult. After three months she packed her things and returned home to her parents in the Cordillera. Then, when Joey was transferred to Ilocos, in the north, she joined him, but again returned home after three months because she could not adjust to the heat. She was then offered the opportunity to set up a community-based health programme in one of the villages in the Cordillera, which she accepted. Joey decided to follow her, and they had been living there for three years when their house was raided by the military, who arrested a visitor suspected of belonging to the New People's Army (NPA). After this, it was not safe for them to stay, so they moved to Baguio City, where they had another three children.

In Baguio, Joey concentrated on organizing mineworkers in the vicinity of the city. Amanda combined child care with organizing and helping to set up new organizations. She started with professionals in the health institutions. Over the years, community-based health programmes had emerged in the different provinces, directed by doctors from Baguio. In 1983, this resulted in one of the first NGOs for community-based health work in the region. Amanda was central in building this NGO, but at the same time she felt her capacity was limited if she worked only in the health sector. So once a director was found for the new NGO, Amanda moved on to organize what were called the 'middle forces', a term that referred to city-based, middle-class professionals. She mainly worked through church channels. She was very effective at this thanks to her background as the daughter of a priest, and because she had built good contacts with the National Council of Churches while organizing students of the seminaries in Manila during her college years.

In 1984, Amanda helped to set up yet another new organization, an NGO for lay church workers. This time she engaged herself full-time and became the programme co-ordinator. Like the other NGOs, the organization was embedded in the National Democratic movement, and she took up the position as part of her political work. Using the NGO format gave them the necessary logistics, since it was the only way to access funding.

> Funding agencies like to see there is a Board of Directors and a staff, and because People's Organizations do not have those things they cannot apply for funding. And we needed the infrastructure. When you just depend on what is there, you cannot control the direction it is going to take. You have to be able to invite a priest and get together for an education session, a workshop, and the only way to do that is by setting up an NGO.

Because Amanda had links with the National Council of Churches, one of the key endorsing bodies for funding agencies, it was not difficult for her to obtain funds.

Starting women's work After two years working for the lay church workers' programme, Amanda set up an NGO for organizing women that would soon become CWNGO. The initial costs of reproducing materials and research were covered by the church workers' NGO. Two years later, CWNGO was in good enough shape to acquire funding of its own (see below). Before starting this work, Amanda had never given much thought to women's questions. Only when tasked to organize women did she start to read feminist literature. This resonated with several of her own ideas about the hardship of life for women in the Cordillera. It also gave new meaning to some of her own experiences in struggling to combine motherhood with political work. She had always tried to be as effective as she could, but had received comments that made her feel that political leaders thought her work trivial and insignificant, and that no account was taken of the demands that motherhood put upon her. She was also confronted with double moral standards in the movement when, after a brief romantic involvement with another man (also married), she was barred from taking on a higher position, while he was allowed to continue his political career without interruption.

Once CWNGO acquired funding, the programme expanded rapidly (see Chapter 3) and soon offices were established in the different provinces. Gradually, Amanda entered a new domain of work: that of international representation and solidarity. As early as 1980, she was invited to a Conference of the World Council of Churches in Australia to talk about her community-based health programme. Then, in 1988, she was asked to represent the national women's coalition, GABRIELA, on a speaking tour as part of the Women and International Debt campaign in the Netherlands. In 1989 she attended her first international conference for indigenous women, in Australia, and became part of the 'continuing committee' that organized the next conference in Norway. By then, CWNGO had organized an international conference in Baguio, at which the Asia Indigenous Women Network (AIWN) was formed. Work on international indigenous women culminated in the 1995 International Women's Conference in Beijing, where Amanda convened, on behalf of AIWN, a number of activities in the NGO Forum resulting in the Beijing Declaration of Indigenous Women.

Moving international Amanda's international involvement with indigenous women soon brought her into UN activities, and before long her international work had snowballed. As an officer of the Cordillera People's Alliance she often represented the region in international events, and increasingly received personal invitations. She was invited to all major UN conferences, played a role in several committees, and received more invitations than she could handle from all over the world to attend national conferences or undertake speaking tours. Her involvement in indigenous affairs led her to specialize in sustainable development, intellectual property rights and a range of issues related to the ordering of the globalized economy, through institutions like GATT and the World Trade Organization (WTO). In 1994, she asked for a year's leave of absence from CWNGO to concentrate on her international work. At the end of that year, a most painful episode followed, after which she parted ways with the political movement she had belonged to for more than 20 years.

Amanda has always defined her activities as being within the National Democratic movement, but she has never wanted to be completely confined to its strict co-ordination and stringent political framework. For several years this worked out satisfactorily. However, the period when Amanda's work moved into ever widening orbits coincided exactly with the regrouping of the National Democratic movement in order to go 'back to its basics' (see Chapter 3). This led to mounting problems. While Amanda enthusiastically explored new ideas and venues, she did not want to submit herself to the long meetings discussing intensified co-ordination structures. She was also being increasingly criticized for taking political positions in international arenas without consulting the organization back home. The local leaders considered her international work 'reformist', and some people suggested that she had deliberately introduced feminist perspectives into women's work in the region in order to divide the movement. Yet Amanda thought her work was still compatible with the National Democratic political movement. She felt that 'having been moulded within the movement, and with her heart in the right issues, and acting in its spirit', she should be trusted. However, she felt she had lost the 'moral authority' to have her ideas seriously considered. Finally, she decided to maintain a working relationship with people in the movement, but to organize her own work outside it.

Parting ways with the National Democratic movement was painful, not least because it changed (at least temporarily) her relationship with most of her siblings, their spouses and many of her friends. By this time, however, she had developed an extensive social network in the international NGO world. With some of these friends she had deliberated for some time about setting up an international NGO to facilitate the activities of indigenous peoples in international arenas and to inform them of the implications of international developments for their situation. Amanda now set up this NGO in Baguio City, and quickly initiated a programme to run with 15 staff members.

Years before, Amanda could not have imagined how her life would change, nor how many changing circumstances she would have to respond to. She adjusted her study plans with the introduction of martial law, and then responded to finding herself pregnant, to having to abandon the local health programme after her house was raided, and to feminist readings redefining her past. Now, she had to recompose her life once again, after stepping away from the political movement that had been her 'home' since high school. This new NGO emerged from the few years of involvement with international work and was organized around an entirely new social network. Yet, at the same time, the NGO was also an unfolding of earlier commitments and ideas, even of earlier social networks. When the programme was established, she drew her staff primarily from among former friends wishing to change jobs, or who had drifted away from the National Democratic movement. Like jazz musicians who create new music by reshuffling familiar chords (Bateson 1990: 2), Amanda *improvised* her life in response to changing circumstances. She built on the experiences, people, knowledge and skills that she had assembled around her in the course of time, and recomposed them in order to reweave the fabric of her life again and again. This life history, then, tells us how Amanda lived her life and in the process gained experience, formed ideas and grew into a leader. It does not explain how she became effective as a respected NGO representative of indigenous peoples, or what we can learn from her story for a sociological analysis of NGO leaders. For this, I turn to a discussion of Amanda's international work and of the way she deals with funding agencies.

The International Delegate

At the first international conferences Amanda attended, she simply aimed to tell the Philippine story to an international audience and to mobilize support for the struggle against the Marcos dictatorship, and then for the structural changes that were needed under Aquino. Later, she found it more important to 'get hold of international processes and the implications of international agreements' in order to report back to the Philippines about what was going on in international institutions. Soon she began increasingly to see her task as actually influencing the outcome of international conferences and policies, and she was not without success.[1] She became integrated into some of the official processes of United Nations policy making and was active in formulating alternative NGO discourses, most notably as part of a core group that drafted an alternative NGO declaration of the 1995 Social Summit. This received hundreds of signatories in the course of a few days, and caught so much attention that a last-minute slot was provided in the Plenary Session of the Summit for Amanda to present the declaration. This was within two years of her first attendance at a UN event. How did she ascend so rapidly in this international arena?

First, I should mention two background elements that facilitated her work: her grassroots experience and her training as a political activist. Her decade-long experience as a political activist honed her sharp analytical mind and provided her with many practical skills that turned out to be very useful in international work. As Amanda says: 'Once you have been there and they sort of know you are effective in terms of writing or lobbying, and you get a reputation for hard work, they ask you back.' Moreover, Amanda was one of the few people in international work who had actually worked for years directly organizing at village level. She represented CWNGO, which is a worldwide pioneer in focusing on women's issues among indigenous peoples.[2] So Amanda had a story to tell that was grounded in experience. This worked in different ways. It gave her confidence, and she found much of value in her own experience to make sense of and evaluate new ideas. It also made her an interesting person to international audiences and, above all, a credible representative of indigenous peoples. As she says:

> our experience in the Cordillera is something that had not often been done on this scale. And it is being done where women are in a highly militarized situation and facing extreme poverty. Our experience is quite novel, you know, for a lot of international audiences.[3]

Mastering languages of development   It helps, then, to have a story that is grounded in experience and which represents a pioneer NGO. But a story is not a thing, it is a *representation*. The previous chapters have amply shown that there are always multiple stories to tell about the same events and organizations. It is not merely that different people have different interpretations: they change their stories according to different times, places and audiences. We all do, but Amanda had developed this into an artful skill. She realized it was a condition for being effective in the kind of work she was doing, and learnt it mostly during speaking tours. Talking of her first speaking tour, she explained:

> You know, this campaign was really quite educational for me because, in the span of a day, we spoke to different kinds of groups, such as church women and then women belonging to communist or socialist parties. And then again you talk to school kids. That was a very good exercise in terms of how to make your language suit the content of what you are going to say so that you will be understood. It made me better equipped to deal with different audiences.

What Amanda had developed was the ability to gauge rapidly the interest of her audience, to adjust her story to bridge different life worlds, and to convey its meaning in such a way that the notion of common experiences and interests could easily evolve. She quickly absorbed the pertinent discourses and everyday practices to deal with specific situations. Within a short space of time, Amanda became as familiar as any UN bureaucrat with the language in which to couch resolutions and United Nations covenants. She became equally skilful in knowing the crucial parts of conferences to attend, in what locales to find the people she wished to speak to, how to get enlisted as a speaker, how to circumvent the bureaucracies and how to get press coverage for a particular viewpoint.

What makes her different from a UN bureaucrat is that her experiences are not confined to United Nations interfaces. Her travels take her to local NGOs, 'grass roots' interfaces, governmental meetings, international think tanks, funding agencies and political groups. The span of her radius of action is rather unique. No one (except me) in CWNGO was surprised, for example, when in the midst of a meeting in which we were discussing details of programme implementation in the villages, Amanda was called away to a telephone call (in Spanish) from Guatemala. Nobel Prize winner Rigoberta Menchu was on the line, asking if she could hop on a plane to join the international indigenous fact-finding mission to Chiapas, in Mexico, where the Zapatistas had just initiated their uprising. Like the village women leaders of Chapter 4, Amanda may rightly be called an interface expert. Informed from different angles, and able to speak in different capacities, often gives her an advantage over the specialists she deals with at any one particular interface. Because she moves in different domains of international development, she provides links that prove to be of particular value in circles of international policy making.

Creating social communities Being an interface expert is only part of the story. Another important part consists of how leaders are made through, and themselves make, social networks. Traversing discourses and domains is not an abstract activity, but happens through social networks. Amanda could not have achieved her integration into international arenas if she had not acquired the necessary contacts. It was in becoming acquainted with specific actors of international NGOs and indigenous peoples that she was introduced, invited and endorsed. However, social networks are not simply resources people possess. They are not some kind of social bank account one can draw on whenever necessary.[4] Instead, I found Amanda and other international NGO actors continuously engaged in *creating* and maintaining personalized relations and social communities. Despite the de-territorialized nature of international arenas, global friendships are forged and social communities flourish. These networks are loosely demarcated and change according to the meeting ground, but they none the less evolve community-like features with their own histories, multistranded relationships, patterned interactions and the development of hierarchies, competing factions and power games. They are *functional* communities of people who meet on different occasions, exchange ideas and co-ordinate on strategies.

Between events, communication lines are continued through the use of e-mail, fax messages and telephone conversations. At the same time, these communities are turned into *social* communities. When meeting, only part of their interaction concerns the official issues of the day. A large amount of time is devoted to discovering each other's background and discussing everyday politics within the NGO communities. Despite the de-labelling and de-institutionalization of political differentiation, an aspect that seems always under scrutiny is whether international NGO colleagues originate from radical or conservative communities. Discussing politics is not limited to spelling out viewpoints, strategies and controversies, but entails a lot of keeping an eye on one another to observe other ways of operating. Information about the kind of hotels people stay in and who sponsored their stay is continually exchanged, and apparently provides (additional) clues in an ongoing process of working out who are valuable and trustworthy partners to link up with for international work and who are better avoided. Sexual innuendo is frequently part of conversation. Several times I heard about a (real or mythical?) woman who, as the story goes, had five children conceived during international events by men of different indigenous backgrounds, thus personally contributing to the 'genetic diversity' of the world. I have no idea how many international actors actually develop frequent sexual relationships during their hectic travel schedules. What I did observe, though, is that gossiping about these kinds of relationships keeps everybody busy and seems to be important in strengthening social ties, and, in many cases, is given political significance as well.

It has been suggested that the availability of electronic means of communication facilitates depersonalized, professional NGO intervention in respect of the contestation of issues of global development and world economic growth. From my observations, however, the selection of precisely what information and messages are read from among the barrage of electronic communications will depend on the identity of the sender. Personal social networks and criteria remain important elements in the use of electronic mail, mailing lists and websites. The ways these are put to use contributes to the forging of social communities. Apart from the business at hand, messages often contain personal information, gossip and exchanges on everyday politics. News can travel around the world in a matter of hours. The types of social communities that are created through a combination of 'virtual communities' and infrequent face-to-face encounters are meaningful. They produce what Appadurai calls neighbourhoods (Appadurai 1995). To a certain extent they become 'life worlds constituted by relatively stable associations, by relatively known and shared histories, and by collectively traversed and legible spaces and places' (ibid.: 215). Appadurai points out that virtual neighbourhoods of international electronic communications can have a significant meaning for struggles taking place in 'real' neighbourhoods. Indeed, ideas and discourses generated in international social communities find their ways to the respective localities of the participants.

It is through the creation of social communities that concerted NGO action is realized, even though different actors only actually meet on brief occasions. In the months building up to the International Women's Conference in Beijing, a core group of six indigenous women evolved almost without deliberation. They knew each other from previous events and through brief exchanges of e-mails, and arrived in Beijing with a similar understanding of what had to be done. They made use of certain shared routines. For example, the first thing they did when meeting was to note down their respective telephone numbers in the hotels where they were staying. Although they found time to chat, their encounters were at the same time characterized by highly efficient, almost shorthand, consultations: 'Let's involve (x) person.' 'Yes, she was also very good at (x) event, do you have her phone number?' 'Can you have a draft declaration ready tomorrow, because I am speaking at (x) forum?' 'Have you heard, (x) requested a slot in the official conference. Imagine, she is not even indigenous. I think we should endorse (y) instead.' 'Are you coming to the rally tomorrow in (x) venue, it's important.' Even though there was no joint meeting, the six women, through numerous small encounters and telephone calls before breakfast, managed to formulate a declaration and mobilize indigenous women present at the NGO forum to endorse it.

Amanda and her colleagues were not interested only in the official part of drafting declarations, they also organized informal activities for indigenous women at the conference. Since UNCED in 1992, the United Nations' preparation of NGO forums automatically includes indigenous peoples as one of the relevant categories. Among the large tents erected on a field at the site of the NGO forum as venues for regional or sectoral NGO representatives and activities, one was designated for indigenous women. Amanda co-ordinated the activities in that tent. There were daily meetings, women just dropped by, and information was exchanged about relevant panels among the thousands of activities. The tent was above all a locality for women to socialize, to find contacts and to exchange often emotional experiences linked to their indigenous identity. Most of the 150 women who regularly attended the ongoing 'caucus' as it was called, were not directly involved in the formulation of the Beijing Declaration of Indigenous Women, but the declaration was debated and found its constituency in the tent.

From this discussion of international work we may conclude several things. Amanda's particular skills and background facilitate her activities in international arenas. This is realized through the two key skills developed during her international experience. She skilfully masters and combines the different discourses that prevail in different domains, and she has the ability (together with her colleagues) to give *social* meaning to infrequent, culturally diversified, professional relations. As I show in the next section, these abilities also played an important role when dealing with funding agencies.

Power at the Funding Interface

At first sight, the relation between NGOs and their funding agencies appears one of inequality, where the NGO depends on funding for its survival and the power rests with the funding agency, which can impose conditions for turning on the money tap. However, the relationship in practice may be quite different. The funding agencies also depend on the NGOs, and power relations at the interface of NGOs and funding agencies evolve in different ways. This is discussed further in Chapter 9, but I now anticipate it by looking into the question of how NGOs deal with their funding agencies. Since most funding comes from international sources, the relation with funding agencies is another instance of an interface over large distances with infrequent encounters.

Some NGOs are much better positioned than others to acquire funding. CWNGO has always been fortunate in this respect (which does not mean that the organization has a large budget). All relations with its four major funding agencies have been initiated by the funding agency and not by the NGO. CWNGO was founded at a time when the topic of indigenous women was rising on the policy agendas of funding agencies, and when relatively few organizations were focusing explicitly on this target group. In addition, the fact of Amanda's visibility in international meetings seems to play some role. It puts her in the picture and perhaps makes her appear trustworthy. Also, some funding agencies are notorious for incorporating the more 'famous grassroots' in their portfolio. At one conference, for example, Amanda was approached by the director of a funding agency who invited her to submit a proposal. When she replied that several proposals of CWNGO had already been turned down by his agency because they were considered too radical, he apparently said: 'So, why don't you make another one and send it to me and then I shall see personally what I can do about it.'

Getting acquainted with a funding agency is only one step. Subsequently, it requires a lot of effort to make the funding relationship work and last. The relation can be viewed as an arena of contestation, where power struggles take place. The parties negotiate the terms of financing, reporting and accountability, in order to define the terms of their relation. Is the NGO a client of the funding agency, or are they partners? Is there one- or two-way accountability? Is it possible to establish a relation that stretches beyond the contractual obligations, in order to facilitate prolonged support? How can the NGO obtain recognition from the funding agency as a trustworthy organization? I explore these questions by analysing how CWNGO, and Amanda in particular, deal with one of the funding agencies.

Establishing a relation   The relationship with CWNGO's major 'funding partner' was established in 1987, when a representative of this agency visited the Cordillera in search of indigenous women with supportable programmes. In Chapter 3 I described how CWNGO managed to get into touch with this person during her visit and give her a proposal. A lot of things had to happen before the proposal was approved. The European Funding Agency (EFA) required church endorsements and CWNGO had to undergo official registration. Most importantly, the desk officer of the EFA wanted them to change the proposal. He felt that there was too much emphasis on research, and preferred to have a larger component for socioeconomic work. When Amanda went to Europe in 1988 on a speaking tour, she made an appointment to see this person.

Naturally, funding agencies try to find out what they can about prospective partners. It appears that this also happens the other way around. NGOs, if possible, do not just learn from agency reports and leaflets what their policies and priorities are; they also gauge how to approach the agency's representative. NGO actors have their own perceptions of cultural differentiation, and express a preference for working with agencies from one nationality over another, according to the way they treat their NGO clients. Moreover, they experiment with and investigate how to relate to particular agency representatives: who among them, for example, is sensitive to flattery, or who prefers a more direct approach. Before going to Europe, Amanda went to visit a Philippine-English couple who lived in Baguio and were familiar with the EFA representative she was going to meet. The couple wondered if she should aim to get funding through this person, because:

They warned me he would want a say on how one managed the project. I think they were intimidated by him. He says what he thinks and is not diplomatic at all. So they asked me if we really wanted to be funded by them. I said: 'Well, considering that we don't have any funds, why don't we explore it?'

Amanda bore in mind the information she had gathered about the representative when dealing with him. During the visit, the EFA representative again questioned the need for research written into the proposal. As Amanda remembers:

Then I really got pissed off. So I said: 'Well, if you are not interested in it, maybe we can look for others who will be interested to really support the thing.' And then he backed off. Maybe he was expecting me to say, 'Sure, if that is what you think.' That is what he would expect, because usually Filipinas are like that [laughs] you know. I think that was one of the things which somehow ... after that we became quite close. I just discovered that when you are very frank with him, when you really tell him what you think, it is okay, because he is also like that.

On the basis of what she had learnt about this agency and person, Amanda decided to 'play it hard' and this strategy paid off. Not only did she acquire the funding, she also negotiated the terms of the 'partnership' by refusing to treat the wishes of the funding agency representative as commands. In the process, the two managed to establish a relationship of mutual appreciation, and the relationship was pursued successfully. EFA continued to fund the organization for several more periods. A relationship thus evolved in which CWNGO obtained finance for three-year programmes, on which regular reports were submitted, after which the new three-year programme had to be proposed and subjected for approval to the funding agency. What did CWNGO do to convince the funding agency that the reality at the basis of their reports was good enough to continue funding?

Maintaining a relation CWNGO stays in touch with the funding agency through reports and occasional visits. Amanda encourages the funding agency representative always to include CWNGO in his itinerary when visiting the Philippines. When she has a schedule in Europe, she will also try to drop by his office. According to her, face-to-face contact is a key element to facilitate the negotiation process. As she explains:

It somehow gives the funding person a chance to really try to get to know you. That's important in that kind of relationship. How do you really know the kind of people you are dealing with? Are these the people you can trust? Are these the people who will really implement what you are talking about? So, I think that is crucial in establishing a relationship with the funding agency. Otherwise, it is just communication, *you can write the best thing but they would never really know what you are.*

Reports, at first sight, represent a different mode of communication with the funding agency. While visits are meant to enrol funding agencies' trust, reports are a mechanism of formal accountability by which the NGO has to answer to the authority. However, a close reading of reports shows that they are also devices for negotiating mutual accountabilities, and interweave formal and moral modes of accountability. CWNGO sends regular financial statements (which are not taken into account here) and annual or biannual narrative reports. The narrative reports are between ten and 20 pages and are organized in a similar format. Most of the pages consist of quantitative summaries of the NGO's activities, followed by a number of qualitative observations, lessons learnt, insights gained and a brief outline of next year's direction. Before giving this information, the reports always start with several pages that describe national and regional processes and events. These pages contextualize CWNGO's work for the year.

The opening pages take the reader, as it were, to the area and give a sense of what has been going on in the last year. They convey some messages too. In the first place, they show that CWNGO defines its work within the sociopolitical context of the region and is sensitive to regional issues. In other words, the NGO makes it a point of principle not always to follow its own programme as planned. It prioritized its obligations to respond to demands from the region beyond the implicit contract in the pre-planned programme. In the second place, the reports serve as a disclaimer for possible shortcomings. The context is never really encouraging for NGO work, and the updates deal in particular with the militarization and human rights abuses in the area. Providing such introductory paragraphs reminds the funding agency that the NGO staff are front-line workers operating in difficult conditions. There is an implicit challenge in the text, saying: 'In case you are disappointed in the outcome, dare to criticize us from your safe, predictable desks.' The opening paragraphs, then, are attempts to dictate a certain reading of the report. They are not merely responses to reporting requirements, but serve to enrol the reader and to negotiate the relation between the funding agency and the NGO.

At this point, I must hasten to add that I am not arguing that NGOs and funding agencies are equal in a process where power evolves. The two parties are in unequal relation. Although NGOs have certain (moral and knowledge) advantages over the funding agencies, there remains a difference. Funding agencies can set out *strategies*, whereas the NGO develops campaigning *tactics*. At the end of the day, the NGO has to play it well and *hopes* to obtain funds, while the funding agency *decides* what to do. Amanda is well aware that no matter how sympathetic a funding agency representative is to an NGO, the agency's interests will usually come first. Although she likes to be as frank as she can, she is careful not to say anything to place the representative in a double bind, since 'In the end, they also have their job to defend, so when they have to draw the line they will take the side of the funding agency.' Notwithstanding the cordial relationships and personal appreciation NGOs may have for funding agency representatives, this cannot entirely compensate for a number of other sentiments they espouse. These range from contempt by the front-line worker for the bureaucrat, to a post-colonial anti-imperialist anger for being at the mercy of Northern agencies and a resentment towards strangers having a right to pry into internal matters. Dealing with funding agency requirements is very time-consuming and can create a lot of anxiety in the NGO, which, after all, depends on funding for its survival. This was very noticeable in CWNGO, when a new term had to be negotiated at a time when many funding agencies were withdrawing support from politically radical NGOs in the Philippines. A nervous and mounting tension reigned in the office for several months and many staff members, afraid of losing their jobs, started to explore exit opportunities. By the time the proposal was approved, the management committee jokingly announced they had to go on sick leave because of FAT – Funding Agency Trauma.

The point I want to make is that acknowledging the existence of inequality does not mean we should overlook the strategizing agency of NGOs in shaping the relationship with funding agencies. NGOs can make a difference, and can become relatively powerful in defining the situation, the role of the NGO and the terms of the relation with the funding agency. Whether they manage to establish a relationship of trust depends on how well they play this game and how well they represent their organization.

NGO Leaders as Brokers of Meaning

What can we learn from Amanda's story for a social analysis of NGO leaders? It appears that, in addition to particular personal skills and talents, two features stand out in successful NGO leadership. These are the ability to bridge different life worlds by mastering a large range of development discourses, and the ability to create social relations and communities. These are abilities, but the question is, of what? Are these indeed the abilities of development leaders who successfully build the organization through their own value-driven, knowledge-based and responsive leadership style, as John Hailey (1999: 3) stipulates? Or are they the abilities of leaders who successfully represent their organization at social development interfaces? To my mind, bridging life worlds and forging social relations are not primarily the abilities of leaders, but of brokers.

In attempting a social understanding of Philippine NGO leaders, Gerard Clarke analyses leadership in terms of patronage. For him, NGO leaders act as patrons to their staff members, who thus become clients through the development of personalized ties (Clarke 1998: 199). At the same time, he conceives of NGO leaders as clients of political patrons in society. NGO leaders, in his view, continually risk being crushed by competing pressures from their staff and constituency on the one hand, and their political patrons on the other. In Clarke's view, NGO leaders have little room for manoeuvre in defining the meaning of their organizations. This does not match at all with the picture evoked by Amanda's story. Although in the Philippines patronage certainly plays a role, the concept falls short of explaining NGO leadership.

Another perspective on NGO leadership in the Philippines is offered by Aldaba, who shows that, on the basis of their educational standing, NGO managers are predominantly middle-class. He views NGOs as 'vehicles for middle-class participation in social transformation' (Aldaba 1993: 51). Aldaba suggests that NGO leaders should maximize their in-between position. Instead of trying to identify with a particular target group, they should recognize the distinct assets that emanate from a combination of their middle-class, educated positions and their experiences with the grassroots. Precisely because they are middle-class professionals, they are 'able to network with other sectors that are also working for social change' (ibid.: 22). In the eyes of Aldaba, this makes them ideally suited to becoming mediators of development. This notion comes closer to Amanda's case, but is still not able to explain how NGO leaders acquire and play out this position in practice.

Olivier de Sardan explicitly views NGO leaders as *brokers* (1995), or development interveners who mediate between different knowledge systems, namely, the language of development and local languages (Olivier de Sardan 1995: 155). In this view, development interveners fulfil a function in bringing together two parties who need each other, but can only get together through the mediation of a broker. They fulfil their brokerage role in exchange for commissions. This perspective acknowledges that NGO leaders have an interest of their own in development, be it some personal project or a cause for which they stand, and recognizes them as strategizing actors. What I find problematic in Olivier de Sardan's approach, however, is that he assumes there is a need for brokerage before the appearance of the broker, that is, the broker fills a gap that already exists between two parties. This follows from his treatment of development languages as incommensurable. He assumes that development agencies and local people can never understand each other unless the development agent acts as go-between. As discussed in previous chapters, I do not think the assumption of incommensurate development discourses is either pertinent or accurate, and it should be replaced with an idea of development discourses as interpenetrating and negotiated.

I think we do more justice to the abilities of actors like Amanda by bringing into the analysis another approach to brokers, namely, that put forward by Cohen and Comaroff, who focus on the management of meaning as a form of political behaviour. According to these authors, the role of broker embodies the essential attribute of power: 'the capacity to construct and purvey meanings concerning a variety of relationships and interactions' (Cohen and Comaroff 1976: 88). They conceptualize the broker as a political actor 'who seeks to make the other parties to brokerage relations – patrons and clients – dependent upon his services' (ibid.). In this analysis, a broker not merely responds to a need, but negotiates relationships by convincing the other parties of the meaning of organizations, events and processes. Following these authors, I suggest we consider an important element of NGO leadership to be the ability to act as brokers of meaning. Successful leadership, to my mind, is contingent upon the capacity of NGO actors to enrol others in accepting their presentations of worthwhile values, of target groups in need, of their own role as disinterested parties, and the services of their organization as indispensable.

Notes

1. Note that the question of the impact of NGO activities on international policy processes is outside this discussion of Amanda's involvement as an NGO representative at the UN. For assessments of the influence of NGOs in international policies, see Wilmer 1993; Kakabadse and Burns 1994; Willetts 1996; Arts and Roozendaal (eds) 1999.

2. The work done on indigenous women (see Tauli-Corpuz and Hilhorst 1995) has attracted little attention in international indigenous work. A 1993 volume (Wilmer 1993), for example, reviewing indigenous movements in world politics, makes not one reference to women or women's activities.

3. I found the international NGO community highly competitive. One of the ways in which NGO actors discredit one another is by claims that they do not represent the 'real' grassroots constituency. Where their roots are indigenous, one might hear the comment that they are not really indigenous, either by blood or by upbringing.

4. For this reason I avoid the concept of social capital.

NINE
Funding Agencies and NGOs: Peeping Behind Paper Realities

The relationship between Southern NGOs and their Northern funding agencies is much debated. Central questions are how much influence funding agencies are entitled to have, and how much influence they actually exercise in practice. The debate is complicated by the diversity among both funding agencies and NGOs. Funding agencies vary in their approaches, policies and styles of intervention, and therefore in the extent to which they can and want to impose on NGOs. Diversity among NGOs regarding their size, leadership, country and fields of work further accounts for large differences in the room for manoeuvre of NGOs *vis-à-vis* their funding agencies. In view of this diversity, Farrington and Bebbington (1993: 188) dismiss the notion that donors are determinant of NGOs' activities and modes of operation. Instead, they maintain that NGOs 'manoeuvre within this diversity' in order to pursue their own strategies, by selectively choosing those funding agencies whose interests coincide with their own and by their ability to repackage their programmes according to donors' desires.

Most authors, however, are inclined to ascribe more power to funding agencies than to NGOs. Hulme and Edwards conceive of the donor–NGO relation in terms of bargaining and negotiation, although at times marked by coercion (1997: 11). In their view, NGOs have varying room for manoeuvre, which defies gross generalizations about donor power. Nevertheless, the authors conclude that there is a process of convergence towards donors among Southern NGOs, that results in increasing upward accountability at the expense of the relationship of the NGOs to their constituencies among the poor (ibid.: 280). Thus, 'while NGOs remain diverse, there is clear evidence that this diversity is being reduced by donor policies' (ibid.: 9; see also Smillie 1995). In like manner, it has also been argued that diversity among funding agencies is declining. In the post-Cold War era, fewer funding agencies are inclined to finance politically radical projects (Biekart 1996) and, notwithstanding variations, they have moved towards an agenda based on neoliberal economics and liberal democratic theory (see Chapter 6).

Donors are considered powerful because their influence stretches well beyond the obvious gateway to finance that they can provide or withhold. Accepting a funding relationship entails entering into agreements about what is to be done, and how it is to be reported and accounted for. Trends in donor preference influence agendas for development. This has been the case, for example, with the focus on gender and environment at the expense of class-targeted interventions (Dietz 1997), or on microcredit aimed at promoting self-employment rather than protecting the public provision of basic needs (Edwards and Hulme 1996: 9). Donor policies also impact on everyday practices. As was discussed in Chapter 6, modes of accountability elicit particular accounts and invite a certain ordering of activities. In other words, practices of funding may have profound implications for how NGO actors give meaning to their organization and its fields of intervention. While strong critique is often voiced against the direct interference of donors in NGO policies (see, for instance, Perera 1997), the more damning objection to donor influence may be that it frames the very terms of what constitutes NGOs, society, development and social change.[1]

However, it is not an easy task to gauge the magnitude and pervasiveness of donor influence on NGO programmes and practices, since this differs by country and case (INTRAC 1998: 82–5). Furthermore, as argued in previous chapters, we should not take at face value NGOs' adoption of certain notions, since these may later be renegotiated in everyday practice. And while agreeing with the above-mentioned trend towards convergence, one can also note certain trends towards divergence, and who can tell how prominent these may become? What indubitably stands out is that funding agencies are important actors in development. But where are the studies necessary for unravelling the actions of these actors? So much focus has been put on research into NGOs (admittedly including this book) that funding agencies seem to have escaped ethnographic scrutiny altogether. It seems that my problem statement regarding NGOs, namely, that we cannot take for granted what these organizations are, do and want, is equally pertinent for funding agencies. If not, the representation of these agencies as neoliberal democratic organizations working towards rational, accountable and transparent development will continue to stand as erect as the Statue of Liberty itself. What is needed, then, is an exercise for funding agencies, similar to the one attempted in this book for NGOs, namely, the lifting of the veils on their representations, revealing the dynamics underneath, and looking at the practices of donor actors with a view to defining the meaning of their organizations and modes of legitimacy.

I wish to make a start on this kind of analysis by elaborating one case of a donor–NGO relationship. It concerns the relation between CWNGO and an organization belonging to the United Nations, which I shall simply call the 'United Nations Agency' (UNA). It will be followed by an account of how this relationship, after a promising start, turned sour to the point where the UNA terminated its funding, because, as the director of the funding agency claimed, the NGO was neither efficient nor accountable to its constituency. The case study, however, shows the vastly more complex, multilayered history underlying this outcome, resulting from the dynamics of political differences, organizational competition and differential interpretations of 'partnership'. I conclude with some notes on a sociopolitical understanding of donor organizations.

The SPRINC Programme

In the early 1990s, an UNA development expert, whom I will call Mr Izmit, conceived of a programme for indigenous women. This became the SPRINC programme: the Self-Help Programme for Indigenous and Tribal Communities.[2] SPRINC started in 1993, and has projects in a number of developing countries, including several in the Philippines. One of its first programmes in the Philippines was conducted by CWNGO. Like most international development programmes, SPRINC involves a number of development actors. It is financed by donors, in particular from Denmark and the Netherlands, who are involved in the programme through regular meetings with project representatives. The Geneva-based SPRINC staff, consisting of Mr Izmit and an assistant, is concerned with funding, producing training material, carrying out monitoring and evaluation and providing general guidelines and advice. At the country level, the programme is managed by a co-ordinator concerned with monitoring and training. The partners of the programme consist of 'indigenous and tribal peoples at the grassroots level' (the People's Organizations, or POs in Philippine jargon). They identify projects, are involved in the selection of local NGOs and project staff, and have to undertake a yearly self-evaluation. Local NGOs are responsible for project design and implementation, hiring of personnel and staff training.

In what follows, the history of CWNGO's involvement with SPRINC is outlined. More precisely, I will explore different narratives about this involvement from the viewpoint of CWNGO and SPRINC respectively. The narratives are based on interviews, correspondence, project reports and my own observations. After a brief chronology of the history of the programme, I focus on issues of contention regarding politics, implementation, and partnership.

Funding Agent Seeks Indigenous Woman, or
Vice Versa?

The question of how the relationship between SPRINC and CWNGO started takes us straight into diverging narratives. Mr Izmit and Amanda, the director of CWNGO, met in 1993 at a meeting organized by the UNA in Manila. As Amanda remembers it, Mr Izmit expressed that he was happy to meet her in person, since he had seen some of her writings. He invited her to submit a proposal. CWNGO then submitted a proposal for research and training, which was approved. It was a project of five months. When it was finished, Amanda consulted Mr Izmit about a possible continuation. He then suggested to her that they incorporate their project into the new SPRINC programme that was about to enter its pilot phase. According to Amanda's story, Mr Izmit went as far as to write the proposal for them. As she recalled several years later:

> We didn't have time to write something down, so we just talked with him, and he wrote the proposal for us. The next time we met he showed it and Minda made some revisions. When he saw these he approved it there and then. In principle of course, it still had to go through the procedures.

According to CWNGO staff, Mr Izmit was so interested in incorporating their project into SPRINC that he sat down and drafted the proposal. When I asked Mr Izmit about this in 1997, he asserted that he had never done any such thing. He remembers the story differently:

> I met Amanda in 1993, when I was on a mission in the Philippines. *She asked me* if we could help to set up training and co-operatives. We then decided together for some case studies. The first phase was more or less okay. I don't remember the contents, but I remember that I was not 100 per cent satisfied. However, as I really liked Amanda and the people she worked with, and since they are a local NGO, I decided to continue with a pilot.

By the time I heard this version, the relationship had already turned sour and ended, and we cannot judge how his critical memory about the first days was influenced by subsequent events. What I find interesting, however, is Mr Izmit's insistence that CWNGO requested his support, and his firm denial that he had a hand in writing the second proposal. Unlike Amanda's presentation of his role, his own narrative clearly fits into SPRINC's discourse of participation, which stipulates that the programme responds to requests of locally formulated programmes. The suggestion of an alternative reading of how the programme started clearly disturbed him.

The different projects Whatever really happened at the start of the relation, the fact is that CWNGO began with a five-month project for research and training, with the primary purpose of collecting baseline data. The budget was US$5,000 for project activities. There was no provision for salaries: staff involvement was CWNGO's counterpart contribution. While Mr Izmit recalls that he was not very enthusiastic about CWNGO's performance, CWNGO staff members remember especially the bureaucratic delays incurred in the implementation. Eight months and a lot of bureaucratic hassle elapsed between the moment of approval and the final go-ahead for this small short-term project. According to CWNGO's reports, the implementation consisted of 14 education cum data collection seminars with local women's organizations. These were orientations for women, pre-membership education seminars for co-operatives, and project and co-operative management training.

The second proposal was submitted in March 1994. It was couched within the frame of the new SPRINC programme, and a larger proportion of its activities had to be devoted to credit for co-operatives – at least one for each of the five provinces. There was also provision for staff salaries: two plus a part-time project co-ordinator. The total amount involved was US$28,500. The project was immediately approved to run from May 1994 to April 1995. The staff involved in SPRINC were two CWNGO organizers from the socioeconomic desk in the Baguio office and a member of the management team, Minda, as co-ordinator. The proposal envisaged co-operative projects for six Women's Organizations. In the course of the year, however, it was realized that this number was too high, and on consultation with the UNA representatives it was reduced to three.

The first organization to avail itself of a revolving credit fund was a village Women's Organization in Luaya in the province of Kalinga (see Chapter 5). This local organization had a longstanding relation with CWNGO and had managed a credit fund before. Initial activities for the SPRINC programme consisted of meetings and training. In May 1995, the local Women's Organization requested a release of money in order to set up a rice fund. There had been a severe drought, and the harvest was further destroyed by an excessive number of mice in the fields. The women wanted to buy rice in bulk to sell in the village. The implementation of the fund went very smoothly, and within a year they were ready to pay back the loan in order that another Women's Organization could make use of the fund. The other two organizations involved in the project were both urban poor Women's Organizations in Baguio City. They wanted to do weaving and needlework projects. The first one started its revolving fund in September 1995, the second in December 1995. As a result of these late starting dates, the project lasted until mid-1996, instead of finishing in May 1995. During this period, the relation between the agencies increasingly deteriorated. Nevertheless, CWNGO submitted a third proposal for a renewed phase under SPRINC. However, in April 1996 Mr Izmit wrote a letter announcing that SPRINC would no longer finance this new phase of the project. This set in motion the end of the relationship between CWNGO and SPRINC.

With this brief history in mind, I shall elaborate on the qualitative aspects of the relation between the two agencies. I start with a meeting that took place in Baguio City in November 1994, when the SPRINC Philippines office had just begun operating. This meeting was organized by Mr Buduyan, usually referred to as Alfredo, the Manila-based co-ordinator of SPRINC. The meeting had a double purpose. It was an occasion for Alfredo to introduce himself and to discuss some of the protocols and procedures of the project with CWNGO staff. In addition, a visiting consultant from UNA-Geneva wanted to meet indigenous peoples' representatives, to discuss a possible UNA-sponsored programme that she was preparing. Let me call her Maria.

I discuss this meeting for two reasons. First, I want to analyse the general flow of the meeting and the conversation that took place, so as to provide a window on everyday relations between funding agencies and NGOs. Words like partnership, participation and learning are easily used in development, and carry the promise of a certain equality among participants. These notions can be put to the test by focusing on the outcomes of capital events, such as decisions about funding or deliberations about the content of programmes. On the other hand, they are also lived out in ordinary events and find expression in the way people treat each other during interaction. In everyday encounters, power relations are forged and inequalities reproduced. Even though the following is only a sample of one such encounter, it hints at the importance of this kind of analysis for understanding donor–NGO relations. Second, I wish to use the meeting as an entry point for discussing the political controversy that continuously lingered in the project relation. This concerned the different attitudes of the 'partners' regarding government policies on indigenous land.

UNA Meets the People of the Cordillera

That Saturday morning, we assemble at nine o'clock in one of the NGO offices in Baguio to attend the meeting with the UNA people. Minda, the project co-ordinator, has summoned all four staff members of CWNGO's project desk. Moreover, one of the Board members of CWNGO – who is at the same time an officer of another NGO working on indigenous issues in the Cordillera – is asked to sit in. I am there at my own request, with permission to observe and tape the meeting. At ten o'clock, one hour late, three people arrive: Alfredo, Maria and an officer of a government organization. The latter is involved because Maria has requested to consultation both with government and non-government actors.

Once all of us are seated around the table in the office, everybody briefly introduces him- or herself and, at the suggestion of Alfredo, expresses their expectations of the meeting. The latter are invariably the same: 'to learn more about the SPRINC programme'. The introductions on the part of the CWNGO people are brief and hardly audible. I wonder if the appearance of Maria makes them shy. She looks impressive: very ladylike (beautifully kept hair, expensive blouse matching the colour of her eyes and an elegant pair of slacks) and has an unmistakable air of confidence. She takes more time to introduce herself and her intended programme in the Philippines. In the transcript of the meeting all participants have only a two-line introduction, while hers extends to 66. She formulates her expectation of the meeting: 'I came here to learn from CWNGO.'

After the introduction, Minda starts to talk in order to set the agenda. When she suggests taking up two hours for sharing ideas, she is interrupted by the government employee, Delma, who announces that she has made other appointments for Maria at some government agencies, the first scheduled for eleven o'clock. This means that suddenly there are only 45 minutes left for the remainder of the meeting with Maria. The SPRINC matters will be left for discussion after her departure. After these deliberations are finished, Maria begins to speak. As can be seen from the statistics shown in Table 9.1, she talks for most of the meeting: some 65 per cent.[3] If we add to this the contribution of Alfredo, then it turns out that the UNA representatives fill up 80 per cent of the speaking time. Although a quantitative analysis of speech does not say much in itself, it certainly gives an indication of the social relations of the meeting.

Table 9.1 Speaking turns of participants at UNA–NGO meeting in Baguio

	Organization	Number of speaking turns	Number of lines in transcript	% of lines in transcript
Maria	UNA Geneva	16	543	65
Alfredo	UNA Manila	11	121	15
Delma	Local Govt	2	4	0
Minda	CWNGO	5	85	10
Yola	CWNGO	12	73	9
5 others	CWNGO	5 (1 each: intro)	10	1

Once the introductions are made, Maria explains the purpose of her visit. She came to the Philippines, she says, to promote her idea that UNA can facilitate the implementation of a new government programme for the management of ancestral lands, called DAO-2. Under the programme, indigenous peoples can register their claims to ancestral land. She talks for a long time, corresponding to 355 lines of uninterrupted speech in the transcript. Rather than wanting to *learn* from CWNGO, it seems that she wants to *convince* the CWNGO representatives of the opportunities involved in DAO-2. Moreover, she claims that she already knows CWNGO's position on the matter. Even before the participants are given the chance to comment, she states as part of her speech that:

> I know that, especially in the Cordillera, DAO-2 is not very successful or, I mean, has encountered significant resistance. I have read about it, and I shared this with Alfredo when we met in Rome. There are certainly a number of weaknesses and gaps. However, I think the whole concept is very interesting.

She then proceeds to explain possible advantages of programmes like DAO-2. While doing so, she uses examples from six different countries that she has visited in person. It is hard to miss the message that, although an Italian national addressing a meeting of indigenous people, she is in fact the expert on indigenous affairs, especially since none of the local participants has had a chance to talk up to that moment. The 'lecture' on schemes for managing ancestral lands ends with Maria saying that she believes that NGOs and POs 'should work with the government'. She concludes:

> Well, I know that in the Philippines, and not only in the Philippines, there is a resistance from NGOs to collaborators ... as soon as you do so, you are looked at and perceived by others as being co-opted by the government, that you have sold yourself to the government. This has been an attitude of several intellectuals I have noticed. And I remember once, I had a discussion with a very good Venezuelan anthropologist. And I said, now the government is more open and willing to get NGOs in to get this sort of advice, why don't you join? And she said: 'No, because I don't want to get my hands dirty, because if things don't work out, I would get the blame in the future.' That is too easy ... .

Through this statement, she not only dismisses those opposing the government as 'intellectuals' (with the implication that they are distant from the experiences of real indigenous peoples), but blames them for choosing an easy way out of a challenge. At this point, for the first time, Yola intervenes. She says: 'It is different here. If you join a government project, sometimes, they just take you in because it is a condition. So, your suggestions and recommendations are not apt ...' But before she can finish her sentence, Maria interrupts her:

> That is why I was thinking if you could have an international organization which was more neutral and which in this case would really work ... I mean there are enough human resources and expertise in the country to be used, there is no need for ... [interrupts herself] my idea is that the UNA would play a role of bringing in different people and co-ordinating the work.

A discussion then evolves, during which the CWNGO representatives are finally able to explain some of their reservations regarding DAO-2. While the meeting goes on, I notice that, apart from Minda and Yola, who get increasingly irritated, the CWNGO staff members gradually detach themselves. One staff member starts to leaf through a book, another busies herself drawing. She will later tell me she has not understood anything of Maria's rapid English. Towards the end of the meeting, Maria inquires from the CWNGO representatives what, in their opinion, should be the priority in the Cordillera. Yola then briefly explains something about research and the resolution of boundary conflicts. Without responding to Yola's considerations, Maria has to leave for her next appointment. Before leaving, she says she wants to hear more from CWNGO and will therefore return for lunch. However, she is apparently overtaken by subsequent events, because she does not return to the meeting and we hear no more from her. Years later, I will find out that Maria did indeed set up some projects in the Philippines, but not in the Cordillera. She never communicated this to the region.

Considering the discussion, in which the CWNGO staff obviously did not agree with Maria, I expect them to be quite sharp about the meeting. However, to my surprise they hardly say a word about it. When I ask Minda what she feels about the meeting, she just shrugs her shoulders and says: 'Well, what can you expect?' She is apparently not very shocked by the way the meeting evolved or about Maria's attitude. I wonder if, perhaps, she would have been more surprised had a consultant actually given them space to formulate their experiences and opinions without imposing his/her own ideas. It seems that the staff who were present consider the meeting a non-event – just one of those things you have to put up with as part of the funding relationship. On the other hand, the issue discussed (DAO-2) is going to be increasingly significant for the way in which the relationship evolves. The visit of Maria presages a mounting discomfort of the NGOs with SPRINC's position regarding this matter.

The pitfalls of land politics DAO-2, the programme that Maria so enthusiastically promoted, was strongly opposed by the NGOs in the Cordillera. The objections raised were many. At the most principled level, the indigenous movement to which the NGOs belonged denied the government's right to acknowledge claims to the land, which belonged to indigenous peoples and thus ought to be outside government jurisdiction. There were also numerous legal and practical objections. There was no single clause or guarantee that the claims registered under DAO-2 would be granted. It was thus felt that the government dangled a carrot in front of the indigenous communities without actually promising any results. While problematic in themselves, the objections against DAO-2 were seriously compounded by the suspicion that the whole programme was no more than a ploy, to facilitate the acceptance of other government policies aimed at exploiting the region's resources in a way that ran exactly counter to the idea of self-determination (see also Chapter 3). One programme was a new dam to be constructed in San Roque, which would be far larger than the dams planned for the Chico river in the 1970s that were successfully thwarted by the indigenous movement (see Chapter 2). Another programme concerned the new mining law, which granted (international) mining companies permission to exploit up to 100,000 hectares of land for the purpose of pit mining. Under this law, companies acquired rights to open mines in the area, to use all the timber and water needed for the exploitation and even to dislocate people whenever necessary (Tujan and Guzman 1998). The opposition to this policy was overwhelming, and united groups of many different political colours.

According to the indigenous movement, the ancestral land programmes were at best hypocritical and probably downright deceitful. They believed that the delineation of ancestral land made land measurement and registration possible, which had not been acceptable to the local communities. It was strongly feared that all land data gathered under 'delineation of ancestral domain claims' would be used to facilitate the entry of foreign mining companies, which would eventually destroy the ancestral land. Once it was clear that SPRINC indeed worked within the framework of DAO-2, this posed a serious problem to CWNGO. Increasingly, actors in the Cordillera NGO Consortium considered the UNA's contribution 'dirty money', meaning money that should not be accepted as a matter of principle. When CWNGO learnt that Mr Izmit was preparing a new programme in the Cordillera, in collaboration with local government, it considered ending its relationship with the UNA. CWNGO management was angry that SPRINC had bypassed the NGO supposed to be its partner in setting up this new programme, which, in addition, had an anticipated budget 15 times larger than the combined budgets for the two

CWNGO projects. Most of all, they felt it would compromise them politically. As Minda said:

> We entered this relationship to maximize our resources. As long as we forward our needs, and their demands are still acceptable, that's it. Now, with the new project, that is very controversial and so we are not keen to pursue it. If Izmit will really push for the [DAO-2 related] CADCI, then we cannot relate to them any more.

A few weeks later, the letter arrived from Mr Izmit saying that he was not going to continue supporting CWNGO. In the same letter, he invited Minda to act as a consultant in the new programme. She wrote back turning down his offer and severing ties with SPRINC.

Problems in Implementation

In the course of the project, SPRINC grew increasingly critical and impatient with CWNGO's performance. The major problem, in the eyes of Mr Izmit and Alfredo, was that the pace of implementation was too slow. The project officially lasted for one year, until April 1995. However, the first revolving fund was only established in May 1995, i.e. after the termination of the project term, followed by funds for the other two organizations in September and December of that year.

CWNGO partly bounced back by criticizing SPRINC for also being slow, because it did not release the money until February 1995. More importantly, Minda felt there was a large gap between the two organizations' conceptions of the project. She stressed that the UNA representatives did not understand the need for social preparation and the importance of context for project implementation. As she explained one day to a new SPRINC staff member (a Dutch development worker) who came to Baguio:

> We cannot just release the money. We need to do social preparation. In our experience it takes several years, and this group we work with only started one year ago. It is difficult to create togetherness. We wanted the organization to mature, so that the project will not create divisiveness. We want to give them skills and projects, but at the same time work for a strong organization. We were there before, we were there during, and we will be there after! And we will be blamed if the money creates problems, because we give it to them, that is why we are very cautious.

This comment referred especially to the two urban poor women's projects. These concerned newly formed groups in migrant communities with little organizational history or social cohesion. CWNGO therefore found it important to set up the organization properly, so that they would be 'ready' to handle a project that involved money.

Who are the experts on indigenous peoples? The problems between CWNGO and SPRINC were also related to different values regarding cooperatives and indigenous knowledge. CWNGO appreciated initiatives that helped women socioeconomically, but not necessarily through income-generating projects. This could apply to projects aimed at forging social security through, for example, emergency credit or, as in the case of Luaya, a rice loan fund. Other projects could enhance women's subsistence or room for manoeuvre, for example, a day-care centre. In addition, it wanted projects that contained elements for strengthening Women's Organizations. Minda felt that SPRINC had a strong preference for projects that involved cash, further monetizing indigenous communities and resembling individual enterprises. As she said:

> The problem is really their [SPRINC's] economic approach, no, their cash-oriented approach ... And then, they have an individual bias. They don't want a project to strengthen organization, only at the family level. In the end, it is the business that they look at. So, they are happier with the weavers than with the rice fund, because the weavers are more like a business.

Minda believed that CWNGO's arguments about indigenous women's cooperatives fell on deaf ears in SPRINC, and that, generally speaking, SPRINC did not take seriously their indigenous knowledge. Instead, SPRINC relied on expatriate academics, much to the anger of CWNGO. As part of SPRINC activities, for example, they were at one point invited for training on indigenous co-operatives. The workshop was facilitated by expatriates who were 'experts' on indigenous peoples. As Minda commented: 'They brought in these experts on Indigenous Peoples [IPs]. So, we have this workshop with experts on IPs talking to *us* about who and what IPs are, on what their culture is and what their values are.'

This example brings me to the next objection of CWNGO to SPRINC, namely, that the programme entailed a lot of bureaucracy and imposed activities. Every two months CWNGO submitted a detailed report following formats designed by Geneva. In addition, there were regular workshops, training activities and meetings that CWNGO staff had to attend, whether they thought them relevant or not. It annoyed the staff that most of these activities were held at very short notice, 'as if they think that we are always available', and were not based on a needs analysis. They often taught them things they already knew. Off the record, a SPRINC staff member acknowledged that not all training was appropriate to the programme, but served other strategic purposes, as was the case, for example, with training provided by a Dutch bank that sponsored SPRINC. As the SPRINC staff member said:

> Well, that is a concession to the donor. They have given money and they also want to score with this project, as with all of them. You have to allow them space to show off with the project, which they also consider their project.

While this training made sense for the continuation of SPRINC, to the participants it just meant another week away from work.

All in all, CWNGO increasingly perceived of SPRINC as a bureaucratic, Geneva-centred, cash-oriented and academically biased programme. The staff felt that they were not taken seriously in their experiential indigenous knowledge, and in particular that SPRINC imposed a bureaucratic method and economic values that ran contrary to what they defined as 'indigenous style'. SPRINC, on the other hand, blamed CWNGO for 'withholding projects from indigenous women' (by postponing the release of funds) and for being 'inefficient and slow' in their implementation.

The Meaning of Partnership

Perhaps the core problem between SPRINC and CWNGO was their different perceptions of the meaning of partnership. SPRINC considered its principal partners to be indigenous and tribal peoples at the grassroots level. Ideally, according to UNA documentation, these People's Organizations identify projects and then select or even set up an NGO to be responsible for implementation. In practice, the way in which NGOs and POs relate, and how SPRINC related to the NGOs, turned out to be much more complicated.

SPRINC, NGOs and the POs

In the case of the Cordillera, SPRINC entered a relationship with CWNGO, which selected the Women's Organizations for the programme. The perception of the programme set-up diverged from the start. According to the UNA, SPRINC stood on its own, and was implemented by village-based staff members over a fixed period of time. For CWNGO, SPRINC was embedded in other activities and co-ordinated with other actors (the local groups and other NGOs in the network). For the NGO, SPRINC represented one chapter in an ongoing history. For the UNA, it formed a history on its own. Illustrative in this respect are the progress reports of SPRINC. Without giving information on the context in which the programme operated, they report on activities as if they had started from 'zero'. The NGO staff, for example, are reported as having been 'recruited and trained', even though they had already been employed by CWNGO for several years. The Kalinga Women's Organization is reported as having been formed with an initial membership of 58, notwithstanding its years of history prior to SPRINC. Through these reports, a myth is sustained of a programme without a history, operating in an institutional void, a point I will come back to later.

Although the starting point differed from the ideal situation represented by SPRINC, Mr Izmit wanted CWNGO to comply with his format. He wanted project staff to be based in the villages and to work full-time on the programme. CWNGO refused to do this. It considered that a staff member in the village would be 'overkill' of supervision and monitoring for small projects. CWNGO, moreover, adapted to the pace of agricultural cycles, meaning that during planting and harvesting time no activities would be organized. In practice, this resulted in a prolonged implementation. The staff did not work full-time as stipulated in the contract, but, on the other hand, they continued with the programme long after it had officially ended. This issue became one of the breaking points between CWNGO and SPRINC. When the third phase proposal of CWNGO again did not incorporate village-based staff, Mr Izmit 'got fed up'. As he said: 'That was it. They want to keep the money for their staff, they don't care.'

During the life of the programme, SPRINC shifted away from NGOs and wanted to work directly with People's Organizations instead. From the way Mr Izmit and Alfredo talked, it appeared that they increasingly considered NGO actors to be self-interested political agitators. During a consultation in Manila with the project holders, for example, a UNA consultant asked *Manang* Lorena from Luaya if her organization had considered working with CADCI, a regulation under DAO-2 for the registration of ancestral domains. *Manang* Lorena replied in Ilokano: '*Haan mi nga kayat, tapno nu sumrek ti CADCI, agbalin nga pubic land ti dagayo.*' Alfredo translated her comment: 'She says that they don't like CADCI, because when you enter CADCI, your land will change into public land,' and added as a comment of his own: 'That is probably what they told her.' *Manang* Lorena does not speak English, but she understands it very well. She thus understood Alfredo's comment, and instantly replied: '*Saan! Nabayag nga ammomi dayta, adu ti kapadasen mi* (No! We have known that for a long time. We have many experiences).' Nevertheless, Mr Izmit maintained the idea that opposition to DAO-2 came from the NGOs and not from the people. When I interviewed him in 1997, he gave me his view:

I know that some progressive NGOs have a problem with DAO-2. But our partners [meaning the local POs] tell me that 'it is only because they fear that they will have no work when our problems are solved'. The NGOs oppose DAO-2 so they can still maintain a role. Our partner organizations complain that the NGOs get all this money, but they don't see what they do with it.

In addition, Mr Izmit felt that the NGOs continued to create a role for themselves in order to protect their jobs:

They are paid for their services, so they serve. If you withdraw your assistance, they withdraw their service, even when they say that they are with the people. POs, as they call them in the Philippines, are real local organizations and accountable to their members. They are there and they will not leave when the project ends. What is built up, what is capacitated will remain in the community. This is not just our idea, this is proposed again and again by the communities.

It is interesting to see how Mr Izmit dealt with DAO-2. He translated the political opposition against DAO-2 into a case of NGOs wanting to keep their jobs (ignoring altogether that the opposition against DAO-2 was not spearheaded by the NGOs, but by the Cordillera People's Alliance, representing some hundred People's Organizations). He then translated this into a lack of accountability on the part of NGOs. Political differences thus got repackaged in the technical development language of accountability. As a result, SPRINC changed its policies regarding NGOs. Whereas in the first phase NGOs were considered implementing partners, this shifted to direct support for People's Organizations, which could hire NGOs as consultants.

The CWNGO people had a different story to tell. They did not respect SPRINC's allegations about their supposed lack of accountability, because they considered the UNA much less accountable to the village women. CWNGO interpreted the whole issue in a different way, namely, that SPRINC itself wanted to take over the facilitating role. In 1995, the SPRINC office in Manila was reinforced by two expatriate development experts. According to Minda:

SPRINC works with NGOs in other countries, but here in the Philippines they don't like to. They have this office in Manila with these foreigners working with them, and they also want to do things. We just completed a training session for the weavers when the Dutch volunteer *insisted* that she give another one, and our staff should just be there.

In the eyes of CWNGO, SPRINC simply used the argument of ac-

countability to appropriate more of the implementation of the programme and to expand its office in Manila. The issue of accountability
and what the people wanted was discussed over the heads of the People's
Organizations. As in the case discussed in Chapter 6, 'the people' were
brought up by both organizations as anonymous supporters. Mr Izmit's
claim that 'the communities themselves proposed this' is difficult to sustain.
His encounters with villagers were sporadic and hardly spontaneous. On
the other hand, CWNGO also partly orchestrated local women's statements, if only because statements during consultations had to be written
up in English and were therefore drafted with the help of project staff.
The differing representations of SPRING and CWNGO may be seen in
Table 9.2.

Of partnership and loyalties There is one more element relevant to
understanding the breakdown between SPRINC and CWNGO. It is the
way that CWNGO began to criticize SPRINC publicly. This was not
part of the partnership that SPRINC had in mind. The first time that

Table 9.2 Differing representations of SPRINC and CWNGO

SPRINC representations of CWNGO	CWNGO representations of SPRINC
'CWNGO asked us to help them'	'UNA wanted a project with us. The UNA representative from Geneva even drafted the project proposal for us'
'SPRINC aims to strengthen the capacities of indigenous and tribal peoples, helping them to design and implement their own development plans and initiatives, and to ensure that their traditional values and culture are safeguarded'	'SPRINC is cash-oriented. What they like is projects that look like businesses, not the projects that help subsistence, although that is also economic. And they have an individual bias; they don't like projects that strengthen the organization'
'CWNGO is too slow in implement-ing the projects'	'UNA does not communicate the schedules. Appointments are always made and changed at the last minute'
'One of the tasks of the SPRINC – Cooperative Branch level (in Geneva) is to produce and disseminate training materials'	'They don't see us as experts on indigenous affairs. They rely on expatriate academics to tell us about indigenousness'
'CWNGO should not have criticized SPRINC in public. As partners we should solve problems internally'	'UNA should not have cancelled the project unilaterally, after all, we are supposed to be partners'

CWNGO publicly criticized SPRINC was in a meeting in Thailand, in December 1994. It was a four-day 'Technical Review' meeting with project holders and representatives of the donors. CWNGO had two participants: Minda and Violet, both from the management team. During Minda's presentation, she included a remark about the Geneva-centredness of the SPRINC programme. This had upset the SPRINC representatives, and Alfredo had immediately asked them to 'clarify their statement'. As she later understood, the meeting was meant to convince the donor representatives of the value of the programme. Instead of playing along with this, they had criticized SPRINC. Minda recalled the experience as follows:

> You know, I think I really hit a raw nerve, because the donors had been invited to get them to fund the second phase of the programme. And they already had their reservations with the UNA for being top-down, so when I said that, it hit them right where they were weakest. But, of course, they never told us that was the purpose of the meeting. They only told us that it was a technical meeting to discuss the programmes and that part of the programme was on how they organized it, so we gave our assessment.

The meeting also gave project holders the opportunity to get to know the donor representatives. The CWNGO participants had particularly liked one of the representatives of the Dutch Ministry of Foreign Affairs, with whom they stayed in touch after the workshop. Six months later, CWNGO received Mr Izmit's letter rejecting their proposal for continuation. Although CWNGO had already been doubtful about continuing with SPRINC, the management was angry about this unilateral decision. That the proposal was turned down without discussing it, or stipulating what had to be changed, to their minds, exposed the 'true nature of SPRINC's sense of "partnership"'. CWNGO started to make some noise about it. They wrote letters of complaint to Geneva and informed their 'friend' in the Dutch Ministry of Foreign Affairs. This man approached Mr Izmit to ask for clarification and to urge him to continue working with CWNGO. His appeal was effective, as Izmit later acknowledged: 'CWNGO has friends, this man from the Ministry was very critical of us.' As a result, Mr Izmit had lunch with Amanda, the executive director of CWNGO, when she was in Geneva for the UN Working Group on Indigenous Peoples, to work out a compromise. But the attempt to renew the relation did not last more than a few days. During the same Working Group meeting, a representative of the Cordillera People's Alliance criticized UNA for imposing its programmes on the communities. Although the statement came from CPA, Izmit blamed it on CWNGO. When the remark was later quoted in an international newsletter covering the Working Group meeting, Mr Izmit felt angry that CWNGO had breached the partnership. As he said: 'It was an internal problem. But then they started to criticize the agency. I tried to keep it internal, but they took it to the international forum.'

Mr Izmit immediately brought the issue to the attention of Alfredo in Manila, who arranged for a letter to be produced by one of the People's Organizations involved with SPRINC. This letter was sent to the donors and to the editor of the newsletter. It denied the accusation, and bounced the ball back by asserting: 'CWNGO is not a PO, who are they to criticize the programme?' Once more in the history of the programme, a PO was brought on stage to back up a development organization. This final conflict meant the definite ending of relations between CWNGO and SPRINC – or did it?

Epilogue on SPRINC When I visited Mr Izmit in Geneva in December 1997, he told me that the project with the Baguio weavers had continued without CWNGO and now worked satisfactorily. The institutional counterpart of SPRINC was now INNABUYOG, the Regional Indigenous Women's Organization. Mr Izmit was very pleased to have a staff member responsible for the project who herself belonged to the People's Organization. When he mentioned her name, I realized I knew this woman. She used to be a staff member of an NGO for the urban poor, belonging to the same Consortium as CWNGO.

Two months later I met Minda in a restaurant at Schiphol Airport, the Netherlands, where she stayed some hours in transit on her way to a conference. Asked about the latest developments, she told me that indeed the new SPRINC staff used to be with the urban poor NGO. This NGO had been dissolved, in order to work directly as part of a People's Organization. Although they had taken on this new identity, they still belonged to the Consortium and continued to work with the same political orientation. Even Minda herself continued to be involved, albeit in a different capacity – as an officer of INNABUYOG. With some satisfaction, she declared: 'You see, UNA cannot get rid of me.' Whether this should be labelled a 'victory' is doubtful, but it brings out the irony of the situation. From the distance of Geneva the problem was neatly solved: the role of the NGO was eliminated and the project became owned by the PO. Seen from nearer by, the situation was more diffuse: the distinction between NGO and PO virtually disappeared, and continuity prevailed in terms of staff, and thus partial 'ownership' of the project, by the political movement of CPA and the NGO Consortium that Mr Izmit so much disliked.

Multiple Realities of Funding Agencies

In the introduction to this chapter I called for an ethnographic analysis of funding agencies. The first question is whether the UNA was in fact a funding agency. There is no easy answer to this. In the first phase of the relationship, during the initial five-month project, the UNA clearly acted as a funding agency. The confusion starts after this period, with SPRINC. SPRINC is a programme financed by external donors. It is not directly implemented by the UNA, but through the relations it enters into with implementing agencies. In the eyes of CWNGO, the UNA therefore continues to be the funding agency. In the Philippines, the situation becomes even more complicated when the Manila office expands and uses the services of two expatriate development experts to assist the programme co-ordinator. At that point, the Philippine SPRINC section becomes more and more of an implementing agency itself. The identity of the agency acquires additional layers when we take into account the actors. For example, the national co-ordinator, Alfredo, had had decades of experience as a government bureaucrat before he joined SPRINC. His ideas have always echoed government positions. This contributed to the fact that SPRINC began to drift away from the NGOs in order to work more through local government structures (as they did in the Cordillera after severing ties with CWNGO).

The case of SPRINC may appear exceptional, but I would argue that multiple realities are part of every funding agency. Many take on several roles or identities: they may be fundraisers in their own society, or depend on government financing. They may take the role of implementing agency and organize conferences, or give training. They may be membership organizations of churches or social movements, branches of political parties or private firms, and compete with other funding agencies. Some even present themselves in international conferences as representatives of their Southern NGO partners. When this is the case, my notion of organizations as fluid entities applies equally well to funding agencies as to NGOs. This has the important implication that we should not mistake the policy statements of funding agencies for the 'real thing'. Such statements are official presentations, drafted to suit particular audiences. The everyday practices of funding organizations are steered more by the multiple realities beneath this surface, just as in NGOs, where their actors balance different domains of work.

The above account reveals the many layers and narratives of the relation between SPRINC and CWNGO. The agencies have a very different understanding of themselves, each other and what happened during the programme's history. What is interesting is that the differences are often expressed in the same language. As can be seen in their accounts, many of the criticisms and claims are mirrored: each agency considers the other ineffective, unaccountable and the breacher of their partnership. What is at stake is not so much the terms of the debate, but the meanings attached to these terms. This underscores the arguments put forward in Chapter 1 on the negotiation of seemingly dominant development discourses. CWNGO and SPRINC seem to agree about the importance of things like indigenous knowledge and participation. However, in the process, the meaning of these concepts is negotiated on the basis of deep-seated differences, for instance about the relative importance of expert knowledge and local knowledge concerning 'indigenousness'.

One of the contested concepts is 'partnership' (INTRAC 1998: 90). Funding agencies have increasingly come to adopt this term to denote their relationship with the NGOs that they support. As Stirrat and Henkel say: 'for the donors, the great advantage of the model of partnership is legitimation in that it allows them to claim a certain authenticity: "we are of and for the people"' (Stirrat and Henkel 1997: 75). But what does partnership mean? Because of the asymmetry between givers and re-ceivers, Stirrat and Henkel point out that partnership should not be understood as legal partnerships but more as the partnership of marriage, involving complementary and different identities: 'as with most marriages, the relationship is as much a site of struggle as a cause of harmony' (ibid.: 76). The nature of partnership and the roles and discretion of the partners involved are always under negotiation, and the way in which the partnership evolves reflects the power processes taking place.

Bickering over effectiveness, accountability and partnership deals with more than semantics. It is about politics, in two ways. First, it is about politics in an ideological sense, as in the controversy around SPRINC's and CWNGO's positions on ancestral land delineation. Both organizations are reluctant to bring this argument out into the open. SPRINC translates the political opposition to DAO-2 in terms of a self-interested lack of account-ability. CWNGO articulates the political undercurrents with audiences in the region, but in international meetings speaks in terms of how the UNA imposes its programme on the community, thereby emphasizing a lack of participation. James Ferguson (1990) likens development to an anti-politics machine. On the surface, this indeed seems to be the case with the history of SPRINC. However, as this chapter makes clear, even though ideological politics disappear from public transcripts, they continue to play a definite role in the minds and actions of the respective stakeholders.

Second, it is about politics in a more narrow, organizational sense. Funding agencies can no more escape questions of legitimacy than NGOs. They have to legitimate themselves in the eyes of their own donors, governments, constituencies and finally the public at large (mediated through the media). As mentioned, the use of the term partnership can be viewed as a device for legitimation. This notion brings Quarles van Ufford (1993: 141) to label project reports and representations of the local scene as *political* statements. This author shows how development agencies carefully balance knowledge and ignorance in order to enhance their legitimation. He discusses an Indonesian project, where: 'everyone involved in the project knew that these notions [about the community] were false, but there was no alternative to upholding the official development ideology' (ibid.: 137). Reports of SPRINC stating that a new organization had been formed, knowing that it had been operating for years prior to the project, can be understood as such a political statement aimed at legitimation.

The argument of accountability turned out to be a particularly strong weapon in this quest for legitimation. Mr Izmit and Alfredo could justify their Manila office's expanding role in the implementation of SPRINC by casting doubt on the accountability of CWNGO. CWNGO likewise defended the need for its prolonged involvement in the programme by accusing SPRINC of being top-down and Geneva-centred, instead of being accountable to indigenous people and values. The role of the People's Organizations in the discussion remained marginal: both agencies mobilized certain PO voices in their representations. Accountability to the local people seems an effective argument, as it is morally high ground and difficult to falsify. When it is used, as in the cases presented here, to settle conflicts between different intervening agencies, it becomes political. Thus, 'you are not accountable to your constituency' is very likely to mean: 'my notions of development are better than yours and I want to expand my influence or take over your clients'. As shown in Chapters 3 and 4, the adoption of dominant discourses is not without danger. However, as this case makes clear, making use of the (depoliticized) dominant development discourse can also be a weapon in the hands of funding agencies that want to impose their agenda. It can also be a weapon in the hands of NGOs that want to resist this imposition and work towards their own agenda.

Notes

1. For the case of the women's movement in the Philippines, this notion was elegantly elaborated by Colette St-Hilaire (1992).

2. As with the Philippine organizations, I have used pseudonyms for the international organizations and programmes. My ethnography aims to reveal processes, which are only partially particular to the organizations under study.

3. This means that 65 per cent of the lines of the transcripts were hers. Actually, her contribution was even greater, since the change of tape that occurred while she was speaking is not taken into account.

TEN
Conclusion: NGO Everyday Politics

This project started from a certain frustration. Non-government development organizations had become a major phenomenon since the 1980s. Their small size, links to the grassroots, sympathetic values and capacities for efficient service delivery were marked advantages over state development institutions. In the early 1990s, however, the glorious image of NGOs became dented. Discussion erupted about their proclaimed effectiveness, their alleged close connections to the grassroots and their possible lack of accountability. Although I found these issues relevant, the discussions, both critical and celebratory, seldom moved away from generalized notions. They often spoke of NGOs as if they were a single phenomenon. It was assumed that one could know what an NGO is by knowing its leaders and reading its mission statements and reports. I did not believe this to be the case.

I wanted to know why certain sets of actors form organizations that they call NGOs, and how they ascribe and negotiate meanings for such an organization. Processes of meaning-making are central to everyday practice, since they underlie the numerous small and big, proactive and responsive, decisions and actions that together make up the organization. In addition, I have a focus on matters of everyday politics. On the one hand, this entails the way in which ideology was important in shaping the organization. On the other, it involves the question of how NGOs acquire legitimation as a development organization *vis-à-vis* other relevant parties, including clients, donors and constituencies. These are questions into organizational processes, which cannot be studied through mission statements, reports, surveys or interviews with managers alone. This book argues the importance of studying everyday practices for understanding, managing and supporting NGOs.

An actor orientation The case for the crucial importance of everyday practices for understanding NGOs is founded theoretically and methodologically in an actor orientation. Such orientation starts with the premise that social actors have agency. People reflect on their experiences and what happens around them, and use their knowledge and capabilities to interpret and respond to development. This means that we cannot study the social without studying the actors, but also that we cannot study people without studying the social. Organizational policies, cultures and accountabilities, just as much as larger processes of law, politics, culture, history and economics that enable or constrain social life, do not work upon people, but through them. They become effective only through the mediation of interpreting actors. Hence, understanding these processes requires studying how actors interpret and act upon them. This takes more than interviews or workshops. We must observe the way NGO actors deal with NGO-ing, and delve into their past and present surroundings, social networks and histories to understand their motivations, ideas and activities. In this way, we can learn how NGO actors find room for manoeuvre to realize their projects.

The concept of room for manoeuvre refers to the social space actors have, or lack, for enabling their ideas and projects. How actors 'expand' their room for manoeuvre depends on their effectiveness in enrolling others in their projects, which is called effective agency. To study this, I followed NGO actors in their different domains of work, studying how NGO practices come about and acquire meaning, through formal manifestations and actions as well as more informal everyday operations. This often took the shape of a social interface analysis. Interface analysis focuses on the linkages and networks that develop between individuals or parties at points where different, and often conflicting, life worlds or social fields intersect (Long 1999: 1), such as in interactions between different stakeholders of NGOs. Interface analysis can reveal important dynamics, concerning the interplay of multiple discourses and the way in which power relations get shaped.

Processes and things, labels and representations One aspect of social life that is turning out to be particularly important for understanding NGO-ing is how people (not just anthropologists) grapple with the relation between processes and things (Baumann 1996). In their everyday practices, people have a practical awareness of the process nature of organizations. Yet they simultaneously adhere to 'thing' notions about the same. Multiple realities of organizations come about because organizations may represent many things for different people both simultaneously and sequentially. One focus of the study is how actors accommodate these different notions in finding meaning; how they use them strategically in processes of legitimating; and how they respond when other people use 'thing' notions about their organization. The latter refers to how NGO actors manage or not to negotiate the labels given to their organization by others, which box them into particular ideological corners (such as those of feminism or Communism), or turn them into utilitarian objects (such as project providers).

My definition of NGOs reflects the complicated relation between processes and things. By most definitions, development NGOs are intermediary organizations that bring about development for poor and marginalized people. The definitions distinguish NGOs from non-NGOs and fake-NGOs, with the result that they do not analyse how such distinctions are constructed and used in practice. I took a different position. Acknowledging the process nature of organization, I did not want to adhere to a normative definition, but to keep an open mind as to why and how NGOs are formed in practice, and how actors accord meaning to their unfolding forms, principles and procedures. Instead, I define the *term* of NGO as a label claiming that the organization does good for the development of poor and marginalized others. The question then becomes why actors take on this identity, and how they find recognition as the 'do-good' organizations implied in the label.

Another class of things of particular interest is representations. Through their accounts and practices, NGO actors convey images about what their organization is, does and wants. By definition, representations are a simplification of the 'real thing'. Unlike the multiple realities and nitty-gritty of everyday practices, representations provide a single understanding and closure. They are narratives that are organized around a specific rationale, based, for example, on the causality between inputs and outputs, or on a reduction of reality to politically opposed interests. The point is that representations are not just a neater and simpler version of reality, but may be completely unrelated to reality. I concur with John Law (1994: 26), who argued that we should abandon a correspondence theory of representation. Instead of asking ourselves whether a representation corresponds to reality, we should be concerned with the workability and legitimacy of a representation. Throughout this book, then, I have elaborated how actors compose different representations, and explored the contests involved in their efforts to enrol others in accepting them.

Duality of discourse My interest in issues of meanings and legitimation took me inevitably to studying discourse. Discourses are more or less coherent sets of references for understanding and acting upon the world around us. As was pointed out by Foucault, discourses intertwine knowledge and power. Just how discourse works, how it exactly links knowledge and power, is a matter for debate. Positions in this debate run along an axis ranging from extremely structuralist to highly voluntaristic. The latter position may be found in interpretations of discourse as merely any kind of conversation, or in views of the world as a marketplace of ideas that actors strategically employ to their liking. The extreme on the structuralist side is found in views of discourse as 'regimes' that constitute us to the extent that we make them true by allowing them to play upon ourselves. I define my position somewhere in between, by speaking of the 'duality of discourse', following Giddens's notion of the 'duality of structure'. Recent literature rejects the notion of a hegemonic development discourse. There are always multiple discourses, and actors find room for manoeuvre to renegotiate them. Discourses do not provide ready-made scripts to act upon but are reshuffled, circumvented and enacted by social actors. Hence, they are actors' constructions. However, the other side of the duality of discourse stipulates that discourses are not innocent and can, indeed, become powerful. The more dominant a discourse, the more it operates as a set of rules about what can and cannot be said and done, and about what. As a consequence, actors, through their discursive practice, may turn these discourses increasingly into reality. Many chapters of this book have looked into the issue of the duality of discourse by asking, on the one hand, how actors strategically use discourse, and on the other, when and how particular discourses become powerful and what that means for NGO practice.

Why NGOs are formed Why do people form NGOs? The NGOs that have been introduced in this book were formed as functional devices both for idealistic and more practical reasons. CWNGO emerged from a political movement, and was formed by activists who found that adopting the label and format of an NGO facilitated the acquisition of funding and, moreover, provided them with a 'neutral' entity through which to operate in politically volatile situations. Another NGO, the Kayatuan Ladies' Association discussed in Chapter 4, was formed to attract projects. It is important to note that, in both cases, becoming an NGO was an identity *added* to ongoing organizing processes. CWNGO continued to be a hardly distinguishable part of the larger whole of the National Democratic political movement it belonged to, and the KLAi was entangled in social networks and organizations in and beyond the village. This supports the idea that one cannot perceive NGOs as entities, but that we have to take into account the notion of multiple realities. Rather than organizations with fixed boundaries, NGOs appear to be composed of overlapping social networks. The fact that these NGOs were formed for particular reasons, and as part of ongoing organizing processes, points out that taking on the identity of NGO is a political act. Adopting this claim-bearing label is a strategy in NGO everyday politics aimed at acquiring legitimation as an organization that does good for the development of others.

How to deal with multiple realities in NGOs Once NGOs are formed, they acquire realities of their own, moving away from their founding rationale and often becoming more important for the actors involved than originally intended. NGOs appear as an amalgam of different discourses, relations and ambitions. This multiplicity is partly related to political opportunities, changing state–society relations and changing discourses in the world's development communities (Tvedt 1998). CWNGO was shaped by opposition to dictatorship and by the struggle against the dams in the Chico river, followed by opportunities and constraints resulting from the restoration of democracy in 1986. It further evolved as it did because it played upon preferences in the international development 'community' for indigenous women, and because part of its values and modes of operation were derived from discourses prevailing in these communities. However, as I have argued throughout this book, the multiplicity of NGOs also stems from organizational features and processes. One particular relevant aspect of NGO-ing is that NGOs operate in a number of different domains, each with their own (but partly overlapping) languages, rules, routines and demands. The result is a situation where a great many 'forces' pull and push NGO actors in different directions, creating incompatible commitments, confusions and contradictions. These discontinuities and segmentations are exacerbated by differences among staff members in the NGO with regard to their politics, origin, kinship, sexuality and livelihoods.

The importance of the notion of multiple realities for researchers is hard to overestimate. Without systematically realizing that there is more to NGO-ing than the single reality displayed in reports or in interviews with managers, one cannot account for changes occurring through time and for inconsistencies taking place in practice. Moreover, taking the identity of NGOs for granted diverts the attention away from power processes in these organizations. It would leave one unaware of conflicting notions, and hence of signals of alternative modes of NGO-ing and prospects for change. Finally, the notion of multiple realities may shift one of the most poignant questions asked in NGO research, which is the question of how and why NGO practice diverts from rhetoric or policy. Rather than asking why NGOs do not live up to their promises, the more relevant question may be how NGO management and staff members arrive at a certain coherence in practice, given the multiple binds and life worlds in which they operate. How do managers and staff deal with multiple realities?

It is by reshuffling and combining the different 'pulls and pushes', in other words, by improvising, that NGO actors attribute meaning to the organization and arrive at a certain coherence in their everyday practices. Management and staff members attach meaning to the NGO by reflecting on the question of what the organization and its environment signify. Because all actors are actively engaged in these ongoing reflections, organizations are decentred: their meanings are not just derived from the wilful manipulation of managers, nor can we distinguish neat competing voices of 'management versus the rest'. Meanings are informed by many elements. They draw on official policies and office procedures, as well as on a range of discourses from within and outside the organization. As a result, staff members attach different values to the diverse meanings the NGO may have, such as a giver of services, a family, an ideological bastion, a source of livelihood, a space for women, a cultural statement of 'unity in diversity', a project bureaucracy and an indigenous institution. Processes of ordering in these multiple realities evolve through everyday practices, for instance, around the symbolic use of locales in the office, through a variety of overlapping social networks and by evoking particular cultural institutions. However, although there are always ordering processes, resulting in patterns, routines and a certain predictability, there is never order. Actors continue to have different understandings of, and continue to negotiate, organizational properties.

Finding room to manoeuvre In order to survive, NGOs need to find legitimation as 'intermediary organizations doing good for the development of others'. This quest for legitimation is complicated because NGOs operate in different domains, where different values and relationships prevail. NGOs deal with different stakeholders. They have to convince their clients that they have something worthwhile to offer, while enrolling them in the (political) projects of the NGO. They have to convince their constituency, such as the social movement or church community, that they maintain their loyalty to it, while doing their development work. They have to convince funding agencies that they are worth putting money into, and persuade their counterparts in international arenas that they are knowledgeable and can represent the ideas of their local clients.

This aspect of legitimation is important for understanding NGO daily politics. As outlined above, it adds to segmentations and contradictions in NGO practice. However, because NGO actors deal with multiple domains that are relatively separated from one another, they also find room for manoeuvre in strategically operating diverse relationships. In Chapters 4 and 8, I elaborated how certain actors, whom I call 'interface experts' – be they village women or international NGO personalities – can become powerful because they master languages prevailing in different domains, and can use this strategic knowledge to advance their interests at different interfaces. In Chapters 5 and 6, I explored how NGO strategies and practices that are seemingly directed to one domain of operation are actually meant to influence another field of action. For example, the policy model of Cordillera NGOs, which was officially meant to steer organizing in the villages, mainly worked as a strategic device in inter-agency conflicts. I want to stress that NGOs, because they link a variety of domains that, at most, partially overlap, have a knowledge advantage over their stakeholders that enhances their power. Because actors in different domains have only fragmented knowledge about one another, they rely on NGO representations to know what happens in the other domains – a characteristic that complicates accountability processes.

How NGOs relate to stakeholders At first sight, the relation between NGOs and their stakeholders appears to be contractual. Stakeholders act as authorities, for whom NGOs fulfil certain explicit or implicit obligations. The analysis in this book highlights how, in practice, relationships between stakeholders and NGO actors are negotiated and evolve into a myriad of ties. The nature of the authority relation, for example, is not as clear-cut as would follow from the idea of NGOs as mere service institutions. Chapter 9 shows how, despite the fundamental inequality between funding agencies and NGOs, the latter can sometimes, if not turn the tables, at least develop a substantial countervailing power, allowing them to secure stable funding and to negotiate the terms of accountability.

Furthermore, we have seen how relations tend to expand into multiple ties binding stakeholders and NGOs. Relations with stakeholders turn out to be multiplex. Villagers, for example, endeavour to bind NGO actors through maximizing their social ties, and they put pressure on NGO actors to make them morally accountable to them. Chapter 8 showed how NGO leaders forge social communities within international arenas to delineate partnership (whom to work with and whom to oppose) and fruitful working relations. They also strategically enrol representatives of funding agencies, through linking with them in social and moral ways. As a result, seemingly contractual relations come to take on different entertwining layers, where contractual obligations are entangled with moral obligations, emotional rewards (generated by gratitude, flattery, observed improvements and other encouraging feedback), friendly favours and ideological statements. Again, this complicates accountability relations.

How and when discourse becomes dominant The notion of duality of discourse has helped me to understand a variety of processes taking place in NGOs. It highlighted how actors strategically deploy a multiplicity of development languages, such as when relating to development interveners (Chapter 4), and to funding agencies (Chapter 9). But it also allowed me to bring out how discourses are one of the structuring elements of development. At most times, I found NGOs articulating a number of multiple 'official' discourses that find their way in policies, analyses, speeches and practices, as well as 'everyday' discourses, based on, among other things, kinship and cultural institutions. Each of these discourses is coherent in itself and provides particular scripts for action. When NGO actors give meaning to their organization they draw, in part, on these discourses. However, at certain points in time, as I stated in Chapter 1, discourses indeed succeed in effecting a 'closure' of alternative readings of situations and relations. More than fashions, these discourses are effective in re-creating the past, stipulating policy for the present, reshaping organizational forms and practices, and including, excluding and recomposing people's relations. One of the questions I have addressed in this book is when and how particular development discourses become dominant by coercing, convincing or seducing people to close options and create new realities.

I found two different kinds of processes through which discourses may turn dominant. The first is when wider political processes pose such threats that actors resort to a single discourse.[1] This has, for example, been observed with discourses on nationalism and gender, where women in crisis situations find certain roles and identities foreclosed to them (Byrne 1996; see also Wilson and Frederiksen 1995). Two such instances were discussed in the present book. In Chapter 2, under the threat of inundation of their ancestral lands, a discourse on 'land is life' quickly gained prominence among alternative notions about land. And in Chapter 3, I followed how a particular ideological discourse gained central importance in a social movement and NGO Consortium when its leadership felt increasingly challenged and marginalized. Note that in these cases the specific discourse became dominant within a short time-span. It was, perhaps, not consciously decided on, but at least in these situations actors were aware of the changes taking place. They were debated, and participants were 'intensely committed to the outcome of these debates' (Smith 1989: 26).

However, there is another way in which discourse becomes dominant. This takes place over longer periods of time, and happens in a far less visible manner. In these cases, powerful discourses are emergent properties. They do not result from immediate crisis situations, but are reproduced through the unintended consequences of everyday routine practices, without the actors being aware of it. For example, this was the case in

Chapter 4, where the numerous actions of village women contributed to the centralization of a modernist discourse at the expense of the status of peasant women. I found this also in Chapter 3, where, in the course of time, a development discourse gained ground and slowly changed values attached to the formal educational requirements for staff members. As a result, the activist founders of NGOs increasingly found themselves displaced, in an outcome partly of their own making, by college degree holders. The irony of the duality of discourse, as this case brings out, is that actors adopt certain discursive strategies to enhance particular interests, but may find themselves eventually caught up in this discourse, leading to undesired consequences beyond their control.

Even though discourses can become dominant (in different ways), this study concurs with the point that they are never hegemonic. Even the rectification discourse that seemed to become hegemonic in channelling the way in which actors experienced development, was, as I discussed in Chapter 3, mediated by actors' agency, and acquired multiple meanings as a result of the differential responses to it by the actors involved. Moreover, there are always multiple discourses. Even in the situation where the rectification discourse was for some time the only acknowledged official discourse, it was contested by informal discourses engrained in everyday practices, in particular those concerning gender and sexuality.

The localizing of meaning One of the reasons why several authors talk about hegemonic discourses in development is that they assume that when actors use particular phrases derived from a dominant discourse, they also adopt its meaning. This idea has been discredited in several recent publications, for overlooking the fact that the meaning of development notions is renegotiated in the local context. So, even when a certain vocabulary is adopted, it may acquire different and often multiple meanings in the localities. The same goes for institutions. Various chapters of this book show that we cannot assume the meaning of organizations and organizational practices from their appearance as modern organizations. In Chapters 4 and 5, I discussed local village organizations that adopted modern, formal modes of organizing but endowed these with different symbolic meanings. One organization had taken on board a full complement of officers in order to divert conflict and competition among women professionals. In another case, villagers politely embraced this form of organization, with its set of separate committees with clear responsibilities and tasks, and held their meetings in highly formal ways as homage to the NGOs. It was both a token of respect and a strategy to confirm the ties and obligations between NGO staff members and themselves. In view of this, we should be cautious not to stop our enquiry once familiar institutions are identified, since they may turn out to have entirely different symbolic meanings. It raises, for instance, some question as to the assumed homogeneity of NGOs worldwide taking on similar properties, ambitions and activities (Tvedt 1998).

Making representations workable and legitimate Since NGOs operate in a variety of social domains, a large aspect of their work consists of providing representations of processes occurring in the other domains. When talking to a representative of a funding agency, an NGO manager will discuss the state of local development, how state policies operate at local level and the alternative projects of social movements. Likewise, NGO staff members present particular readings of the country's political economy and state–society relations to local villagers. In this book I paid considerable attention to how such accounts or representations are formed and how they become workable and legititmate.

Legitimation centres around making certain representations more acceptable than others. Representations of development NGOs, therefore, have everything to do with power. Competing understandings often lead to conflicts. Chapter 2 showed how three parties developed and defended particular discourses on a movement for regional autonomy, in a vicious conflict over leadership of the movement and 'ownership' of its history. In Chapter 6, I described another conflict over local development, involving two NGOs that had to account for their interventions in an NGO Consortium. In many cases, however, accounts become workable through processes of enrolment. This happens relatively unnoticed and without (open) conflict. In these cases, the account-giver has mustered enough effective agency to enrol others into accepting his or her understanding and adopting his or her projects. As I found, enrolment efforts work through addressing the different layers of relationships outlined in this book, and by combining various modes of operation. Illustrative of this is the nature of reports the CWNGO sent to its funding agency. As discussed in Chapter 8, these reports were more than mechanisms of formal accountability. They were also devices for negotiating mutual accountabilities, and attempts to enrol the funding agency through interweaving the formal records with moral claims.

I wish to emphasize the role of local people in the everyday politics of legitimation of development interveners. Participation of local NGO stakeholders in policy discussions and accountability processes is often given primary importance. In practice, I found the influence of local people in these processes negligible. Instead, time and time again I found that local people, indicated by their orchestrated presence or merely by quoting them anonymously, were depicted as supporters of claims by outsiders competing over access and power in development and seeking their own legitimation. This was the case for NGOs as well as for funding agencies. As I concluded in Chapter 9, principled discussions over account-ability to local clients of development are likely to hide competition over outsiders' notions of development and influence over these local people. What happens in the domain of local development is drawn into other domains, where it acquires a different meaning as a weapon in conflicts or competition.

Since representations are constructions, they reveal the agency of the account-giver. A 'good representation' (that is, one that works and legiti-mates), as I stipulated, is a skilful improvisation that combines fragments of actual experiences and discourses with bits of knowledge about the party for whose sake it is delivered or enacted. For this reason, I have stressed that NGO leaders are *brokers of meaning*. Rather than filling pre-defined gaps for intermediation, they negotiate relationships by convincing the other parties of the meaning of events, processes and needs and their own roles. At the same time, however, we must realize that the social construction and working of representations are not one-way processes. Interfaces with stakeholders are better viewed as arenas, and representations as the out-comes of negotiated processes influenced by both parties at the interface. The two-way nature of constructing representations is, first, apparent from the ways in which NGO actors are influenced by experiences with and ideas from their stakeholders in constructing their representations. This point is illustrated by the history of the movement for regional autonomy, where experiences with local villagers brought activists to change their own projection of the situation (see Chapter 2). Second, NGO actors have to negotiate their identity in relation to the notions and expectations that stakeholders have about them. In many cases, as we have seen, NGOs lose this battle for their identity.

In Chapter 5, several case studies made clear how local villagers, by fostering a certain image of the NGO and responding accordingly, re-shaped considerably the NGO and its interventions. In one case, the NGO was not able to overcome the kinship-based tactics employed by the villagers; in another they were confronted with reluctance as soon as they stepped out of the role of an alternative government accorded to them by the villagers. Likewise, in other domains NGOs had to deal with political labels attached to them (as in the case of CECAP in Chapter 3), as well as with general claims regarding NGOs by international agencies, government representatives or the media. Making representations work is a process reflecting *and* effecting power relations in development.

Everyday Politics

In this final section, I would like to reiterate some implications of this study for issues of NGO everyday politics, both for legitimation and ideology.

Politics of legitimation: issues of accountability The accountability of development NGOs is considered a problematic issue. My analysis corroborates this. NGOs are accountable to different stakeholders. The substance of their accountability is mainly directed to their local development work. It forms the backbone of NGO legitimation in other domains. As the case studies have demonstrated, the room for manoeuvre of NGOs for steering development in villages or poor urban areas varies, but should not be overestimated. Development processes are constituted by many things, including historically produced associational patterns, the ensemble of development interventions and local resources, and wider processes of inclusion, exclusion and marginalization. In the interface between staff members and villagers, I found villagers in all cases appropriating development interventions by redefining meanings and redistributing benefits. This resulted in a variegated picture of unpredictable processes with a large diversity of outcomes.

Indeed, it is clear that accounts of these local processes are necessarily partial, simplifying, and but one interpretation among many possible narratives. It is therefore important to take on the study of how particular narratives are constructed and gain legitimation in accountability relations. In Chapter 6, I followed an accountability process and discussed some pertinent literature. I found accountability processes to reflect negotiation and power struggles in the context of the everyday politics of legitimation, and competing development interveners, as well as the struggles between donors and NGOs, rather than what happened in the actual development process. I concluded that this turns transparency into a myth: instead of revealing what really happens in the localities, accounts are permeated by what happens in the accountability process.

In the face of increasing criticism of NGO accountability, several alternatives have been proposed for improving practice. A number of authors have suggested that NGOs should clarify and redefine their core values in order to have a more stringent frame of reference for accountability processes (Fowler 1997; Edwards 1999). Others have sought to devise alternative tools for more comprehensive and more participatory accountability (Zadek and Gatward 1996). Although these new approaches perhaps represent a major change in accountability practices, they should not be considered a panacea for the accountability problem, and are as liable as more traditional forms of accountability to be used as weapons in the everyday politics of legitimation. There does not seem to be a single solution or methodology to realize accountability. We shall always need critically to improvise, combine methods and make the best of them.

For those who demand accountability, in particular donors, I think it would help to acknowledge different modes of accountability, instead of relying solely on formal accountability. Perhaps, when international organizations and donor agencies begin to realize and acknowledge the social nature of accountability, they might invest more in trust and less in disciplining by means of detailed accountability demands. What I mean is not that they should trust development NGOs, but rather that they should invest in becoming trustworthy partners with development NGOs, thereby forging the moral commitment of NGOs to live up to their promises.

Notwithstanding my reservations, I am not pessimistic about accountability. The everyday politics of legitimation that tend to corrupt accountability also contain the necessary pressures to move towards more meaningful accountability. NGOs are vulnerable to losing their good name, by which their legitimation stands or falls. The easiest way to protect one's good name is by living up to one's proclaimed standards. This is the case for individual NGOs, but also for the entire sector. Development NGOs have become aware that the reputation of their sector is increasingly at stake with policy makers and the public at large (the latter through critical reporting by the media). As a result, NGOs risk losing the respect that they so easily commanded in the 1980s and 1990s. This provides additional grounds for critical reflection within NGOs. Considering the nature of NGOs as intermediary organizations, they have to show stakeholders that they are doing a reasonably good job with their clients. If they don't succeed, they risk losing their appeal for funding agencies, their legitimacy as advocates, their credibility in the eyes of media people and, eventually, their status as organizations that are seen to do good for the benefit of others.

Everyday politics of development   It has been suggested that there is a tendency among development NGOs in the South to converge towards variations of Western-dominated neoliberal and liberal-democratic development agendas. I have already stipulated that I do not agree with this notion of a hegemonic development discourse. Here, I want to address the underlying concern of those authors debating this matter, namely, that such convergence leads to the 'depoliticization' of development, or as Ferguson (1990) aptly put it, that development has become an 'anti-politics machine'. For the case of the NGO Consortium recounted in this book, this is clearly not true. They are influenced by development agendas, but have also deliberately chosen to take their own political positions. Are they just exceptions? I do not think so. Other NGOs working among indigenous peoples, for example in Guatemala, Bangladesh and Peru, have undergone similar histories of tension between revolutionary, indigenous and development discourses and agendas, with varying outcomes. Numerous other NGOs identify with alternative ideological notions or are actively engaged in political, social or religious movements. The observed convergence is, to my mind, therefore an exaggeration.

How can this exaggeration be explained? First, it may result from a lack of acknowledgement of the multiple realities of NGOs. NGOs may adopt particular development agendas at certain interfaces, but endow them with their own meanings, while at the same time propagating other agendas elsewhere. Second, it may result from a Western-centric perspective. The announcement of the end of ideology in the West (among certain groups) has, to my mind, framed the observations regarding global processes and trends. As a result, manifestations of ideology are not recognized, or are relegated to the margins by considering them remnants of a bygone era. Third, ideological variations are more difficult to appreciate today than in the days when the world of development was neatly divided between Marxists, modernists and traditionalists, each with their own institutional bastions. Nevertheless, they continue to exist and their resurgence can be observed in many places. Since the anti-globalization movements provide new rallying points for NGOs, their ideological involvement may become increasingly more visible (Smith et al. 1997, Guidry et al. 2000).

The future of development NGOs is thus likely to be much more diversified than the observers of convergence expect. With or without the label of NGO, organizing processes will continue to shape differential development outcomes. There is always the risk, of course, that such situations turn ugly and that NGOs may exacerbate violent conflicts, promote exclusion and accentuate marginalization. But I expect that working towards closing the enormous and growing gap in the quality of living conditions, socioeconomic welfare and life expectancy in an increasingly global but unequal world will also continue to be a major concern for NGOs. Commitment to values that advance public and collective interests and that radically side with the poor will continue to be an important element in the ideological visions of many NGOs.

Note

1. Wider political processes can just as suddenly enable discourses as was for instance the case just after the fall of the Berlin Wall (Statham 1998).

EPILOGUE
The Politics of Research

In a politicized environment, research becomes part of political struggle. Research and politics are both about representation, and lines of analysis are bound to find their way into political arenas as statements of controversy, challenge or support. This happened to the project detailed by this book as well. This book is a revision of a thesis completed in November 2000 (Hilhorst 2000). In response, CWNGO, the central NGO in the book, wrote a report while I was reworking the thesis into a manuscript. Part of this report consisted of detailed comments, which I was able to accommodate in the book. Much of the report, however, was about politics and the ethics of research. It denounced my use of theory and ethnography and charged me with having manipulated and abused my research subjects. The report raised many of the major questions that have worried anthropologists and their subjects in recent decades: the association with (neo-)colonialism, the 'ownership' of research and the use of ethnography.

History of the Project

During the last few decades, anthropology has struggled to find ways to study and represent people who are not as 'Other' as the preferred subjects of yesteryear. Different roads have been taken in searching for alternatives. Some anthropologists deliberately refrain from presenting ethnographic detail and resort to more theoretical and abstract forms of analysis. Others have in various ways reduced the distance between the ethnographer and his or her subjects by making themselves part of the analysis, seeking dialogue with the people under study or devising ways of organizing ethnography in participatory ways. I have sought to resolve this issue in a number of research projects by working simultaneously *with* and *on* organizations. Likewise, in this project I worked for three years as research volunteer for the NGO, while at the same time researching into its everyday practices.

My first encounter with Philippine NGOs dates back to 1986, when I did fieldwork with the women's coalition GABRIELA. This project started with the idea of going back there to work for a few years. Thus in 1992, through the mediation of one of my friends in GABRIELA, I was offered a three-year job as researcher with the Cordillera Women NGO. The NGO supported the idea that I would combine this with my own research on the ways NGOs operate in their different fields of activity.

At that moment I could not have anticipated the dramatic turn of events that would follow a conflict in the National Democratic movement over issues of leadership and strategies. When I arrived in the Philippines, a split in the underground movement had spilled over to the NGOs and sectoral organizations. When the NGOs in the Cordillera opted to re-affirm their loyalty to the National Democratic movement, I therefore found myself on that part of the political map belonging to the Reaffirmist camp. In the first year, this made little difference in practice and my work evolved as planned. In the course of time, however, politics became increasingly important and stringent for the NGOs, which set out to realign their work with the political movement. Towards the end of my stay in 1996, many of my initial contacts had left and little space was left for me to work *with* the organization.

Critique

A central problem of my work, according to the NGO report, is its constructivist approach. The report objects to a representation of identities, social movements and other categories as constructed and negotiated. It is stated that I should have 'let the Cordillera situation speak for itself'. My account is a misrepresentation of the Cordillera and the National Democratic movement. According to the report:

> Documentation of the people's movement articulates that national democratic politics has taken root in the Cordillera precisely because it has correctly handled the particularity of Cordillera peoples, their struggles and aspirations, in relation to the overall Filipino struggle for national democracy. The historic gains of Cordillera peoples in assertion of their rights […] were gains as part of the National Democratic movement. If Ms Hilhorst does not accept Cordillera realities, she should at least respect it. She may not impose her misplaced theorizing on us.

A second major objection is the use of ethnography. The use of personal details is considered a breach of confidence, and it is suggested they are being used to 'spice up the scholarly engagement'. The use of ethnography adds to the misrepresentation:

By mentioning only trivial things about CWNGO, using disjointed and isolated events and conversations, she makes a misrepresentation of CWNGO, giving only small snapshots of the whole reality to make her case. What she presents is a distorted picture, far from the whole reality of CWNGO. Too much meaning is given to informal, trivial conversations, while no information is accorded to what CWNGO stands for, what it has achieved, its programmes and what it hopes to achieve.

The third major objection concerns the ethics of a research project where the outcome is considered damaging to the organization under study. Having chosen to work with the network of National Democratic organizations, the report considers it unethical to base the analysis on concepts adverse to this network. In addition, it is asserted that I have not been transparent about the full extent and methodology of my research and that I use and abuse subjects without their free and prior informed consent. 'Why', the report asked, 'didn't Ms Hilhorst allow these very same people the chance to validate her "representations" of their realities?' Finally, it is stated: 'These judgements about "us" by an "other" is reminiscent of colonial ethnographers during the colonial period under Spain and the United States.'

Studying social movements Should anthropologists always agree with their subjects, especially when these subjects represent social movements involved in struggles against oppression? The report states that I should not have studied the NGOs in the Cordillera when my concepts were adverse to the movement to which they belonged. Hence it rightly brings out the major difference to be one of paradigm: where this book maintains a constructivist approach, the National Democratic movement at this point in history builds on the idea of one single truth. That has not always been the case. As I elaborated throughout the book, the NGOs had taken on a more eclectic approach in the 1980s, and the process by which they reverted to their basic ideology in the 1990s is one of the major developments that took place in the course of my fieldwork. One of the consequences of this development was indeed a growing conceptual distance between my project and the NGOs and their movement. Although I readily acknowledge the importance and relevance of the National Democratic movement in the Philippines, I do not agree that they provide the only real and united representation of the situation and people in the country.

More than seeking identification with the NGOs, what motivated my research in the end was my conviction that there was an important story to tell about them. The research formed a unique opportunity to study how NGOs dealt with the ideological struggle in the National Democratic movement, which had for decades been a major player in Philippine politics. I was one of the few, if not the only, independent researcher able to observe what happened with NGOs and the women's movement during this time. The relevance of the experience stretched beyond the individual case: this was one of those rare moments when theoretically important processes of ideological identification are rendered visible and history is explicitly remade. Noticing that people outside of the National Democratic movement usually had – partly due to a lack of information – extremely reductionist ideas of what was going on, it seemed highly relevant to document and analyse the motivations, understandings and practices of actors engaging in this process. As an ethnographer, then, I do not feel obliged to agree with the people I study, so long as I can provide insights into the question of why and how they take on certain ideas and act as they do.

This book provides a narrative on Cordillera NGOs. This means that it presents an interpretation of events and processes. It hopes to be plausible and convincing, but does not attempt to claim the hegemony of truth. The National Democratic movement in the Cordillera claims to represent and thus speak for the people in the Cordillera, denying legitimacy to any other voice. The remark that the book is reminiscent of colonial ethnography is clearly meant to hit the raw nerve of every Westerner involved in development issues, but should not be understood as implying that the same text by a Filipino would be acceptable. Throughout this book, I have put the hegemonic claim of the National Democratic movement in its historical context, pointed out the diversity observed within and around the movement and analysed the everyday politics of representation. Realizing that every interpretation is selective, I do not, however, claim to present a competing truth. The narrative simply hopes to provide readers with some alternative ways of looking at familiar things, like NGOs and social movements.

Consent and ownership I have been transparent about my double agenda. Before coming to the Philippines I had communicated the idea of doing a thesis with the management of CWNGO and presented my proposal. Most people were aware that I was working on a thesis, and my interest in the importance of everyday organizing practices was explicit in reports, everyday conversations and public lectures. It is true, however, that people were not aware of the exact direction of my analysis and the precise way in which I was going to use the data I was collecting.

The notion of prior consent does not easily tally with the nature of ethnography, where the lines of analysis evolve over time. My interest in concepts like multiple realities, representations and discourse rose after noticing how different stories of what the NGO was, wanted and did were being told and used. While certain interests evolved during the fieldwork and started to guide the data gathering, most of the analysis did not take shape until I returned to the Netherlands to begin writing and do more reading. What makes a 'case' is not its empirical properties, but the way in which it is constructed by the researcher. Consequently, what 'something is a case of' may continuously change and can even be re-defined long after the data are gathered (Walton 1992: 121–37). Hence, although people were generally aware of my research interest, I could not seek prior consent about the outcome.

How ethical it is to study movements without extending to them the right to preview the resulting draft is not just a matter of principle. It is contextual and depends on how one perceives the movement under study. Discussions are, for instance, evolving on the question of how anthropologists should deal with 'dangerous others' (Mahmood 2002). Likewise, the anthropologist alone cannot determine the level of dialogue. As Caplan (1994) remarked, the level of identification is not a matter of choice for the ethnographer, but is also set by the people with whom one works. Considering the rigid ideological control within the movement, I could hardly expect appreciation for a book not written from this framework. By the time I was finishing my fieldwork, a single 'truth' about the situation in the Cordillera and the social movement had been defined that precluded discussion with other or multiple realities. Thus, a situation had occurred where I found the ground for dialogue gone missing.

The importance of everyday practices The use of ethnography – participant observation of everyday life – rests upon human relationships, engagement and attachment, and hence involves the risk of manipulation and betrayal by the ethnographer (Stacey 1988: 22). Like most anthropologists, I have tried to minimize these negative effects by refraining from explicit references and using pseudonyms. Nevertheless, ethnography remains the major pillar on which this book rests. My ethnography on everyday practices is not just illustration added to the arguments of the book. The ethnography brings out the major point of the book: that everyday practices are central for understanding NGO realities.

As I argued in Chapter 1, publications on NGOs rarely take everyday practices into account in discussing the policies and performance of these organizations. The same goes for publications on social movements in the Philippines that are mostly written from the perspective of political science. This book sets out to present a more sociological understanding of organizational politics, concurring with authors like Leftwich (1984), Scott (1985) and Kerkvliet (1991) that politics is encapsulated in everyday practices. I hope to have made a strong case for meticulous observation of actors in and around organizations, since only in this way can one understand the making and remaking of discourses and politics.

A focus on everyday practices has also allowed me to bring out the power processes in NGOs and their relations with wider domains. The National Democratic movement claims there is a united 'we' in the Cordillera, a collective consciousness based on shared experiences and aspirations. However, as demonstrated throughout this book, I encountered much differentiation among people in the Cordillera and found relations within organizations and with their clients in some ways problematic. In the larger perspective of resource exploitation and oppression of people in the Cordillera, the National Democratic movement appears as 'David', fighting 'Goliath' with immense dedication and stamina. But on zooming in on the situation, power differentiation becomes strikingly apparent within the movement itself. Hence this ethnography can be read as a cultural critique (Morgen 1989, in Forsythe 1999) on what appears, in this context, as a powerful institution.

Finally, by bringing in ethnographic detail and personal stories, I have tried to counteract prevailing distancing discourses about Third World movements. As Lila Abu-Lughod puts it, she writes women's stories because 'focusing on individuals encourages familiarity rather than distance and helps to break down "otherness". (Abu-Lughod 1993: 30). Bringing out the ordinariness of NGOs and social movements may counteract reductionist and terrifying prejudices against political movements in the South. This has taken special importance in view of post-September 11 discourses on terrorism. In the Philippines, as in many other countries, political movements today risk being erroneously and misleadingly labelled as (supporters of) terrorist organizations. Authorities or vested political parties thus ride on sentiments of anti-terrorism, creating an excuse to oppress and silence political opposition. The accounts of everyday practices and dilemmas of NGOs may also counterbalance blind expectations of supporters of social movements in the North, who may find in the strength of Southern movements an excuse for themselves to refrain from global struggles. As such, it may be that the book will have an effect not by betrayal but by gathering support for social movements in a more honest way.

Bibliography

Abu-Lughod, L. (1993) *Writing Women's Worlds: Bedouin Stories*. Berkeley, CA, University of California Press.

Aldaba, Fernando T. (1993) 'The Role of NGOs in Philippine Social Transformation', in *Philippine Politics and Society*, January 1993. Quezon City, Ateneo Center for Social Policy and Public Affairs.

Alegre, Alan (ed.) (1996) *Trends and Traditions, Challenges and Choices. A Strategic Study of Philippine NGOs*. Quezon City, Ateneo Center for Social Policy and Public Affairs/Philippines-Canada Human Resource Development Program.

Amnesty International (1992) *Philippines: The Killing Goes On*. London, Amnesty International Publications.

Anderson, Benedict (1991/1983) *Imagined Communities*. Revised Edition. London/New York, Verso Books.

Andres, Tomas D. (1988) *Managing People by Filipino Values*. Quezon City, Our Lady of Manaoag Publishers.

Angeles, Leonora Calderon (1989) 'Getting the Right Mix of Feminism and Nationalism: The Discourse on the Women Question and Politics of the Women's Movement in the Philippines'. MSc Thesis, Quezon City, University of the Philippines.

Anti-Slavery Society (1983) *The Philippines: Authoritarian Government, Multinationals and Ancestral Lands*. Indigenous Peoples and Development Series, Report no. 1.

Appadurai, Arjan (1995) 'The Production of Locality', in Richard Fardon (ed.) *Counterworks: Managing the Diversity of Knowledge*. London/New York, Routledge.

Apthorpe, Raymond and Des Gasper (eds) (1996) *Arguing Development Policy: Frames and Discourses*. London, Frank Cass/Geneva EADI.

Arce, Alberto (1989) 'The Social Construction of Agrarian Development: A Case Study of Producer–Bureaucrat Relations in an Irrigation Unit in Western Mexico', in Norman Long (ed.) *Encounters at the Interface. A Perspective on Social Discontinuities in Rural Development*. Studies in Sociology 27, Wageningen, Wageningen Agricultural University.

— (1993) *Negotiating Agricultural Development: Entanglements of Bureaucrats and Rural Producers in Western Mexico*. Studies in Sociology 34, Wageningen, Wageningen Agricultural University.

Arce, Alberto and Norman Long (1992) 'The Dynamics of Knowledge. Interfaces between Bureaucrats and Peasants', in Norman Long and Ann Long (eds) *Battlefields of Knowledge. The Interlocking of Theory and Practice in Social Research and Development*. London, Routledge.

— (2000) 'Reconfiguring Modernity and Development from an Anthropological

Perspective', in Alberto Arce and Norman Long (eds) *Anthropology, Development and Modernities. Exploring Discourses, Counter-Tendencies and Violence.* London and New York, Routledge.

Arellano-López, Sonia and James F. Petras (1994) 'Non-Governmental Organizations and Poverty Alleviation in Bolivia', *Development and Change* 25 (3): 555–68.

Arts, Bas and Gerda van Roozendaal (eds) (1999) *The Influence of Non-Governmental Organizations on International and Transnational Politics.* Nijmegen, Amsterdam School for Social Science Research and Nijmegen Centre for Business, Environment and Government.

Baig, Qadeer (1999) 'NGO Governing Bodies and Beyond: A Southern Perspective on Third Sector Governance Issues', in David Lewis (ed.) *International Perspectives on Voluntary Action: Reshaping the Third Sector.* London, Earthscan Publications.

Bailey, F. G. (1971) *Gifts and Poison. The Politics of Reputation.* Oxford, Blackwell.

Bakhtin, M. M. (1981/1935) 'Discourse in the Novel', in Michael Holquist (ed.) *The Dialogic Imagination: Four Essays by M. M. Bakhtin.* Austin, University of Texas Press.

Balmaceda-Gutierrez, Chit (1992) 'Ka Lita: Sa Pakpak ng Amihan', *Laya, Feminist Quarterly*, 1992 (1).

Barnett, Tony (1977) *The Gezira Scheme: an Illusion of Development.* London, Frank Cass.

Barth, Fredrik (ed.) (1969) *Ethnic Groups and Boundaries: The Social Organization of Culture Difference.* Boston, MA, Little, Brown.

Barton, R. F. (1949) *The Kalingas. Their Institutions and Custom Law.* Chicago, IL, University of Chicago Press.

Basu, Amrita (ed.) (1995) *The Challenge of Local Feminisms. Women's Movements in Global Perspective.* Boulder, CO/San Francisco, CA/Oxford, Westview Press.

Bate, S. P. (1997) 'Whatever Happened to Organizational Anthropology? A Review of the Field of Organizational Ethnography and Anthropological Studies', *Human Relations* 50 (9).

Bateson, Mary Catherine (1990) *Composing a Life.* New York, Plume/Penguin.

Bauman, Gerd (1996) *Contesting Culture: Discourses of Identity in Multi-Ethnic London.* Cambridge, Cambridge University Press.

Benedito, Roberto M. (1994) 'The Kalinga Bodong: An Ethnographic Moment in Legal Anthropology'. PhD Thesis, State University of New York.

Berg, Paul van den (1996) 'Analyse van de Opkomst, Ontwikkeling en Gevolgen van een Tribale Beweging in de Cordillera, Noord Luzon, Filipijnen, 1964–1987'. MSc Thesis, University of Amsterdam.

Bertaux-Wiame, Isabelle (1981) 'The Life History Approach to the Study of Internal Migration', in D. Bertaux (ed.) *Biography and Society: The Life History Approach in the Social Sciences.* Beverly Hills, CA/London, Sage Publications.

Biekart, Kees (1996) 'European NGOs and Democratization in Central America: Assessing Performance in Light of Changing Priorities', in Michael Edwards and David Hulme (eds) *Beyond the Magic Bullet. NGO Performance and Accountability in the Post-Cold War World.* Connecticut, Kumarian Press.

— (1999) *The Politics of Civil Society Building. European Private Aid Agencies and Democratic Transitions in Central America.* Amsterdam/Utrecht, International Books and Transnational Institute.

Biggs, Stephen D. and Arthur D. Neame (1996) 'Negotiating Room to Manoeuvre: Reflections Concerning NGO Autonomy and Accountability within the New Policy Agenda', in Michael Edwards and David Hulme (eds) *Beyond the Magic Bullet. NGO Performance and Accountability in the Post-Cold War World*. Connecticut, Kumarian Press.

Borgh, Chris van der (1999) *Wederopbouw in Chalatenango, El Salvador. Ontwikkelingsorganisaties in een Naoorlogse Maatschappij*. Amsterdam, Thela Thesis.

Boudreau, Vincent (2001) *Grass Roots and Cadre in the Protest Movement*. Manila, Ateneo de Manila University Press.

Brett, E. A. (1993) 'Voluntary Agencies as Development Organizations: Theorizing the Problem of Efficiency and Accountability', *Development and Change*, 24: 269–303.

Brillantes, A., Jr (1992) *Essay on the Local Government Code of 1991 and NGOs*. CSC Issue Paper No. 1. Baguio City, Cordillera Studies Center, UPCB.

Brown, David and Jonathan Fox (1998) 'Accountability within Transnational Coalitions', in Jonathan Fox and David Brown (eds) *The Struggle for Accountability. The Word Bank, NGOs and Grassroots Movements*. Cambridge, MA and London, MIT Press.

Bryman, Alan (1996) 'Leadership in Organizations', in Stewart R. Clegg, Cynthia Hardy and Walter R. Nord (eds) *Handbook of Organization Studies*. London/New Delhi/Thousand Oaks, Sage Publications.

Byrne, B. (1996) 'Towards a Gendered Understanding of Conflict', *IDS Bulletin*, 27 (3): 31–40.

Caplan, P. (1994) Distanciation or Identification: What Difference Does It Make? *Critique of Anthropology*, 14 (2): 99–115.

Cariño, Jessica K. (1990) *Summary Report. Case Studies of the Role of Non-government Organizations in the Development of Selected Cordillera Communities*. Baguio City: Cordillera Studies Center, UPCB.

— (1992) 'People's Organizations, Non-government Organizations and Open-pit Mining in the Cordillera'. Paper prepared for the Fourth International Philippine Studies Conference, 1–3 July 1992. Canberra, Australian National University.

Cariño, Joanna (1980) 'The Chico River Basin Development Project: A Case Study in National Development Policy', *Agham-Tao*, III.

— (1987) 'Discussion Paper for the CSC-sponsored Academic Conference: Issues in Cordillera Autonomy', in Steven Rood (ed.) *Issues on Cordillera Autonomy. Conference Proceedings, 22–24 May 1987*. Baguio City, Cordillera Studies Center, UPCB.

Casambre, Athena Lydia (1991) 'Interpretations of the Debate on Cordillera Autonomy', *Issues on Cordillera Autonomy, General Summary*. Baguio City, Cordillera Studies Center, UPCB.

Castro, Nestor (1987) 'The Zigzag Route to Self-Determination' , *Diliman Review*, 35 (5) and (6): 26–35.

CDP (1987) *A Consolidated Proposal on the Implementation of the CEC (EEC) – Financed Central Cordillera Agricultural Program (CECAP)*. Baguio City, Consortium of Non-Governmental Organizations Cordillera Comprehensive Development Plan (CDP).

— (1991) *Some Perspectives on NGO Work*. Quezon City, Council for People's Development.

CECAP (1992–94) *Annual Report to the Central Cordillera Public*. Banaue, Central Cordillera Agricultural Programme.

Clark, J. (1991) *Democratizing Development: The Role of Voluntary Organizations*. London, Earthscan Publications.

Clarke, Gerard (1998) *The Politics of NGOs in South-East Asia*. London, Routledge.

Clayton, Andrew (ed.) (1996) *NGOs, Civil Society and the State: Building Democracy in Transitional Societies*. INTRAC NGO Management and Policy Series No. 5. Oxford, INTRAC.

Clegg, Stewart (1998) 'Foucault, Power and Organizations', in Alan McKinlay and Ken Starkey (eds) *Foucault, Management and Organization Theory. From Panopticon to Technologies of Self*. London/New Delhi/Thousand Oaks, Sage Publications.

CODE-NGO and DILG (1998) 'Six Years in Retrospect. Reflections on Local Governance under the Ramos Administration'. Proceedings of the National Policy Dialogue entitled *Local Governance Under the Ramos Administration: A Multi-Sectoral Assessment*. Quezon City, The Caucus of Development NGO Networks (CODE-NGO) and the Department of Interior and Local Government (DILG).

Cohen, A. and J. Comaroff (1976) 'The Management of Meaning: On the Phenomenology of Political Transactions', in Bruce Kapferer (ed.) *Transaction in Meaning: Directions in the Anthropology of Exchange and Symbolic Behaviour*. Philadelphia, PA, Institute for the Study of Human Issues.

Colebatch, H. K. (1998) *Policy*. Minneapolis, University of Minnesota Press.

Constantino-David, Karina (1992) 'The Philippine Experience in Scaling-up', in Michael Edwards and David Hulme (eds) *Making a Difference. NGOs and Development in a Changing World*. London, Earthscan Publications.

— (1998) 'From the Present Looking Back: A History of Philippine NGOs', in G. Sidney Silliman and Lela Garner Noble (eds) *Organizing for Democracy. NGOs, Civil Society and the Philippine State*. Manila, Ateneo de Manila University Press.

Coronel, Sheila (ed.) (1998) *Pork and Other Perks. Corruption and Governance in the Philippines*. Quezon City, Philippine Center for Investigative Journalism.

CPA (1989) *What is Genuine Regional Autonomy?* Baguio City, Cordillera People's Alliance.

CRC (1989) *Sourcebook on the Central Cordillera Agricultural Program*. Baguio City, Cordillera Resource Center for Indigenous Peoples' Rights.

Crewe, Emma and Elizabeth Harrison (1998) *Whose Development? An Ethnography of Aid*. London/New York, Zed Books.

Czarniawska-Joerges, B., 1992: *Exploring Complex Organizations: A Cultural Perspective*. London, Sage Publications.

Dacanay, Cynthia (1998) 'The Lessons We Learned', *Chaneg*, 7 (3): 6–11.

Dietz, Ton (1997) 'Particuliere Ontwikkelingssamenwerking. De Medefinancieringsorganisaties en Steun aan NGOs', in Kristoffel Lieten en Fons van der Velden (eds) *Grenzen aan de Hulp. Beleid en Effecten van Ontwikkelingssamenwerking*. Amsterdam, Het Spinhuis.

Douglas, Mary (1987) *How Institutions Think*. London, Routledge.

Dozier, Edward P. (1966) *Mountain Arbiters. The Changing Life of a Philippine Hill People*. Tucson, University of Arizona Press.

Duffield, M. (1998) 'Aid Policy and Post-Modern Conflict: A Critical Review'. *Occasional Paper 19*, University of Birmingham, School of Public Policy.

Dusseldorp, D. van (1992) *Projects for Rural Development in the Third World: Preparation and Implementation*. Department of Sociology of Rural Development, Wageningen, Wageningen Agricultural University.

— (1990) 'Planned Development via Projects, Its Necessity, Limitations and Possible Improvement', *Sociologia Ruralis*, 30 (3/4): 336–52.

— (1995) *Is Onze Samenleving Maakbaar? Tussen Goden en Menselijke Arrogantie*. Voordracht bij het afscheid als hoogleraar in de Sociologische Aspecten van de Ontwikkelingsplanning in niet-Westerse Gebieden aan de Landbouwuniversiteit te Wageningen op 26 oktober 1995.

Eagleton, Terry (1991) *Ideology. An Introduction*. London/New York, Verso.

Edwards, Michael (1999) 'Legitimacy and Values in NGOs and Voluntary Organizations: Some Sceptical Thoughts', in David Lewis (ed.) *Voluntary Action. Reshaping the Third Sector*. London, Earthscan Publications.

Edwards, Michael and David Hulme (eds) (1996) *Beyond the Magic Bullet. NGO Performance and Accountability in the Post-Cold War World*. Connecticut, Kumarian Press.

— (1992) *Making a Difference. NGOs and Development in a Changing World*. London, Earthscan Publications.

Ekins, Paul (1992) *A New World Order. Grassroots Movements for Global Change*. London/New York, Routledge.

Elwert, Georg and Thomas Bierschenk (1988) 'Development Aid as an Intervention in Dynamic Systems', *Sociologia Ruralis*, 28 (2/3): 99–112.

Escobar, Arturo (1995) *Encountering Development. The Making and Unmaking of the Third World*. Princeton, NJ, Princeton University Press.

Escobar, Arturo and Sonia E. Alvarez (1992) *The Making of Social Movements in Latin America*. Boulder, CO/Oxford, Westview Press.

Esman, Milton J. and Norman T. Uphoff (1984) *Local Organizations. Intermediaries in Rural Development*. Ithaca, NY/London, Cornell University Press.

Ethnic Studies and Development Center Research Team (1997) *Policy Influence: NGO Experiences*. Manila, Ateneo Center for Social Policy and Public Affairs.

Fabros, Wilfredo (1987) *The Church and its Social Involvement in the Philippines, 1930–1972*. Manila, Ateneo de Manila University Press.

Fairclough, Norman (1989) *Language and Power*. London/New York, Longman.

Fals Borda, Orlando (1992) 'Social Movements and Political Power in Latin America', in Arturo Escobar and Sonia E. Alvarez (eds) *The Making of Social Movements in Latin America*. Boulder, CO/Oxford, Westview Press.

Farrington, John and Anthony Bebbington with Kate Wellard and David J. Lewis (1993) *Reluctant Partners? Non-Governmental Organizations, the State and Sustainable Agricultural Development*. London/New York, Routledge.

Feeney, Patricia (1998) *Accountable Aid. Local Participation in Major Projects*. Oxford, OXFAM.

Ferguson, James (1990) *The Anti-Politics Machine. Development, Depoliticization and Bureaucratic Power in Lesotho*. Minneapolis/London, University of Minnesota Press.

Fielding, Helen (1994) *Cause Celeb.* London, Picador.

Finin, Gerard Anthony (1991) 'Regional Consciousness and Administrative Grids: Understanding the Role of Planning in the Philippines' Gran Cordillera Central'. PhD Thesis, Cornell University, NJ.

Fisher, W. (1997) 'Doing Good? The Politics and Antipolitics of NGO Practices', *Annual Review of Anthropology*, 26: 439–64.

Florendo, Nela (1994) 'Ideology and Inter-ethnic Images: Igorot Participation in the Revolution', in Tolentino Delfin Jr (ed.) *Resistance and Revolution in the Cordillera*. Baguio City, University of the Philippines.

Forsythe, D. E. (1999) 'Ethics and Politics of Studying up in Technoscience', *Anthropology of Work Review*, 20 (1): 6–11.

Foucault, Michel (1980) *Power/Knowledge: Selected Interviews and Other Writings 1972–1977* (ed. C. Gordon). Brighton, Harvester Press.

— (1995/1975) *Discipline and Punish. The Birth of the Prison.* New York, Vintage Books.

Fowler, Alan (1997) *Striking a Balance. A Guide to Enhance the Effectiveness of Non-Governmental Organizations in International Development.* London, Earthscan Publications.

Fox, Diana Joyce (1998) *An Ethnography of Four Non-Governmental Development Organisations.* Mellen Studies in Sociology, Vol. 16. Lewiston, Queenston, Lampeter, Edwin Mellen Press.

Fox, Jonathan (1992) 'Democratic Rural Development: Leadership Accountability in Regional Peasant Organizations', *Development and Change*, 23 (2): 1–36.

Fumerton, Mario Antonio (1995) 'The Construction of a Women's Liberation Discourse in the Context of the National Democratic Revolution in the Philippines'. MSc Thesis, University of Oxford.

GABRIELA (1993) 'Ramos Government: Perpetrator of Sexual Violence against Women', *GABRIELA's Women's Update*, 8 (1).

Gardner and Lewis (1996) *Anthropology, Development and the Postmodern Critique.* London, Chicago, IL/Pluto Press.

Garfinkel, Harold (1967) *Studies in Ethnomethodology.* New Jersey, Prentice Hall.

Gasper, Des (1998) 'The Logical Framework Approach: Notes Towards Applications to Relief Evaluations', *Development Issues*, No. 12: 42–53.

Gasper, Des and Raymond Apthorpe (1996) 'Introduction: Discourse Analysis and Policy Discourse', in Raymond Apthorpe and Des Gasper (eds) *Arguing Development Policy: Frames and Discourses.* London, Frank Cass/EADI.

Geertz, Clifford (1973) *The Interpretation of Cultures.* New York, Basic Books.

George, Terrence R. (1998) 'Local Governance: People Power in the Provinces?', in G. Sidney Silliman and Lela Garner Noble (eds) *Organizing for Democracy. NGOs, Civil Society and the Philippine State.* Manila, Ateneo de Manila University Press.

Giddens, Anthony (1984) *The Constitution of Society. Outline of the Theory of Structuration.* Cambridge, Polity Press.

Goffman, Erving (1961) *Asylums. Essays on the Social Situation of Mental Patients and Other Inmates.* London, Penguin Books.

Gray, Andrew (1998) 'Development Policy – Development Protest: The World Bank, Indigenous Peoples and NGOs', in Jonathan Fox and David Brown (eds)

The Struggle for Accountability. The World Bank, NGOs and Grassroots Movements. Cambridge, MA/London: MIT Press.

Grillo, R. D. (1997) 'Discourses of Development: The View from Anthropology', in R. D. Grillo and R. L. Stirrat (eds) *Discourses of Development. Anthropological Perspectives.* Oxford/New York, Berg Publishers.

Grillo, R. D. and R. L. Stirrat (eds) (1997) *Discourses of Development. Anthropological Perspectives.* Oxford/New York, Berg Publishers.

Guerrero, Amado (1979/1970) *Philippine Society and Revolution.* Oakland CA, International Association of Filipino Patriots.

Guidry, John, Michael Kennedy and Mayer Zald (eds) (2000) *Globalization and Social Movements. Culture, Power, and the Transnational Public Sphere.* Michigan, University of Michigan Press.

Hailey, John (1999) 'Charismatic Autocrats or Development Leaders: Characteristics of First Generation NGO Leadership'. Paper presented to the Development Studies Association Conference, University of Bath, UK, September 1999.

Hale, C. R. (1997) 'Consciousness, Violence, and the Politics of Memory in Guatemala', *Current Anthropology,* 38 (5): 817–38.

HAMIS (1995) *The Federation of HAMIS Winners in the Philippines.* Manila, Health and Management Information System, DOH/GTZ.

Handelman, Don (1990) *Models and Mirrors: Towards an Anthropology of Public Events.* Cambridge, Cambridge University Press.

Heritage, John (1984) *Garfinkel and Ethnomethodology.* Cambridge, Polity Press.

Herzfeld, Michael (1992) *The Social Production of Indifference. Exploring the Symbolic Roots of Western Bureaucracy.* Oxford/New York, Berg Publishers.

Hilhorst, Dorothea (1997) 'Discourse Formation in Social Movements: Issues of Collective Action', in Henk de Haan and Norman Long (eds) *Images and Realities of Rural Life. Wageningen Perspectives on Rural Transformations.* Assen, Van Gorcum.

— (2000) 'Records and Reputations: Everyday Politics of a Philippine Development NGO'. PhD Thesis, Wageningen University.

— (2001a) 'Interface Experts and Meanings of Development: Progress in a Philippine Igorot Village', *Human Organization,* 60 (4), 401–14.

— (2001b). 'The Power of Discourse: NGOs, Gender and National Democratic Politics', *Asian Studies,* 37 (1 and 2), Quezon City, University of the Philippines.

Hilhorst, Dorothea and Mathijs van Leeuwen (2000) 'Emergency and Development: The Case of Imidugudu, Villagisation in Rwanda', *Journal of Refugee Studies,* 13 (3).

Hilhorst, Dorothea and Nadja Schmiemann (2002) 'Humanitarian Principles and Organisational Culture: Everyday Practice in Médécins Sans Frontières – Holland' in *Development in Practice,* forthcoming.

Hirschmann, A. O. (1970) *Exit, Voice and Loyalty: Responses to Decline in Firms, Organizations and States.* Cambridge, MA, Harvard University Press.

Hobart, Mark (ed.) (1993) *An Anthropological Critique of Development, The Growth of Ignorance.* London, Routledge.

Hulme, David and Michael Edwards (eds) (1997) *NGOs, States and Donors. Too Close for Comfort?* New York, St Martin's Press.

Hulme, David and Jonathan Goodhand (2000) *NGOs and Peace Building in Complex Political Emergencies: Final Report to the Department for International Development.* Peace

Building and Complex Political Emergencies, Working Paper Series, Paper No. 12, Manchester, IDPM, University of Manchester.

Ibana, Rainier R. A. (1994) *Six NGO Terminologies: Their Philosophical Contexts*. Quezon City, Ateneo Center for Social Policy and Public Affairs, Ateneo de Manila University.

INTRAC (1998) *Direct Funding from a Southern Perspective: Strengthening Civil Society?* Oxford, INTRAC NGO Management and Policy Series, No. 8.

Jayawardena, Kumari (1986) *Feminism and Nationalism in the Third World*. London/New Jersey, Zed Books.

Johnson-Odim, Cheryl (1991) 'Common Themes, Different Contexts: Third World Women and Feminism', in Chandra Talpade Mohanty, Ann Russo and Lourdes Torres (eds) *Third World Women and the Politics of Feminism*. Bloomington/Indianapolis, Indiana University Press.

Jones, Gregg R. (1989) *Red Revolution. Inside the Philippine Guerrilla Movement*. London, Westview Press.

Kakabadse, Yolanda N. and Sarah Burns (1994) 'Movers and Shapers: NGOs in International Affairs', *Development*, 4.

Kane, Samuel E. (1933) *Thirty Years with the Philippine Headhunters*. New York, Grosset & Dunlap, n.d., reprinted from *Life and Death in Luzon*, 1933.

Kasarinlan (1993) 'Special Issue', *Kasarinlan*, 8 (4).

Keesing, Felix M. and Marie Keesing (1934) *Taming Philippine Headhunters. A Study of Government and of Cultural Change in Northern Luzon*. California, Stanford University Press.

Kerkvliet, Benedict (1977) *The Huk Rebellion: A Study of Peasant Revolt in the Philippines*. Berkeley/Los Angeles, University of California Press.

— (1991) *Everyday Politics in the Philippines. Class and Status Relations in a Central Luzon Village*. Quezon City, New Day Publishers.

Klandermans, Bert and Sidney Tarrow (1988) 'Mobilizing into Social Movements: Synthesizing European and American Approaches', in Bert Klandermans, Hanspeter Kriesi and Sidney Tarrow (eds) *International Social Movement Research, Vol 1. From Structure to Action: Comparing Social Movement Research Across Cultures*. London, JAI Press.

KMP (1994) '*Development Divergence. Reform in the Philippine NGO Community*'. Quezon City, Peasant Update Philippines.

Labayen, Bishop Julio X. (1995) *Revolution and the Church of the Poor*. Manila, Socio-Pastoral Institute/Claretian Publications.

Lamphere, Louise (1987) 'Feminism and Anthropology: The Struggle to Reshape Our Thinking About Gender', in Christie Farnham (ed.) *The Impact of Feminist Research in the Academe*. Bloomington/Indianapolis, Indiana University Press.

Latour, Bruno (1986) 'The Power of Association', in John Law (ed.) *Power, Action and Belief: A New Sociology of Knowledge?* London/Boston, MA/Henley, Routledge.

— (1987) *Science in Action*. Cambridge, MA, Harvard University Press.

Law, John (1994) *Organizing Modernity*. Oxford/Cambridge, Blackwell.

— (1996) 'Organizing Accountabilities: Ontology and the Mode of Accounting', in Rolland Munro and Jan Mouritsen (eds) *Accountability. Power Ethos and the Technologies of Managing*. London, International Thomson Business Press.

Leftwich, Adrian (1984) *What is Politics?* Oxford, Basil Blackwell

Lehmann, David (1990) *Democracy and Development in Latin America. Economics, Politics and Religion in the Postwar Period.* Cambridge, Polity Press.

Lewis, Martin W. (1992) *Wagering the Land. Ritual, Capital and Environmental Degradation in the Cordillera of Northern Luzon, 1900–1986.* Berkeley/Los Angeles/Oxford, University of California Press.

Liwanag, Armando (1992) 'Reaffirm Our Basic Principles and Rectify the Errors', *Compilation*, pp. 282–334.

Long, Norman (1992) 'From Paradigm Lost to Paradigm Regained? The Case for an Actor-Oriented Sociology of Development', in Norman Long and Ann Long (eds) *Battlefields of Knowledge. The Interlocking of Theory and Practice in Social Research and Development.* London/New York, Routledge.

— (1997) 'Agency and Constraint, Perception and Practices. A Theoretical Position', in Henk de Haan and Norman Long (eds) *Images and Realities of Rural Life. Wageningen Perspectives on Rural Transformations.* Assen, Van Gorcum.

— (1999) 'The Multiple Optic of Interface Analysis: Development Intervention as a Socially and Culturally Contested Process'. UNESCO Background Paper on Interface Analysis, Wageningen University, the Netherlands (unpublished).

Long, Norman (ed.) (1989) *Encounters at the Interface. A Perspective on Social Discontinuities in Rural Development.* Studies in Sociology, 27, Wageningen, Wageningen Agricultural University.

Long, Norman and Jan Douwe van der Ploeg (1989) 'Demythologizing Planned Intervention: An Actor Perspective', *Sociologia Ruralis*, 29 (3/4): 226–49.

— (1994) 'Heterogeneity, Actor and Structure: Towards a Reconstitution of the Concept of Structure', in David Booth (ed.) *Rethinking Social Development. Theory, Research and Practice.* Essex, Longman.

Loste, Manuel (n.d.) 'The Popular Movement for Regional Autonomy in the Cordillera: A Preliminary Assessment'. Unpublished document.

Mahmood, C. (2002) 'Anthropological Compulsions in a World in Crisis', *Anthropology Today*, 18 (3).

Makibaka (1995) 'The Gender Trap', in *Kababaihan at Rebolusyon* (unsourced document).

Malkki, Liisa H. (1995) *Purity and Exile. Violence, Memory, and National Cosmology among Hutu Refugees in Tanzania.* Chicago, IL/London, University of Chicago Press.

Marx, Anthony (1995) 'Contested Citizenship: The Dynamics of Racial Identity and Social Movements', *International Review of Social History*, 40, Supplement 3: 159–83.

McKay, Deirdre Christian (1993) *Transformations of Gender, Tenure and Forest.* MSc Thesis, Nova Scotia, Dalhousie University.

Melucci, Alberto (1988) 'Getting Involved: Identity and Mobilization in Social Movements', in Bert Klandermans, Hanspeter Kriesi, Sidney Tarrow (eds) *International Social Movement Research, Vol 1. From Structure to Action: Comparing Social Movement Research Across Cultures*, pp. 329–48. London, JAI Press.

Miller, Peter (1994) 'Accounting as Social and Institutional Practice: An Introduction', in Anthony Hopwood and Peter Miller (eds) *Accounting as Social and Institutional Practice.* Cambridge, Cambridge University Press.

Miralao, Virginia and Cynthia Bautista (1993) 'The Growth and Changing Roles of NGOs and the Voluntary Sector', *Philippine Sociological Review*, 41 (1–4).

Moghadam, Valentine M. (ed.) (1994) *Identity Politics and Women. Cultural Reassertions and Feminisms in International Perspective.* Boulder, CO/Oxford/San Francisco, CA, Westview Press.

Mohanty, Chandra, Talpade (1991) 'Introduction. Cartographies of Struggle: Third World Women and the Politics of Feminism', in Chandra Talpade Mohanty, Ann Russo and Lourdes Torres (eds) *Third World Women and the Politics of Feminism.* Bloomington/Indianapolis, Indiana University Press.

Molyneux, Maxine (1986) 'Mobilization without Emancipation? Women's Interests, the State and Revolution', in Richard Fagen, Carmen Diana Deere and José Luis Coraggio (eds) *Transition and Development: Problems of Third World Socialism.* New York, Monthly Review Press,.

Mongbo, Roch L. (1995) 'The Appropriation and Dismembering of Development Intervention: Policy, Discourse and Practice in the Field of Rural Development in Benin'. PhD Dissertation, Wageningen, Wageningen Agricultural University.

Moore, Henrietta L. (1988) *Feminism and Anthropology.* Oxford, Polity Press.

— (1994) *A Passion for Difference. Essays in Anthropology and Gender.* Cambridge, Polity Press.

Morgan, Gareth (1986) *Images of Organization.* Beverly Hills, CA/Newbury Park/London/New Delhi: Sage Publications.

Morgen, Sandra (1989) 'Gender and Anthropology: Introductory Essay', in S. Morgen (ed.) *Gender and Anthropology: Critical Reviews for Research and Teaching.* Washington, DC, American Anthropological Association.

Moser, Caroline O. N. (1993) *Gender Planning and Development. Theory, Practice and Training.* London/New York, Routledge.

Munro, Rolland (1996) 'Alignment and Identity Work: The Study of Accounts and Accountability', in Rolland Munro and Jan Mouritsen (eds) *Accountability. Power Ethos and the Technologies of Managing.* London, International Thomson Business Press.

Nauta, Wiebe (2001) 'The Implications of Freedom. The Changing Role of Land Sector NGOs in a Transforming South Africa'. PhD Dissertation, Amsterdam, Amsterdam Free University.

Nuijten, Monique (1998) 'In the Name of the Land. Organization, Transnationalism, and the Culture of the State in a Mexican Ejido'. PhD Dissertation, Wageningen, Wageningen University.

O'Brien, Robert, Anne Marie Goetz, Jan Aart Scholte, Marc Williams (2000) *Contesting Global Governance. Multilateral Economic Institutions and Global Social Movements.* Cambridge, Cambridge University Press.

Olivier de Sardan, Jean-Pierre (1988) 'Peasant Logics and Development Project Logics', *Sociologia Ruralis*, 28 (2/3): 216–26.

— (1995) *Anthropologie et Développement. Essai en Socio-Anthropologie du Changement Social.* Marseille, APAD/Paris, KARTHALA.

Ong, Aihwa and Michael G. Peletz (1995) 'Introduction', in Aihwa Ong and Michael G. Peletz (eds) *Bewitching Women, Pious Men. Gender and Body Politics in Southeast Asia.* Berkeley/Los Angeles, University of California Press.

Ouden, J. H. B. den (1979) 'Social Stratification as Expressed Through Language: A Case Study of a South Indian Village', *Contributions to Indian Sociology*, 13 (1).

Pearce, Jenny (1993) 'NGOs and Social Change: Agents or Facilitators?' *Development in Practice*, 3 (3).

— (1997) 'Between Co-option and Irrelevance? Latin American NGOs in the 1990s', in David Hulme and Michael Edwards (eds) *NGOs, States and Donors. Too Close for Comfort?* New York, St Martin's Press.

Perera, Jehan (1997) 'In Unequal Dialogue with Donors: The Experience of the Sarvodaya Shramadana Movement', in David Hulme and Michael Edwards (eds) *NGOs, States and Donors. Too Close for Comfort?* New York, St Martin's Press.

Pettigrew, Andrew (1979) 'On Studying Organizational Cultures', *Administrative Science*, 24 (4).

PIA (1989) *Baseline Survey on the Cordillera Autonomous Region*. Baguio City, Public Opinion Research Division, Philippine Information Agency.

Pigg, Stacy Leigh (1992) 'Inventing Social Categories Through Place: Social Representations and Development in Nepal', *Comparative Studies of Society and History*, 34 (3): 491–513.

Po, Blondie and Cristina Montiel (1980) *Rural Organizations in the Philippines*. Manila, Ateneo de Manila University Press.

Porter, D., B. Allen and G. Thompson (1991) *Development in Practice. Paved with Good Intentions*. London/New York, Routledge.

Power, Michael (1994) 'The Audit Society', in Hopwood, Anthony and Peter Miller (eds) *Accounting as Social and Institutional Practice*. Cambridge, Cambridge University Press.

Preston, P. W. (1994) *Discourse of Development: State, Market and Polity in the Analysis of Complex Change*. Aldershot, Avebury.

Prill-Brett, June (1989) *Indigenous Experience of Autonomy in the Cordillera*. Baguio City, CSC Working Paper 10. Cordillera Studies Center, UPCB.

Princen, Thomas and Matthias Finger (1994) *Environmental NGOs in World Politics. Linking the Local and the Global*. London, Routledge.

Put, Marcel (1998) 'Innocent Farmers? A Comparative Evaluation into a Government and an NGO Project Located in Semi-Arid Andhra Pradesh (India), Meant to Induce Farmers to Adopt Innovations for Dryland Agriculture'. PhD Dissertation, Amsterdam, University of Amsterdam.

Putnam, Robert D. (1993) *Making Democracy Work: Civic Traditions in Modern Italy*. Princeton, NJ, Princeton University Press.

Quarles van Ufford, Philip (1993) 'Knowledge and Ignorance in the Practices of Development Policy', in Mark Hobart (ed.) *An Anthropological Critique of Development. The Growth of Ignorance*. London/New York, Routledge.

Raedt, Jules de (1987) *Similarities and Differences in Life Styles in the Central Cordillera of Northern Luzon (Philippines)*. CSC Working Paper 03. Baguio City, Cordillera Studies Center, UPCB.

Ragin, Charles C. and Howard S. Becker (1992) *What is a Case? Exploring the Foundations of Social Inquiry*. Cambridge, Cambridge University Press.

Ramirez, M. (1984) *Understanding Philippine Social Realities Through the Filipino Family*. Manila, Asian Social Institute.

Resurrección, Bernadette P. (1999) 'Transforming Nature, Redefining Selves. Gender and Ethnic Relations, Resource Use, and Environmental Change in the Philippine Uplands'. PhD Dissertation, The Hague, Institute of Social Studies.

Reyes-Boquiren, Rowena, Elena Regpala, Geoffrey Nettleton and Ricardo E. Torres (1990) 'Non-government Organizations' Initiatives and Prospects for Development Work in the Cordillera, Northern Luzon'. Paper for the GPP Conference, UP-Baguio.

Riddel, R. and Robinson, M. (1992) *The Impact of NGO Poverty Alleviation Projects: Results of the Case Study Evaluations.* London, Overseas Development Institute, Working Paper 68, November.

Rizal, Jose (1887) *Noli Me Tangere.* Berlin, Berliner Buchdruckerei Aktien-Gesell- schaft.

Roberts, John (1996) 'From Discipline to Dialogue: Individualizing and Socializing Forms of Accountability', in Rolland Munro and Jan Mouritsen (eds) *Accountability. Power Ethos and the Technologies of Managing.* London, International Thomson Business Press.

Robinson, M. (1993) 'Governance, Democracy and Conditionality: NGOs and the New Policy Agenda', in A. Clayton (ed.) *Governance, Democracy and Conditionality: What Role for NGOs?* Oxford, INTRAC.

Rocamora, Joel (1979) 'The Political Uses of PANAMIN', *Southeast Asia Chronicle*, 67.

— (1994) *Breaking Through. The Struggle within the Communist Party of the Philippines.* Manila, Anvil Publishing.

Roe, Emery (1991) 'Development Narratives, or Making the Best of Blueprint Development', *World Development*, 19 (4): 287–300.

Rood, Steven (1994) 'Issues Surrounding Autonomy: Insights from the Work of the University of the Philippines Cordillera Studies Center on Regional Auto- nomy', in Arturo Boquiren (ed.) *Advancing Regional Autonomy in the Cordillera – A Source Book.* Baguio City, Cordillera Studies Center, UPCB.

— (1998) 'NGOs and Indigenous Peoples', in G. Sidney Silliman and Lela Garner Noble (eds) *Organizing for Democracy. NGOs, Civil Society and the Philippine State.* Manila, Ateneo de Manila University Press.

Rood, Steven (ed.) (1987) *Issues on Cordillera Autonomy. Conference Proceedings, May 22– 24 1987,* Baguio City, Cordillera Studies Center, UPCB.

Rovillos, Raymundo D. (1996) 'Continuities and Discontinuities in Gender Roles: The Case of the Central Cordillera Agricultural Programme (CECAP) in Ifugao'. MSc Thesis. Baguio City, University of the Philippines College Baguio.

Russell, Susan (1983) 'Entrepreneurs, Ethnic Rhetorics and Economic Integration in Benguet Province, Highland Luzon, Philippines'. PhD Thesis. University of Illinois.

Rutherford, Stuart (1995) *ASA. The Biography of an NGO. Empowerment and Credit in Rural Bangladesh.* Dhaka, Brac Printers.

Rutten, Rosanne (2000) 'High-Cost Activism and the Worker Household: Interests, Commitment, and the Costs of Revolutionary Activism in a Philippine Planta- tion Region', *Theory and Society*, 29 (2).

— (2001) 'Revolutionary Specialists, Strongmen and the State: Post-Movement Careers of CPP-NPA cadres in a Philippine Province, 1990s–2001', in *South East Asia Research*, 9 (3): 319–61.

St-Hilaire, Colette (1992) 'Canadian Aid, Women and Development: Re-baptizing the Filipina', *Philippines Development Briefing*, No. 3, December 1992.

Sajor, Edsel E. (1999) 'Upland Livelihood Transformations. State and Market

Processes and Social Autonomy in the Northern Philippines'. PhD Dissertation, The Hague, Institute of Social Studies.

Salamon, L. M. (1994) 'The Rise of the Nonprofit Sector', *Foreign Affairs*, July/August: 109–22.

Santiago, Lilia Quindoza (1995) 'Rebirthing Babaye: The Women's Movements in the Philippines', in Amrita Basu (ed.) *The Challenge of Local Feminisms. Women's Movements in Global Perspective*. Boulder, CO/San Francisco, CA/Oxford, Westview Press.

Schlanger, John (1996) 'Private Aid Agencies in Brazil', in David Sogge (ed.) with Kees Biekart and John Saxby, *Compassion and Calculation. The Business of Private Foreign Aid*. London/Chicago, IL, Pluto Press with Transnational Institute.

Schutz, A. and T. Luckmann (1973) *The Structures of the Life-World*. Evanston, IL, Northwestern University Press.

Scott, Alan (1990) *Ideology and the New Social Movements*. London/Boston/Sydney/Wellington, Unwin Hyman.

Scott, James C. (1985) *Weapons of the Weak. Everyday Forms of Peasant Resistance*. New Haven/London, Yale University Press.

— (1990) *Domination and the Arts of Resistance. Hidden Transcripts*. New Haven/London, Yale University Press.

Scott, William Henry (1993/1972) *Of Igorots and Independence: Two Essays*. Baguio City, ERA.

— (1997) *Barangay*. University of Hawaii Press.

Scurrah, Martin J. (1996) 'NGOs, Civil Society and Democracy in Peru: Ideas and Experiences', in Andrew Clayton (ed.) *NGOs, Civil Society and the State: Building Democracy in Transitional Societies*. INTRAC NGO Management and Policy Series No. 5. Oxford, INTRAC.

Severino, Howie (1994) *The European Community in the Philippine Highlands: The Central Cordillera Agricultural Programme (CECAP) and the Politics of Development*. Manila, Philippine Center of Investigative Journalism.

Siapno, Jacqueline (1995) 'Alternative Filipina Heroines: Contested Tropes in Leftist Feminisms', in Aihwa Ong and Michael G. Peletz (eds) *Bewitching Women, Pious Men. Gender and Body Politics in Southeast Asia*. Berkeley/Los Angeles, University of California Press.

Sidel, John Thayer (1999) *Capital, Coercion and Crime: Bossism in the Philippines*. California, Stanford University Press.

Silliman, G. Sidney and Lela Garner Noble (eds) (1998) *Organizing for Democracy. NGOs, Civil Society and the Philippine State*. Manila, Ateneo de Manila University Press.

Sison, Jose Maria and Rainer Werning (1989) *The Philippine Revolution. The Leader's View*. New York, Crane Russak.

Smillie, Ian (1995) *The Alms Bazaar. Altruism Under Fire – Non-Profit Organizations and International Development*. London, Intermediate Technology Publications.

Smircich, L. (1983) 'Concepts of Culture and Organizational Analysis', *Administrative Science Quarterly*, 28 (3): 339–58.

Smith, Gavin (1989) *Livelihood and Resistance. Peasants and the Politics of Land in Peru*. Berkeley/Los Angeles/Oxford, University of California Press.

Smith, Jackie, Charles Chatfield and Ron Pagnucco (eds) (1997) *Transnational Social*

Movements and Global Politics. Solidarity Beyond the State. New York, Syracuse University Press.

Smith-Sreen, Poonam (1995) *Accountability in Development Organizations. Experiences of Women's Organizations in India.* New Delhi/Thousand Oaks/London, Sage Publications.

Snow, David and Robert Benford (1988) 'Ideology, Frame Resonance, and Participant Mobilization', in Bert Klandermans, Hanspeter Kriesi, Sidney Tarrow. *International Social Movement Research, Vol 1. From Structure to Action: Comparing Social Movement Research Across Cultures.* London, JAI Press.

Sogge, David (ed.) (1996) *Compassion and Calculation. The Business of Private Foreign Aid.* London/Chicago, Pluto Press with Transnational Institute.

Stacey, J. (1988) 'Can There be a Feminist Ethnography?', *Women's Studies International Forum,* 11 (1): 21–7.

Statham, Paul (1998) 'The Political Construction of Immigration Politics in Italy: Opportunities, Mobilisation and Outcomes'. *Wissenschaftszentrum Berlin Discussion Paper Series,* FS III-102: 1–60.

Stephen, Lynn (1997) *Women and Social Movements in Latin America. Power from Below.* Austin, University of Texas Press.

Stirrat, R. L. and Heiko Henkel (1997) 'The Development Gift: The Problem of Reciprocity in the NGO World', *Annals, AAPPS,* 554, November.

Stogdill, R. M. (1950) 'Leadership, Membership and Organization', *Psychological Bulletin,* 47: 1–14.

Street, B. (1993) 'Culture is a Verb: Anthropological Aspects of Language and Cultural Process', in D. Graddol, L. Thompson and M. Byram (eds) *Language and Culture.* Clevedon, Avon, British Association for Applied Linguistics in Association with Multilingual Matters.

Stuurgroep Impactstudie Medefinancieringsprogramma (1991) *Betekenis van het Medefinancieringsprogramma: Een Verkenning.* Utrecht, Libertas.

Suzuki (1998) *Inside NGOs. Managing Conflicts between Headquarters and the Field Offices in Non-Governmental Organizations.* London, Intermediate Technology Publications.

Taguiwalo, Judy (1994) 'From Red to Purple Banner: Notes on the Contemporary Women's Movement in the Philippines', *Laya, Feminist Quarterly,* 4.

Tandon, Rajesh (1996) 'Board Games: Governance and Accountability in NGOs', in Michael Edwards and David Hulme (eds) *Beyond the Magic Bullet. NGO Performance and Accountability in the Post-Cold War World.* Connecticut, Kumarian Press.

Tandoh, Yash (1996) 'An African Perspective', in David Sogge (ed.) *Compassion and Calculation. The Business of Private Foreign Aid.* London/Chicago, Pluto Press with Transnational Institute.

Tarrow, Sidney (1994) *Power in Movement. Social Movements, Collective Action and Politics.* Cambridge, Cambridge University Press.

Tauli-Corpuz, Victoria and Dorothea Hilhorst (1995) 'Indigenous Women and the Beijing Conference', Baguio City, *Chaneg,* 4 (2 and 3).

Tigno, Jorge V. (1993) 'Democratization Through Non-governmental and People's Organizations', *Kasarinlan. A Philippine Quarterly of Third World Studies,* 8 (3): 58–73.

Tilly, Charles (1995) 'Citizenship, Identity and Social History', *International Review of Social History*, 40, Supplement 3: 1–17.

Tujan, Antonio and Ros-b Guzman (1998) *Globalizing Philippine Mining*. Manila, IBON Foundation Inc.

Tvedt, Terje (1998) *Angels of Mercy or Development Diplomats? NGOs and Foreign Aid*. Trenton/Asmara/London, Africa World Press Inc., James Currey Ltd.

Uvin, Peter and David Miller (eds) 'Paths to Scaling-up: Alternative Strategies for Local Nongovernmental Organisations', *Human Organization*, 55 (3): 179–85.

Van Ufford, Philip Quartes (1993) 'Knowledge and Ignorance in the Practices of Development Policy', in Mark Hobart (ed.) *An Anthropological Critique of Development: The Growth of Ignorance*. London/New York, Routledge.

Velsen, J. Van (1967) 'Situational Analysis and the Extended-case Method', in A. L. Epstein (ed.) *The Craft of Anthropology*. London, Tavistock Publications.

Villarreal, Magdalena (1994) 'Wielding and Yielding: Power, Subordination and Gender Identity in the Context of a Mexican Development Project'. PhD Dissertation, Wageningen, Wageningen Agricultural University.

Vries, Pieter de (1992) 'Unruly Clients. A Study of How Bureaucrats Try and Fail to Transform Gatekeepers, Communists and Preachers into Ideal Beneficiaries'. PhD Dissertation, Wageningen, Wageningen Agricultural University.

Walton, J. (1992) 'Making the Theoretical Case', in Charles C. Ragin and Howard S. Becker (1992) *What is a Case? Exploring the Foundations of Social Inquiry*. Cambridge, Cambridge University Press.

Watts, Michael J. (1993) 'Development: Power, Knowledge, Discursive Practice', *Progress in Human Geography*, 17 (2): 257–72.

Weekley, Kathleen (2001) *The Communist Party of the Philippines 1968–1993. A Story of Its Theory and Practice*. Quezon City, University of the Philippines Press.

Wieringa, Saskia (ed.) (1996) *Subversive Women: Women's Movements in Africa, Asia, Latin America and the Caribbean*. London, Zed Books.

Willetts, Peter (1992) *Pressure Groups in the Global System*. London, Frances Pinter.

Willetts, Peter (ed.) (1996) *'The Conscience of the World'. The Influence of Non-Governmental Organisations in the UN System*. Washington, DC, Brookings Institution.

Wilmer, Franke (1993) *The Indigenous Voice in World Politics: Since Time Immemorial*. Newbury Park, CA/London/New Delhi, Sage Publications.

Wilson, Fiona and Bodil F. Frederiksen (ed.) (1995) *Ethnicity, Gender and the Subversion of Nationalism*. London, Frank Cass/EADI, Geneva.

Winnacker, Martha (1979) 'The Battle to Stop the Chico Dams', *Southeast Asia Chronicle*, 67, October.

Wolf, Eric (1990) 'Distinguished Lecture: Facing Power – Old Insights, New Questions', *American Anthropologist*, Vol. 92.

Wolters, Willem (1983) *Politics, Patronage and Class Conflict in Central Luzon*. The Hague, Institute of Social Studies.

Wood, Geof (1985) 'The Politics of Development Policy Labelling', *Development and Change*, 16: 347–73.

— (1997) 'States without Citizens: The Problem of the Franchise State', in David Hulme and Michael Edwards (eds) *NGOs, States and Donors, Too Close for Comfort?* New York, St Martin's Press.

Woost, Michael (1993) 'Alternative Vocabularies of Development? "Community" and "Participation" in Development Discourse in Sri Lanka', in R. D. Grillo and R. L. Stirrat (eds) *Discourses of Development. Anthropological Perspectives.* Oxford/ New York, Berg Publishers.

Wright, Susan (1994) '"Culture" in Anthropology and Organizational Studies', in Susan Wright (ed.) *Anthropology of Organizations.* London, Routledge.

Zadek, Simon (1996) 'Interlude: Looking Back from 2010', in David Sogge (ed.) *Compassion and Calculation. The Business of Private Foreign Aid.* London/Chicago, Pluto Press and Transnational Institute.

Zadek, Simon and Murdoch Gatward (1996) 'Transforming the Transnational NGOs: Social Auditing or Bust?', in Michael Edwards and David Hulme (eds) *Beyond the Magic Bullet. NGO Performance and Accountability in the Post-Cold War World.* Connecticut, Kumarian Press.

Zialcita, Fernando et al. (eds) (1995) *People's Participation in Local Governance. 4 Case Studies.* Quezon City, Center for Social Policy and Public Affairs, Ateneo de Manila University.

Index

About the author

Dorothea Hilhorst is Lecturer at the Centre for Rural Development, Wageningen Agricultural University, The Netherlands, with specializations in development and disaster studies. She has been research and evaluation officer of the Cordillera Women's Education and Resource Centre (CWERC) in Baguio City in the Philippines (1993–96) and Desk Officer at the Asia Desk of Cebemo, Oegstgeest, the co-financing agency of projects of NGOs in developing countries (1989–90). She has published widely in academic journals and papers in her field.